944.07   Aronson, Theo
A   The fall of the third Napoleon.
c.2   Bobbs [1970]
                271 p.   illus., ports.

          1. Napoleon III, Emperor of the French,
          1808-1873   2. Franco-German War, 1870-1871
          I. Title

7.50

THE FALL OF
THE THIRD
NAPOLEON

Also by Theo Aronson

THE FALL OF THE THIRD NAPOLEON

—

THEO ARONSON

THE BOBBS-MERRILL COMPANY
INDIANAPOLIS / NEW YORK

THE BOBBS-MERRILL COMPANY, INC.
Indianapolis – New York
Library of Congress catalog card number 74-81295

Printed in Great Britain

For Dudley Frasier

CONTENTS

Author's Note   xiii

Prologue: Imperial Paris 1870   3

PART ONE

    Chapter One: The Dynasty   15

    Chapter Two: The Liberal Empire   42

    Chapter Three: Summer   65

PART TWO

    Chapter Four: The Hohenzollern Candidature   77

    Chapter Five: Metz   97

    Chapter Six: The Change of Crew   115

    Chapter Seven: The Crisis   127

PART THREE

    Chapter Eight: The Road to Sedan   145

    Chapter Nine: Sedan   162

    Chapter Ten: The Fourth of September   183

    Chapter Eleven: Into Exile   202

PART FOUR

    Chapter Twelve: The Peacemaking   215

    Chapter Thirteen: Exile   222

    Chapter Fourteen: Post-mortem   242

Epilogue: Sedan 1940   253

Bibliography   255

Index   265

ILLUSTRATIONS

following page 130

1 Napoleon III, Emperor of the French
2 Eugenie, Empress of the French
3 Eugenie, by Winterhalter
4 Louis, the Prince Imperial, aged thirteen
5 'The Four Napoleons.' Napoleon I and his son, and Napoleon III with the Prince Imperial
6 Prince Napoleon ('Plon-Plon')
7 The Emperor and the Prince Imperial leaving for the front
8 A cartoon of Napoleon III and King Wilhelm, each protesting his innocence before John Bull
9 A *Punch* cartoon showing the ghost of the Great Napoleon cautioning Napoleon III
10 Count Otto von Bismarck
11 King Wilhelm of Prussia
12 Crown Prince Frederick of Prussia
13 Uniforms of the Prussian Infantry during the Franco-Prussian war
14 Uniforms of the French Infantry during the Franco-Prussian war
15 Napoleon III and his generals
16 Marshal Bazaine, Commander-in-Chief of the French Army
17 The Paris crowd in the Place Vendôme demanding news of the war
18 'Two Mothers': a *Punch* cartoon
19 Marshal MacMahon
20 General Trochu
21 French troops trying to force their way into Sedan
22 The white flag being waved above the walls of Sedan, 1 September 1870

23 General Reille delivering Napoleon III's letter to
    King Wilhelm
24 Napoleon and Bismarck on the morning after the
    battle of Sedan; from a painting by Camphausen
25 Napoleon III escorted by Bismarck; from a painting
    by Camphausen
26 The Republican leader, Jules Favre, proposing the
    deposition of the Emperor Napoleon III
27 A caricature of Napoleon III after the fall of the
    Second Empire
28 Napoleon III and the Prince Imperial, photographed
    in England in 1871
29 Camden Place, Chislehurst, Kent. Exile home of the
    Imperial family
30 The Emperor Napoleon III on his death-bed

MAPS

Plan of the campaign from Saarbrücken to Sedan   102
The Battlefield at Sedan   164

It is all very beautiful—for the moment,
but I would not give two sous for the last act!

Alfred de Musset,
at a ball at the Tuileries
during the Second Empire

AUTHOR'S NOTE

The year 1970 marks the centenary of one of the great watersheds in the history of the world—the outbreak of the Franco-Prussian War and the resulting fall of the French Second Empire. For centuries, until the débâcle of 1870, France had been mistress of Europe, and Paris the capital of the civilized world. Then suddenly, in a matter of weeks, culminating in the Prussian victory over the Emperor Napoleon III at Sedan, Germany became the dominant country on the Continent, and the centre of European gravity swung from Paris to Berlin. For the following three-quarters of a century, Germany held the centre of the European stage. It took the two greatest wars that mankind has ever known and a combination of almost every major power in the world to oust her from this position.

I have always been fascinated by this dramatic turning-point. As long as fifteen years ago, as a student, I put a pack on my back and walked the road which the luckless Napoleon III had followed during the war of 1870. In that same month of August, I tramped from Saarbrücken—scene of the first ephemeral French victory, to Sedan—scene of the final ignominious defeat. However, I have not set out to write a military history; this book does not pretend to be a study of the Franco-Prussian war. Nor have I attempted a detailed political analysis of the Empire in its final, liberal stage. This is an account of events during the last days of the French Second Empire and, more particularly, of the fall from power of those two most controversial of nineteenth-century characters—the Emperor Napoleon III and the Empress Eugenie. As much as anything, this is the story of their personal fortunes during those six terrible weeks.

I have received a great deal of help during the writing of this book but my chief debt is to Mr Brian Roberts. Without his practical encouragement, it would have never been written.

xiii

I am indebted for information, material and advice to M. Louis-Napoleon Bonaparte-Wyse; Dr Anna Benna of the Haus-Hof-und Staatsarchiv, Vienna; M. Pierre Blanchard; Miss Y. d'Orleans; Mr Alfred Vital and Mr Brocas Harris. I owe thanks to those many people who have given me assistance during my visits to the battlefields of 1870. I am grateful for all the help that I have received from the Bibliothèque Nationale, Paris; the Library of Congress, Washington; the British Museum, London; and the many libraries and newspaper libraries in London and Paris. Three recently published books which have proved invaluable are *The Franco–Prussian War* by Michael Howard, *The Empress Eugenie* by Harold Kurtz, and *The Fall of Paris* by Alistair Horne. I should like also to thank the publishers of the following books for permission to quote copyright material: Hutchinson, *The Tragic Empress*, Marie de Garnier, Comtesse Des Garets (Skeffington, 1929); and Emperor Frederick's *War Diaries* (Stanley Paul, 1927). Empress Frederick's *Letters*, edited by Ponsonby (Macmillan, 1928). *The Letters of Queen Victoria*, 2nd series, edited by George Earle Buckle (John Murray, 1926).
1969

Imperial Paris
1870

The Emperor Napoleon III, in his efforts to revive the splendours of the reign of his uncle, the Great Napoleon, achieved at least one spectacular success: he transformed Paris into the most magnificent city in Europe. Of all the capitals on the Continent, none was more beautiful, more sophisticated, more cosmopolitan or more animated than Paris during the French Second Empire. It was truly *la ville lumière*, the Queen of Cities, the undisputed centre of the civilized world.

From the very start of his reign, in 1852, Napoleon III had turned his attention to the matter of aggrandizing his capital. The crowded medieval city was to become an imperial metropolis; Paris, decreed the new Emperor, must be 'the most beautiful city in the world'. To this end he had appointed the energetic Georges Haussmann as *préfet* of the Seine department and, for the following sixteen years, the so-called Haussmannization of Paris had been carried out with ruthless dedication. Wide boulevards were cut through the slums, whole areas of decaying houses cleared away and existing monuments stripped of surrounding clutter that they might be seen to better advantage. Palaces were enlarged, parks landscaped and new *quartiers* proclaimed. The city was embellished with trees, fountains, bridges, statuary, squares and thousands upon thousands of new buildings. The great glass domes of newly built theatres, emporiums, hotels and railway stations rose glittering into the sky. By 1870 Paris was a city of elegant thoroughfares, long vistas and triumphal arches; it was the matchless city one knows today. It became the model, not only for the other cities of France, but for capitals throughout the world. Rome, Madrid, Brussels, Stockholm and Mexico City owe their nineteenth-century refashioning to the example of Napoleon III's Paris.

No city has ever formed a more appropriate setting for the life of its period. The new Paris matched the mood of the Second Empire exactly. For one thing it made the ideal background for the parades and processions which were such a feature of the re-established Napoleonic régime. Few days passed without some swaggering cavalcade. One might see the Emperor's carriage, escorted by flamboyantly uniformed *Cent Gardes*, returning to the Palace of the Tuileries. Or the beautiful Empress Eugenie, with her *piqueurs* in green and gold and her postilions in powdered wigs, might be driving to the Château of Saint-Cloud. The young Prince Imperial, attended by a troop of white-robed Algerian horsemen, might be setting out for his daily drive to the Bagatelle. And there were less august processions than these. Helmets flashing, plumes fluttering, swords thudding and accoutrements all a-jingle, a detachment of cavalry might suddenly emerge through some archway to go jogging down the broad, chestnut-lined avenues towards the Champ de Mars. 'There seemed to be bands and banners or military displays almost every day . . .' wrote one enraptured visitor, 'congresses of *Orphéonistes* with gorgeous lyres on their standards, or of *Pompiers* with magnificent brass helmets . . . religious processions with choirs and hundreds of little girls in blue sashes, and statues of the Virgin Mary, or other saints, borne aloft. . . .'

On certain afternoons the crowds thronging the Champs Elysées and the Avenue de l'Impératrice would be diverted by the sight of an altogether more worldly cavalcade as a line of carriages bearing the *haut-monde*, and the *demi-monde*, made its way towards the Bois de Boulogne. They were headed for the fashionable drive around the Lac Inférieur—the larger of the two lakes in the newly laid-out park. A seemingly endless procession of coupés, victorias, phaetons, landaus, calèches, daumonts and barouches would go bowling along under the trees, their occupants ranging from the hat-tipping Emperor himself to the latest and most skittish *demi-mondaine*. In fact, it was the *demi-monde* that stole this particular show. In their brilliantly coloured, satin-upholstered carriages, their extravagant clothes, their flashing jewellery and their dyed hair, they paraded themselves—haughtily or provocatively—before the astonished eyes of foreign sightseers. Indeed, in such profusion did the courtesans of the Second Empire crowd the drive around the Lac Inférieur that they became known as the Ladies of the Lake. To one onlooker, remembering, in his old age, that line of gleaming carriages stretching all the way from the Place Grande-Cascade in the Bois to the Place de la Concorde in front of the Tuileries—'all flooded with purple light by the setting sun'—it seemed like a fairytale.

At night, the scene was no less memorable. Even without the cascade of fireworks that invariably marked the visit of some royal guest (and they came thick and fast) the city seemed ablaze with light. The miracle of gaslighting turned night into day; as the 'Hour of Absinthe' approached, the city was said to look like a scene from the Arabian Nights. At the famous pleasure gardens, the Jardin Mabille, no fewer than five thousand multi-coloured gas jets illuminated the open-air dance floor. To the wonderment of the patrons, glass globes, shaped and coloured like fruit, gleamed garishly amidst the gilded zinc foliage of imitation palm trees. When, on the occasion of a ball at one of the embassies, the Emperor and Empress entered the completely refashioned ballroom, a battery of red and green lights suddenly illuminated a cascade of real water tumbling over stucco rocks. 'The water looked like a torrent of fiery lava *en miniature*,' noted one enchanted guest. 'It was thrilling.'

Most spectacular of all were the great State balls at the Tuileries. Huge bonfires would be burning in the Place du Carrousel for the benefit of the waiting carriages and every window in the façade of the palace would be blazing with light. The gardens would be festooned with coloured lanterns and the terrace adazzle with the latest invention—electric light. Motionless *Cent Gardes*, in the splendour of their sky-blue tunics and silver cuirasses, would line the State entrance and the grand staircase. In the Salon Louis XIV, under a painting of the Grand Monarque himself, the Emperor and Empress would receive any royal guests and the members of the *corps diplomatique* 'The Emperor,' noted one guest, 'did not appear to advantage in his white silk tights and stockings,' but the Empress, in white tulle, spangled all over with silver stars and with diamonds glittering

5

in her red-gold hair, looked superb. The presentations over, a procession would form up and make its way to the Salle des Maréchaux where the rest of the guests were assembled. Behind the sovereigns and their royal visitors would come the various Bonaparte princes and princesses, the foreign ambassadors and envoys, the marshals of France, the presidents of the senate and the *corps législatif*. There would be masters of ceremony in violet, prefects of the palace in amaranth, chamberlains in scarlet, equerries in green, orderlies in pale blue and officers of the hunt in green and silver. The aides-de-camp would be in full military uniform, the ushers in brown and gold, the footmen in green and gold and scarlet, the beadles in plumed hats and broad red baldrics embroidered with imperial eagles.

Through the Salle du Trône, the Salon d'Apollon and the Salon du Premier Consul this impressive cortège would pass and, at the entrance to the Salle des Maréchaux, hung with gold and crimson, the chief usher would cry out, '*L'Empereur! L'Impératrice!*' His cry would be echoed by the beadles, striking the marble floors with their staves. As the company entered the immense hall, hung with chandeliers, banked with hydrangeas and filled with a brilliantly dressed crowd, the band would strike up the anthem of the Second Empire, 'Partant pour la Syrie'. The imperial procession would wind through the throng of bowing men and curtsying women to take its place on the canopied dais at the far end of the hall. The Emperor would offer his hand to a princess, the Empress hers to a prince and the dancing would open with a *quadrille d'honneur*.

Outside, on the boulevards, the scene was hardly less brilliant. Here the movement was continuous. Over twelve thousand carriages passed along the Boulevard des Italiens each twenty-four hours; the pavements were thronged until well after midnight. In her home in the Rue de Courcelles, furnished in self-consciously Bohemian fashion, the statuesque Princess Mathilde Bonaparte might be giving a soirée. 'Here is the true salon of the nineteenth century,' enthused her most frequent guests, the Goncourt brothers, 'for its mistress is the perfect type of modern woman.' Her brother, Prince Jerome Napoleon, amidst the 'Pompeian-style' decorations of his new home in the

Avenue Montaigne, might be indulging in a rather different sort of entertainment. One of his many mistresses once complained that the audible presence of his wife, the saintly Princess Clotilde, in the next room, was *too* embarrassing. At the Austrian Embassy, the vivacious Princess Pauline Metternich would be giving a masked ball. That Paris had become, in the Princess's own phrase, 'the cabaret of Europe', was in no small measure due to her lively example.

There would be a continuous coming and going at the great clubs. At the Jockey would be the men of fashion, at the Union the old *noblesse*, at the Chemins de Fer the stockbrokers, at the Baby and the Sporting the wildest of the wild young men. The famous cafés and restaurants—Tortoni, the Maison Dorée, the Grand Seize—were crowded. At the Café Riche one might see Offenbach, Flaubert, Courbet, Dumas *fils* or, until his death in a madhouse in 1867, Baudelaire. At the Café de Madrid gathered the opponents of the imperial régime, such as the lion-headed Gambetta or the lanky Rochefort. To the Helder came the moustachioed officers of the imperial army in the glamour of their gold-laced, epauletted, frogged, braided and befurred uniforms. Down the stairs of the Maison Dorée the Duke of Hamilton, agreeably wined and dined, tumbled one night to his death.

While the strains of Strauss and Waldteufel might float across the boulevards from the great houses, from the cabarets would come the raucous voice of such singers as Thérésa, whose risqué songs would affect her wildly cheering audiences like 'garlic and spiced brandy'. At the *bals publics*—the Jardin Mabille, the Château des Fleurs, the Closerie des Lilas—the style of dancing was abandoned to the point of delirium. It was the Second Empire (not the *fin de siècle*) that saw the hey-day of the *cancan*. The astonished Mark Twain, visiting Paris a few years earlier, explained that to do the *cancan* was 'to dance as wildly, as noisily, as furiously as you can; expose yourself as much as possible if you are a woman; and kick as high as you can no matter what sex you belong to'. *Cancan* dancers such as the celebrated Rigolboche, who once crossed a boulevard stark naked to gratify a whim of the Duke de Gramont-Caderousse, were fêted like queens.

At the theatre things were scarcely less outrageous. 'We have been each night to the play,' wrote a visiting Englishwoman in 1870, 'and are much disgusted with the badness of the morals they exhibit. I hope real life is not as bad.' It was worse. The actresses themselves were more renowned for the looseness of their morals than for the extent of their talent. Hortense Schneider, star of Offenbach's *La Grande Duchesse de Gerolstein*, was referred to, with good reason, as *le passage des princes*. Blanche d'Antigny earned enough off-stage, not only to bedeck herself in diamonds, but to buy, and decorate in the most excruciating taste, a huge house in the Avenue de Friedland. Cora Pearl made far more successful appearances than in her shortlived role as Cupid in Offenbach's *Orphée aux Enfers*; once, to a party of appreciative gentlemen at the Maison Dorée, she had herself served up on a huge silver salver, quite naked but for a sprinkling of parsley.

Indeed, it was for its licentiousness, as much as for anything else, that Second Empire Paris became renowned. The claim of Dumas *fils* that 'we are marching towards universal prostitution' was hardly an exaggeration. From the Emperor, down through every level of society, to ragged little girls who sold themselves for a few sous, the Empire seemed given over to the pursuit of sexual gratification. The foremost caterers for these appetites were the great courtesans, those *grandes horizontales* who weer such a feature of life in the Second Empire. This was their golden age. The *vieille garde*, the dozen or so courtesans who formed the topmost rank of the *haute bicherie parisienne*, earned, and squandered, the most enormous sums of money. Cora Pearl, who charged up to 10,000 francs a night, was said to have spent £16,000,000 during her hey-day. La Paiva, who lived in a house of almost unbelievable opulence in the Champs Elysées, once set fire to a client's 12,000 francs and promised that while the notes burned, she would be his. He took advantage of the situation, says the diarist Viel-Castel, 'like a man that knows that time is money'. Their dresses were sumptuous, their jewels were priceless, their houses a dazzling amalgam of onyx, marble, bronze, alabaster and gilt. The decanters in La Paiva's Mauguin-designed drawing-room were, regrettably, too heavy to lift.

8

When some Jeremiah complained that 'spirituality and grace have yielded to flesh triumphant and the worship of banknotes', and that it was the *demi-monde* that now 'set the pace and tone of good society', he was not being too fanciful. The difference between the *haut-monde* and the *demi-monde* was becoming less noticeable by the year; duchesses were as immoral as courtesans and courtesans as rich as, if not a good deal richer than, duchesses. To society women, no less than to their menfolk, the courtesans were a source of endless fascination. On the occasion of a *bal masqué* given by Cora Pearl the insatiably curious Princess Pauline Metternich, leading a party of ladies from the Tuileries—all safely masked—invaded the famous *demi-mondaine*'s home. On leaving the ball, during which she had given full play to her acid tongue, Princess Metternich gave Cora's maid a generous hundred-franc tip. The courtesan revenged herself on her guest's insolent behaviour a day or two later by touring the Austrian Embassy during the Princess's absence and giving her housekeeper a thousand-franc tip.

This overlapping of different worlds manifested itself in other ways as well. The once firmly drawn lines between the various social classes were becoming increasingly hazy. Society was fast losing its old rigidity. Not only was the ruling family *nouveau royale*, but the *beau monde* was full of new titles, of people whose money, looks or wit had earned them an entrée. Sons of the old *noblesse* were marrying the daughters of the *nouveaux riches*; beautiful actresses were becoming duchesses. Nor was it enough to have money; one must be amusing also. Glitter was becoming hardly less important than gold.

Even the differences between the sexes seemed to be blurring. To the unfeigned delight of the imperial circle, Princess Metternich would swagger on to the stage at Compiègne disguised as a Parisian cabby, while the son-in-law of the Duke de Bassano, dressed as the gravel-voiced Thérésa, would give a saucy rendering of her celebrated 'Rien n'est Sacré pour un Sapeur'. The young Duke de Mouchy, husband of the Emperor's cousin Princess Anna Murat, was once arrested for dancing naked for the loudly applauding soldiers at the Pepinière Barracks. It was no wonder that Queen Victoria did everything she could to discourage her sons from visiting Paris, and that her daughter, the earnest Crown Princess of Prussia, complained of the mischief which the French Court 'and still more, that very attractive Paris, has done to English Society, to the stage and to literature! *What harm* to the young and brilliant aristocracy of London!'

This scintillating society was not, of course, representative of all France, or even Paris. The countryside was still full of aristocratic squires and hardworking peasants, the towns still full of simple clergy and stolid bourgeois, the cities still full of dedicated professional men, of honest shopkeepers and of underfed and sullen workers. There were men in serious discussion on questions of religious philosophy; there were writers of the calibre of Flaubert, Gautier, Sainte-Beuve and Renan; there were painters—unappreciated by either the régime or the general public—who were eventually to win fame as the Impressionists.

Nor were the results of Napoleon III's transformation of Paris all beneficial. Haussmann, in his passion for size and symmetry, had destroyed much that was old, beautiful or simply picturesque. Screens of swiftly growing chestnut trees could not entirely hide the tastelessness of some of the new houses. And if, by the creation of this system of grandiose roads cutting through the poorer quarters, Haussmann had lessened the chances of barricade-building by the mob, the higher rents which were the natural results of this aggrandizement had simply led to the creation of new, and still more dangerous, slums, farther afield. The Boulevard de Sébastopol was notable, not so much for its grandeur, as for the fact that it was a dividing line between the moneyed districts to the west and the workers' quarters to the east. If Napoleon III had indeed made Paris more beautiful, he had not, as originally intended, made it any safer or more content.

But to the casual visitor, spending a few weeks in Paris in that cloudless spring of 1870, none of this was apparent. He could judge only by what he saw. And coming from countries where the tone was set by such staid courts as Windsor, Berlin and Vienna, he seemed to have strayed into another world. Even to Frenchmen, Second Empire Paris had something of the fantasy, and the impermanence, of a dream.

'Eighteen years of luxury, pleasure, recklessness and gaiety, of gallantry and incomparable elegance,' remembered the Count de Maugny. 'It was for a short time—alas, too short a time!— like an apparition of the dazzling splendours of the eighteenth century.'

Part One

CHAPTER ONE

The Dynasty

1

By the spring of the year 1870, Napoleon III had been Emperor of the French for almost eighteen years. In the capricious France of the nineteenth century, this was no mean achievement. When, in December 1852, this dreamy-eyed nephew of the Great Napoleon had been proclaimed Emperor of the French, few had imagined that he would last so long. So little, in fact, had his fellow sovereigns given for his chances of staying the course, that they had hesitated to grant him official recognition. The Tsar of Russia could not even bring himself to refer to this upstart as *Sire, mon frère*—the form reserved for legitimate sovereigns—and had addressed him simply as *notre très cher ami*. To this studied insult the brand-new Emperor had replied, with characteristic dryness, that whereas one put up with one's 'brothers', one chose one's 'friends'. It had been left to Queen Victoria, alone among Europe's more sceptical monarchs, to show some perspicacity. 'It will however, perhaps be more difficult to get rid of him again,' she had written to her Uncle Leopold, King of the Belgians, 'than one may at *first* imagine.'

And Queen Victoria had been right. Contrary to all predictions, Napoleon III had indeed stayed the course. And not only had he stayed it but he had turned himself into the most powerful monarch on the Continent of Europe. In less than a decade, the Emperor Napoleon III, once looked upon as nothing more than a lucky adventurer, had forced the world to take him and his Empire very seriously indeed.

The going had never, of course, been easy. It had taken him half a lifetime of endeavour to make himself an Emperor in the first place. With the imperial succession passing to him on the early death of the Great Napoleon's only son—known as Napoleon II—he had dedicated himself to the restoration of the Napoleonic Empire. Starting with no apparent advantages other than the name Louis Napoleon Bonaparte (his father, whom Napoleon I had once made King of Holland, had been Napoleon's brother, Louis; his mother had been Josephine's daughter by her first marriage, Hortense de Beauharnais), he had refused to give up until his ambition had been realized. Two youthful and daring attempts at gaining the throne by force having failed, he had turned, at the age of forty, to a less flamboyant method. He had presented himself, in 1848, as a candidate for the Presidency of the newly proclaimed French Republic. Despite all his shortcomings—he was physically unimpressive and, because of a lifetime spent in exile, almost unknown to most of his countrymen—he had won the election by an overwhelming majority. To Frenchmen thirsting, some for glory, some for order and some for an embodiment of the continuing spirit of the Great Revolution, the name Napoleon had meant far more than all the electioneering promises of his rival candidates. Thus, in December 1848, this seemingly unassuming young man had been inducted as President of the Second French Republic.

From this point on there had been no turning back. There was an iron hand, it seemed, in the new President's velvet glove. By a bloody *coup d'état* in 1851 he had seized absolute power and a year later the French nation had been asked to vote on whether or not they wished to replace the Republic by a 're-establishment of the Imperial dignity in the person of Louis-Napoleon Bonaparte'. The answer had left little room for doubt. Almost 8,000,000 had voted YES; some 250,000 NO. On 2 December 1852, on the anniversary of the first Napoleon's great victory at Austerlitz, Louis Napoleon Bonaparte was proclaimed Napoleon III, Emperor of the French.

He could now give France all the order and the glory (if not much of the continuing revolutionary spirit) that she craved. By his marriage, early in 1853, to the Spanish aristocrat, Eugenie de Montijo, the country gained the most beautiful and spirited Empress in Europe. The birth of a son, known as Louis, Prince Imperial of France, ensured that the Empire would have an heir. His foreign policy was no less rewarding. In alliance with England, the Emperor's armies beat the Tsar of Russia in the Crimea, and in alliance with Sardinia, he freed northern Italy from the rule of the Emperor of Austria. Encouraged by his Empress, who had always had a taste for grandiose schemes, he transformed republican Mexico into a Catholic Empire, with Maximilian, the brother of the Emperor of Austria, as his puppet Emperor. He raised France to heights of prestige unknown since the days of Louis XIV and the Great Napoleon and by the brilliance of his Court, made Paris once more the capital of the world. By the tenth year of Napoleon III's reign, Second Empire France stood predominant in Europe.

Yet, for all the splendour of his achievements, the Emperor himself remained an enigma. Never, in fact, has a more controversial figure sat upon the throne of France.

Swept into power on a wave of nostalgia for the glories of the Great Napoleon's day, Napoleon III was one of the least Napoleonic of men. Victor Hugo called him *Napoléon le Petit* and, when set against his dynamic uncle, he seemed little indeed. For the inheritor of a great military tradition, he appeared singularly lacking in martial qualities; he neither looked nor behaved like a soldier. He was squat and, as the reign progressed, so did he become more paunchy. His legs were too short and his head, which lolled a little to the left as he walked, too large. His complexion, which had always been sallow, was becoming grey and puffy. His moustache, with its ends waxed to cat's-whisker points, tended to sag as the day wore on and his hair, for all the youthful auburn of its dye, was thin and ragged. His eyes, pale beneath their heavy, half-closed lids, seemed almost opaque. With his grave, immobile features he looked, they say, more like a sphinx than a Man of Destiny.

This same lack of animation marked his manner. 'Nothing,' he used to quote, 'is great that is not calm', and if there was ever any doubt about his greatness, there was none whatsoever about his calm. It was phenomenal. More often the listener than the talker, he would sit twirling the ends of his moustaches or stroking his little pointed imperial, leaving his companions to wonder whether he was taking in anything that was being said. He so seldom voiced his opinion and so rarely reacted visibly that it was almost impossible to know what was going on behind that blank façade. The words one spoke to him, complained one of his Ministers, were like stones flung down a well: one heard their sound but one never knew what happened to them. 'To fathom his thoughts or divine his intentions,' reported the British Ambassador, Lord Cowley, 'would try the powers of the most clearsighted.'

He never lost his temper. 'It's absurd!' was about as derogatory an exclamation as he would ever allow to escape him. When a clumsy servant once squirted a jet of seltzer water down his neck, he merely moved his glass to a more accessible position, without betraying so much as a flicker of irritation. On the sole occasion that he was known to have shown anger in public—when he rebuked an officer whose carelessness had led to a serious accident—the lapse so upset him that he remained wretched until, that evening, he sent for the officer and spoke to him with the utmost kindness.

The Emperor, declared Lord Normanby, was a gentleman 'from the crown of his head to the sole of his foot' and indeed, the Duke of Wellington's complaint that Napoleon I's main failing was that he was no gentleman, could never have applied to Napoleon III.

His charm, when he chose to exercise it, could be prodigious. To the melancholy, meditative manner inherited from his father, Louis Bonaparte, he brought all the seductiveness of his mother, Queen Hortense. His sincerity, his attentiveness, his rare flashes of humour were guaranteed to captivate any companion. Guests, arriving to criticize, came away enchanted. Even that normally acidulous diarist, Charles Greville, had to admit that the Emperor was perfectly *comme il faut*, with excellent manners and easy, pleasant, fluent conversation'. One of his earliest conquests had been Queen Victoria. His quiet charm, coupled with his somewhat buccaneer looks (he had been much younger then) had completely bowled her over. 'He is endowed with a wonderful *self-control*, great *calmness*, even *gentleness*, and with a power of *fascination*, the effect of which upon all those who become more intimately acquainted with him is most *sensibly felt* . . .' she had written in breathless fashion at the end of their first encounter. It was an opinion which was to be echoed time and again by those with whom he came in intimate contact. An ogre to some of his political enemies and a hypocrite to others, Napoleon III remained a man of unvarying warmth of heart to his intimates.

'The more I see of this man,' wrote Dr Barthez after seven years of close association with the imperial family, 'and the more closely I study him, the more attached I become. . . . It is really curious to see how strongly he was the instinct of practical benevolence, and the satisfaction he feels in doing good incessantly, wherever he goes.'

Stories of his kindness, his modesty and his generosity are legion. 'Gentleness,' wrote the Countess de Mercy-Argenteau, who claimed to be the last of the long line of women he loved, 'was the distinguishing feature of his character. . . . One could not be admitted into the Emperor's intimacy without becoming his enthusiastic admirer.'

Yet even the closest of his associates did not really know what to make of him. 'I love and admire him, but who can say he knows him?' declared the Countess Tascher de la Pagerie, who had been a friend since his boyhood. 'I believe that if I had married him,' his cousin Princess Mathilde Bonaparte once cried, 'I should have broken his head open to see what was inside it.' And the woman whom he did marry—the transparently honest Empress Eugenie—was often driven to near-distraction by the tortuousness of his mind and his methods.

What, in fact, went on behind that mask-like face? Did his silence denote strength of character or was it simply that he did not know what to say? Was he as astute as some imagined or merely a dreamer who had been lucky? Was Bismarck right in calling him 'a sphinx without a riddle' and in claiming that he was 'from afar something, near at hand nothing'? To his enemies his inscrutability was taken as a sign of callousness and duplicity; to his friends it denoted wisdom and sincerity.

And in a way, both friends and enemies were right. Lord Cowley knew what he was saying when he declared that the Emperor was 'a strange mixture of good and evil'. His opinion was echoed by the Austrian Ambassador, Baron Hubner. 'What a singular man!' exclaimed Hubner. 'What a mixture of opposites! Calculating and naïve, pleasure-loving and fond of marvels, sometimes sincere, sometimes impenetrable, ever a conspirator.'

There was contained in Napoleon III's character a wealth of conflicting traits: his mind was an amalgam of almost every opposing quality. He was a combination of tyrant and humanitarian, of strategist and drifter, of realist and idealist, of soldier and philosopher, of despot and democrat. He was a peace-loving man who was to lead France into three wars. He was an enthusiastic inventor of weapons who could not bear the sight of the wounded on the battlefield. He was a military dictator with an almost sentimental regard for the sufferings of the poor. He was an autocrat who professed a love of liberalism. He was a child of the Revolution and a son of the Church. He would set out to achieve the most praiseworthy results by the most disreputable methods. He seized power by a skilfully planned and ruthlessly executed *coup d'état* yet believed in stars and omens and portents. He was a man of simple personal tastes who presided over the showiest and most opulent Court in Europe.

While his luck held—which it did for the first decade of his reign—so was this duality of his mind assumed to be a strength rather than a weakness. He was pronounced to be calculating, subtle and far-sighted, a man of many parts. Misfortune, coming later in the reign, revealed otherwise.

It was the year 1859, the year in which he returned in glory from his campaign against the Austrians in northern Italy, which marked the turn of the tide. After this, as things began to go wrong, so did his ambivalence—his tendency to be all things to all men—cease to be an advantage. This very lack of definition, in fact, was responsible for the troubles which now began to close in on him. In the triumphs of the first half of the Second Empire were buried the seeds that were to grow into the disasters of the second half. The *coup d'état* of 1851, by which the Emperor had made himself absolute master of France, earned him the undying hatred of the republicans. The War of Italian Liberation, so seemingly successful, cost him the friendship, not only of conquered Austria, but of England, who took alarm at this resurgence of Napoleonic military glories; of the Pope, who saw in the establishment of an independent Italy the diminution of his own powers; and of the Italian patriots themselves, who resented the fact that, by concluding a hasty peace with Austria, he had not freed all northern Italy from Austrian domination as originally promised. Then, to placate an increasingly apprehensive Catholic opinion at home, the Emperor—so equivocal had his position become—was obliged to keep a French garrison in Rome to protect the Pope against the very Italian nationalists whose cause he had so recently championed. This, in turn, lost him the support of French liberals.

This same belief in the 'pri nciple of nationalities', in the development of 'completed nation states', which had led him into the Italian campaign, lured him into deeper waters still. It caused him to show sympathy for the insurgent Poles (thus losing him Russia's goodwill) and to sit helplessly by while Prussia, putting this principle into practice, set about unifying Germany. In 1866, in the fourteenth year of Napoleon III's reign, Prussia, in a campaign of unprecedented speed and brilliance, beat the Austrians at Sadowa, thus clearing the way for Prussian hegemony in Germany. Almost overnight, France was faced with a new and formidable rival, and Napoleon's fumbling efforts to extract some sort of compensation from Prussia as a reward for his neutrality were treated with contempt by the victorious Prussians. Count Otto von Bismarck, the Prussian Chancellor, was beginning to get the Emperor's measure. 'I have the impression,' he had earlier reported to his master, King Wilhelm of Prussia, 'that the Emperor Napoleon is a judicious and amiable man, but not so shrewd as the world thinks him.' Now, after Sadowa, he was sure of it.

In Mexico, too, Napoleon's earlier achievements were turning to ashes. The attempt to create a Catholic Empire in the New World came to grief when the growing threat of Prussia forced Napoleon III to withdraw his protecting troops from Mexico, abandoning his protégé Maximilian to the mercy of the Mexican nationalists. The Emperor Maximilian was captured, tried and executed. The news of the tragedy was confirmed on the very day that Napoleon was attending the distribution of awards at one of the Second Empire's most magnificent set-pieces—the *Exposition Universelle* of 1867. The Mexican disaster, claimed the Austrian Ambassador, was to the Second Empire what the Retreat from Moscow had been to the First.

It was thus becoming obvious, by the end of the 1860s, that the Emperor Napoleon III, so recently the master of Europe, was now floundering from one crisis to the next. His foreign policy was in ruins, his Empire was without allies and opposition to the régime within France itself was becoming stronger and more voluble by the day. Ageing, ill and irresolute, he was drifting, it was said, 'like a ship without a rudder'.

'So it all comes back,' complained one of his most devoted but outspoken adherents, the Duke de Persigny, 'to his character. It is impossible not to love and respect him, but he lacks a quality essential to great princes—severity, the faculty to punish as well as to reward. To see him at close quarters, as simple and modest in his brilliant fortune as the least of his subjects, the perfect gentleman without a shadow of personal pride or vanity, applying to every topic the greatest good sense, the most intrepid of men in moments of peril, it is impossible not to be charmed and conquered, and one understands the grandeurs of his reign. But if one looks deeper into his nature and witnesses the strife between his reason and his kindly heart, one pities this prince, so generous, so indulgent, for being unable to punish those who deserve punishment. How easily can this noble spirit be the victim of intrigue! Hence the errors, weaknesses and frustrations at home and abroad. . . .'

A less partisan, and more trenchant, summing-up came from that veteran French politician, Adolphe Thiers, who had been in opposition to the Emperor throughout his reign. France, said Thiers, had made two mistakes: the first when she took Napoleon III for a fool, and the second when she took him for a genius.

By the spring of 1870 the Emperor Napoleon III had indeed reigned for almost eighteen years. How much longer, it was wondered, could he possibly last?

2

The Empress Eugenie had come a long way in the seventeen years that had passed since her marriage to Napoleon III in

1853. Then she had been looked upon as little more than a strikingly beautiful *femme du monde* who had been lucky, or clever, enough to land a somewhat spurious Emperor. Now, at the age of forty-four, she could consider herself to be one of the leading figures on the European scene, very much of a personality in her own right.

Acceptance, for her, had come even more grudgingly than it had for the Emperor. He, at least, had been royalty of a sort, whereas she, by the standards of Europe's more established monarchs, had been very much a parvenue. It was true, of course, that her father, the Count de Montijo, had been a Spanish grandee of ancient lineage, but then her mother's ancestry had been decidedly less illustrious. The Countess de Montijo had been the daughter of William Kirkpatrick, a Scots wine merchant who had acted as Consul for the United States at Malaga. Although the young Eugenie had adored her father, his retiring disposition, coupled with his relatively early death, had ensured that it was in the care of her bustling, vivacious and ambitious mother that she had grown up. From spa to spa, from capital to capital, the Countess de Montijo had flitted with her two lovely daughters—the dark, modest Paca and the chestnut-haired, high-spirited Eugenie. When Paca was married off, most gratifyingly, to the rich and distinguished Duke of Alba in 1844, the Countess de Montijo turned her full attention to finding a husband for her second daughter. With the less pliable and somewhat unconventional Eugenie, her task was not quite so easy. It was not until five years later, when Eugenie was already in her twenty-third year, that the two Montijo ladies, on a visit to Paris, were presented to Louis Napoleon, at that stage still President of the Second French Republic. Eugenie, whose father had been an ardent Bonapartist, was immediately drawn to this grave and romantic prince; he, in turn, was captivated by her luminous beauty and independent manner. If he imagined, however, that he could win her by any means other than fair, he was mistaken: Eugenie, for all the free and easy cosmopolitanism of her ways, was one of the most virtuous of women. The more Napoleon came to know her, moreover, the more did he come to appreciate her many good qualities. She had, in addition, something of his own self-consciously heroic attitude towards life. She was certainly more than just a flashy adventuress. She seemed, in fact, to have the makings of an admirable Empress.

As Napoleon's plans towards re-establishing the Empire matured, so did his love for Eugenie deepen. Always a superstitious man, he became convinced that their destinies were meant to be linked. When one or two oblique attempts at finding himself a royal bride failed, he made up his mind to marry her. He proposed and Eugenie, more in love with Napoleon's career than with Napoleon himself, accepted. They were married, amidst scenes of garish splendour, in Notre Dame on 30 January 1853. The Second Empire was then less than two months old.

Eugenie's story, since those days, had been one of growing ascendancy; ascendancy not only over the prejudices against her background but over the conviction that she was nothing more than a beautiful woman with a flair for fashion. Somewhat overshadowed by the Emperor during the early years of the reign, it was she who by 1870 appeared to be overshadowing him. With her passion for politics, her lively intelligence and her assertive manner, the Empress Eugenie had gradually developed into one of the most fascinating and controversial women of the age. By the mid-1860s she was far and away the most notable royal consort on the Continent of Europe.

Her beauty was by now in full flower. The approach of middle age had done little towards dimming those celebrated looks. It is extremely difficult, at this distance in time, to appreciate Eugenie's rather special beauty; it had to be seen, they say, to be fully realized. Hers was essentially a beauty of colouring and mobility, all but impossible to record in paintings or photographs. Her skin was like faintly glowing alabaster. Her hair was as rich and lustrous as burnished copper. Her large, downslanting eyes, as variable in mood and colour as the sea and never without their boldly pencilled outline, had a peculiar, heavy-lidded attractiveness. Her profile had the aquiline perfection of an antique cameo. It was a sensitive, aristocratic and particularly Spanish face. In repose, it was a sad one.

But she was seldom in repose. It was her animation, in fact, that brought her beauty to life. Possessing a wonderfully natural grace, her every movement was a delight. Every tilt of that red-gold head, every turn of that slender neck, every flutter of those tiny hands, was an enchantment. She seemed incapable of making an inelegant gesture. Yet there was nothing studied about her demeanour; she was usually far too occupied with what she was doing to be aware that she was doing it with extreme elegance. When Augustin Filon, the Prince Imperial's tutor, first saw her at close quarters at Biarritz in the autumn of 1867, he was amazed at her lack of affectation. She stood there on the terrace of the Villa Eugenie, her face exposed to the ravages of the blazing sun, while she outlined the new tutor's duties. 'There was no posing, no striving after effect,' noted the young man, 'she was far simpler and more natural in her movement and in her speech than any of the ladies who surrounded her, and she seemed to think no more of playing the part of a pretty woman than of assuming the role of an Empress.'

When occasion demanded it, of course, no one could queen it better than she. By far the best-dressed woman in Europe, she wore her clothes with great authority, and on those gala occasions—the state visits, the balls, the soirées—which were such a feature of the Second Empire, she always looked magnificent. She had by now developed the stock traits of royalty: the ability to put people at their ease and the mind trained to remember faces, places and things. She was also a gracious and accomplished hostess. The passing of time, moreover, had brought an increasing awareness of her position and responsibilities. She was no longer *la Reine Crinoline*—the Empress with the exaggerated reputation for frivolity, extravagance and high-handedness. She was still a woman of great verve and energy but she was more dignified these days, and a shade disillusioned.

Her married life had not been happy. Where Napoleon III was one of the most sensual of men, Eugenie had little taste for the sexual side of marriage. She remained always cold and unresponsive. So chaste herself, she could neither understand nor forgive what the Emperor called his *'petites distractions'*. But not even his most devoted apologist could claim Eugenie's frigidity as the sole cause of Napoleon's philanderings; it was his most persistent weakness and he never made the slightest effort to cure it. 'As a rule the man makes the attack,' he once sighed, 'but I defend myself and sometimes I surrender.' In fact, he always surrendered. And each time Eugenie found out about a fresh surrender, she made a scene. As the Empress angry was not a pretty sight, Napoleon came to dread these attacks. It was her pride, far more than her heart, which suffered from her husband's frequent liaisons and, being so virtuous herself, she never could adopt the happy-go-lucky attitude towards infidelity so common amongst the licentious society of the Second Empire.

Nor was this the only point of disagreement between husband and wife. They were unalike in so many ways. Where Napoleon was indolent, tranquil and laconic, she was energetic, excitable and talkative. Where he was vacillating and devious, she was resolute and almost embarrassingly honest. Where he was circumspect, she was indiscreet. In the political sphere too, their creeds were utterly different. The Emperor, in his hazy way, favoured aspiring nationalists and had ideas of liberalizing his own régime; Eugenie, in her dogmatic fashion, championed the Pope against the Italian patriots, favoured the legitimate monarchies, and was all for Napoleon keeping power firmly in his own hands. As the reign progressed, so did he seem to be veering ever more steadily to the Left and she to the Right. That these differences of temperament and ideology should lead to frequent disagreements between them was inevitable.

But the theory, widely believed at the time—and since—that Napoleon III allowed Eugenie more and more say in affairs of State in order to avoid these harrowing domestic scenes, is much too facile. Nor is it true that the Empress turned to politics as a compensation for the failure of her married life. She had married Napoleon with a very lofty conception of their joint obligation towards France and it was a conception which never weakened. She had always known, she claimed, that she was destined to make her mark in the world. When, during her girlhood, someone had once said that women existed to mend stockings, she had felt confident that the remark could not possibly apply to her: 'I felt that there was a different *métier* in me,' she afterwards declared. She was cast, she did not doubt, in a more heroic mould. 'I was born during an earthquake . . .' she once told Augustin Filon. 'What would the ancients have thought of such an omen? Surely they would have said I was destined to convulse the world.' Eugenie, who always took herself very seriously indeed, took her politics no less seriously. She looked upon it as her duty, not only to play a part in affairs of State, but to keep the Emperor on what she considered to be the right road.

Napoleon, for a variety of reasons, encouraged her political activities. For one thing, he had a high opinion of her capabilities. She had acquitted herself very well as Regent during the Emperor's Italian campaign of 1859 and, on his return from Italy, he had arranged for her to attend all ministerial meetings. Trusting so few of his subordinates (he could never quite shake himself free of the lone habits of a conspirator) he was pleased to have someone so close at hand whose devotion to the imperial cause was unquestioned. However different their methods might be, they were both determined that the imperial crown should be passed on to their son. Her firmness, her honesty, her very outspokenness provided a refreshing relief from the aura of duplicity with which he surrounded himself. In the shifting sands of political compromise, Eugenie stood like a rock. In a way she had become his *alter ego*, personifying, as she did, the despotic rather than the democratic side of his nature. It has even been suggested that the Emperor encouraged the growing belief that the Empress was an arch-conservative; with his consort championing the clericals and the traditionalists, he was free to attend to the liberals. In the struggle between conservatism and radicalism, he would then be seen as steering a middle course.

Whether or not this was the Emperor's intention, the Empress certainly came to be looked upon as a reactionary firebrand. Although her political influence was never as real as a great many people imagined, she gradually came to be identified with all the régime's more disastrous ventures. The blame for the Mexican fiasco, for instance, was always laid squarely at her door. Indeed, it was she who, dazzled by the prospect of doing something for Catholicism, the Habsburgs and the prestige of the imperial régime, had encouraged the Emperor to undertake the foolhardy adventure. With her assertive manner and passionately expressed opinions it was easy to believe that she was a political force and that she now ruled, not only her husband but France as well. 'The Emperor yields to her in all,' announced Queen Sophie of Holland to Lord Clarendon in 1867 and professed herself shocked at the Empress's unpopularity. 'Hers is not a superior mind,' noted the Queen on another occasion. 'She is full of grace, she has high and noble inspirations but she is very fragile in mind, incapable of reflection, though for her own concerns she is shrewd and cunning.' In time, it was for her less attractive features—her arrogance, her impetuosity and her pride—rather than for her many admirable traits, that the Empress became renowned. As the French had always referred to the hated Marie Antoinette as 'the Austrian woman', so did Eugenie become known as *l'Espagnole*.

A contributory factor to the Empress's air of ascendancy over the Emperor was the worsening state of his health. Never really strong, he had been suffering increasingly from pains in the bladder during the last few years. Although his doctors had once diagnosed a stone, no treatment had been carried out, and the discomfort experienced by the Emperor during subsequent ministrations had made him ever more loath to be examined. His nature, moreover, was of a type that prefers a quick alleviation of the symptoms to a thorough treatment of the cause. As a result, his pain became worse. This in turn sapped his energy, clouded his brain and weakened his resolve. His tendency to evade, to procrastinate, to drift with the tide, became more pronounced as the years went by. At council meetings, he was often in a state of drugged and hopeless apathy.

Eugenie, on the other hand, was blessed with splendid health and on the rare occasions that she did not feel well, always took, and followed, expert advice. Her energy remained a source of amazement to the members of her entourage; in middle age she could still walk any girl off her feet. Just as Napoleon's poor health made him unsure and indecisive, her vigour gave her confidence. The contrast between their attitudes—hers resolute, optimistic and aggressive, his wavering, pessimistic and cautious—was clearly illustrated during the Sadowa crisis of 1866.

With Prussia's lightning victory over Austria at Sadowa establishing her as a new and powerful force in Europe, many considered it essential for France to assert herself now if she wished to avoid a future conflict with her aggressive young neighbour. At a hurriedly arranged council meeting on the morning after Sadowa, Eugenie enthusiastically supported the idea of massing troops on the Rhine while there was still time to gain some territorial compensation from Prussia as a reward for France's neutrality. Napoleon, racked with pain, hesitated to take so bold a step. None the less Eugenie's strong and impassioned arguments carried the day and the council decided on mobilization. The decision was to be published in the official *Moniteur* the next day.

It never was. During the night, away from Eugenie's insistent presence, the Emperor (swayed, declared Eugenie, by 'other influences') changed his mind and countermanded the council's decision. He could not face the risk of war. As a result, Prussia's military victory at Sadowa became a crushing diplomatic defeat for imperial France.

Although the Emperor had sound reasons for his change of heart, Eugenie tended to put it all down to the state of his health. 'I assure you,' she told Prince Metternich, the Austrian Ambassador, 'we are moving towards our fall. . . . He can't sleep or walk, and he can hardly eat. For two years he has been living in utter prostration, has not occupied himself with the government. . . .' It was at this stage that she began thinking in terms of her husband's possible abdication, with herself succeeding him as Regent for the young Prince Imperial. She was never one to doubt her own abilities. Whether or not she discussed the idea with the Emperor is not known. If she did, he probably responded to the suggestion in his usual fashion: he would postpone the decision until later.

Thus, as the 1860s drew to their close, so did Eugenie seem to grow in stature. At the *Exposition Universelle* of 1867, when the Emperor and Empress played host to all the crowned heads of Europe and half the world seemed to have come to Paris, it was she who was the cynosure of all eyes. While Napoleon, looking tired and uneasy (this show of magnificence was meant to fool others, not himself) chatted quietly in corners to visiting princes, Eugenie dazzled her royal guests by her beauty, her grace and her assurance. If there was any doubt about Napoleon's powers, there was none whatsoever about hers. A young Englishman visiting Paris the following year saw her at a little ceremony in the Tuileries Gardens at which the twelve-year-old Prince Imperial was drilling a company of cadets. 'On a bench overlooking the gravel in front of the Tuileries sat a very tired old gentleman, rather hunched together, and looking decidedly ill. I do not think I should have recognized him but for his spiky moustache. He was anything but terrifying . . .' noted the observer. 'Behind him stood the Empress Eugenie, a splendid figure, straight as a dart, and to my young eyes the most beautiful thing I had ever seen . . . wearing a zebra-striped black and white silk dress, with very full skirts—the crinoline was just going out—also a black and white bonnet. But it was the way she wore her clothes, and not the silks themselves, that impressed the beholder. . . . The Empress was a commanding figure, and dominated the whole group on the terrace—the Emperor, huddled in his seat, was a very minor show.'

Towards the end of 1869 the Empress went to Egypt to represent France at the opening of the Suez Canal. With so many of the projects championed by Eugenie turning to dust, here was one which had turned to gold. For many years, like a latter-day Queen Isabella of Spain, Eugenie had encouraged *her* Columbus—her cousin Ferdinand de Lesseps—in his determination to cut a canal through the isthmus of Suez. When the Khedive of Egypt invited her to the inauguration, she accepted without hesitation. She was an enthusiastic traveller and the ceremony itself would be exactly the sort of *grande geste* she adored. She sailed for Egypt, by way of Venice, Athens and Constantinople, that autumn, and on 16 November, her yacht led the first line of ships through the Suez Canal.

Many years later, when someone once asked the Empress to name the four most brilliant memories of her reign, she put the opening of the Suez Canal as one of the most 'dazzling' moments of her career. 'There was a real Egyptian sky,' she remembered, 'a light of enchantment, a dreamlike resplendence. I was awaited by fifty vessels, all beflagged. . . . My yacht, *l'Aigle*, at once took the head of the procession, and the yachts of the Khedive, the Emperor Franz Josef, the Prince Royal of Prussia,

Prince Henry of the Netherlands, followed at less than a cable's length. The spectacle was so supremely magnificent, and proclaimed so loudly the greatness of the French régime, that I could contain myself no longer: I was exultant!'

It was, in many ways, the crowning moment of her life.

3

As the Emperor grew yearly more irresolute and the Empress more unpopular, so did the hopes of the Bonapartists centre on the heir to the throne—Louis, the Prince Imperial.

In March 1870, the Prince turned fourteen. Small and slender, with his mother's features if not her beauty, he was a charming boy. Dressed, on gala occasions, in a black velvet suit with red silk stockings, a floating red tie and the Grand Order of the Legion of Honour aslant his chest, he made a delightful picture. In spite of having been raised in an atmosphere of the utmost artificiality, and of being not only a prince, but the only child of an elderly and doting father, he had developed into a surprisingly unspoilt youngster. This was largely Eugenie's doing. To counteract the Emperor's indulgence and the courtiers' petting, the Empress had been compelled to take a firm line with the boy. He could so easily have developed into an idle, arrogant and conceited little prince, demanding adulation as a matter of course. *'Plus héroique que tendre'* was how someone— much to Eugenie's gratification—had once summed up her character and it was a definition which could very easily have applied to her attitude towards her son. With Louis having inherited much of his father's softness of heart and dreaminess of temperament, she was determined to make a man of him. To some, in fact, her treatment of the boy seemed almost too harsh. Inevitably—for almost everything that Eugenie did was misrepresented—it was whispered that she cared nothing for Louis, that she loved him as the heir to the throne rather than as her own son. 'There are three of us who love that child,' said Napoleon III's outspoken cousin, Princess Mathilde, referring to the Emperor, the Empress and herself, 'two of us with our hearts, *et la troisième avec son devoir*'. The claim was nonsense

31

and, as the years went by, so did Eugenie have the satisfaction of seeing her son grow into a well-mannered, modest and good-natured youngster.

It was not entirely due to Eugenie's firm handling, however, that the boy had turned out so well. There was an innate goodness about him which no amount of training could have produced. He was naturally kind and had a tactfulness far in advance of his years. He never sulked and he never lost his temper. Like his father, he was extremely well-meaning and would never voluntarily hurt anyone's feelings. Even in his mimicry, for which he had a marked talent, he was careful not to give offence. He had a rich vein of humour but he never laughed at another's expense.

He was not, unfortunately, as intelligent as could have been wished. Augustin Filon, taking up his duties as tutor in 1867, when the Prince was eleven, described him as positively backward. He was lively enough, with his high spirits bordering on hysteria at times, but when it came to his lessons, he seemed to have no powers of concentration whatsoever. 'I should say our only trouble with the Prince was an incessant restlessness,' complained Filon, 'an excessive nervousness that never allowed his limbs or his imagination an instant's repose. His body and his mind alike had a dread of the quietude we were forced to impose upon him. . . .' It was almost impossible to capture or hold his interest; his attention was so easily distracted. He would sit in his study in the Pavillon de Flore of the Tuileries, with beyond the windows the incomparable view of the tree-lined Champs Elysées, driving his tutor to near-despair by his inability to fix his attention on his work. He seemed to be in a state of perpetual absent-mindedness. The only indoor occupations for which he showed any enthusiasm were artistic: he had a passion, and a real talent, for drawing, modelling and amateur theatricals. For the world of books he showed no enthusiasm whatsoever. 'When, in order to re-animate his interest,' wrote the long-suffering Filon, 'I did my best to make him foresee the [literary] discoveries that were near at hand, wide horizons soon to be descried, his blue eyes became vague and lustreless, with that distressed look that comes from non-comprehension. I then used to have doubts as to the intellectual future of this boy, charming and good and pure as he was. Was he going to prove inferior to his destiny?'

Whether he was to prove inferior or not, however, it was a destiny of which he was fully aware and inordinately proud. That he was the heir to the triumphant Napoleonic tradition was something about which he needed no reminding. In a corner of his study stood the Great Napoleon's travelling library, its well-thumbed volumes once housed in that shabby villa on St Helena; in a glass-fronted cabinet were displayed those sacred dynastic relics—the famous hat, the grey redingote and the sword of Austerlitz; from the windows, across the sparkling waters of the Seine, could be seen the gilded dome of Les Invalides beneath which the great man lay buried. Once, at Biarritz, when the boat in which the imperial party was returning after a day's excursion struck a rock and started to sink, Eugenie cried out, 'Don't be frightened, Louis!'

'*Je m'appelle Napoléon!*' the boy answered magnificently.

In one important respect he was worthy of the name: he adored soldiering. Almost as soon as he could walk he had been bundled into uniform. At eight months he was a grenadier, at two years a corporal. At three he attended a review on his own pony and he was not yet four when he sat on the saddle-bow of his father's horse, watching the victory parade of the troops returned from Italy. The following year he accompanied his father to the great military camp at Châlons and there, among the bluff-voiced, fiercely moustached veterans, he felt thoroughly at home. When asked to propose the toast one evening, he leaped to his little feet and shouted '*à l'Armée!*' He had only to be told that his behaviour was 'a disgrace to his uniform' for him to mend his ways immediately. Unable to concentrate for five minutes on his books, he would spend what Filon considered tedious hours with his riding-master, Bachon, perfecting his horsemanship. 'I have never heard him complain of the length of those lessons . . .' sighed the tutor. In this field the boy's concentration certainly paid dividends. 'No other prince could match him, passing along the lines of infantry on a full-grown horse, moving at an even pace without the slightest deviation, despite the clash of the military bands and the reflection of the sun on the bayonets,' claimed one witness.

His games were all of war. On Sunday afternoons he and his friends would thunder across the terraces at the Tuileries, their 'scientific' military operations quickly degenerating into riotous hand-to-hand fighting, with Louis becoming so feverish that there was nothing to be done with him. When his blood was up he was completely out of control. He 'would have gone through a glass partition, a closed door, or jumped out of a window,' says Filon. 'He lost all idea of the possible, all idea of reality.' At the age of eleven he was given a 'military household' and so passed into the care of a governor, General Frossard, and four aides-de-camp. With the exception of Augustin Filon, there was hardly a man in the Prince's circle who did not wear uniform. It was no wonder that the boy looked upon soldiering as the only possible profession and on himself as a soldier first and foremost. Raised on tales of the *Grande Armée*, surrounded by gorgeously uniformed troops, escorted, on his afternoon drives, by bronze *spahis* in their billowing robes, he saw in soldiering a glamour and a romanticism that was sadly lacking in the schoolroom. Once, when on a visit to Toulon, his governor gave him an account of the famous siege which had set the young General Bonaparte on the road to glory. Much to the governor's surprise (for he shared Filon's estimate of Louis's mental abilities) the boy knew all about it. He even went so far as to break into the governor's narrative here and there in order to finish what he was saying. 'I was stupefied . . . and delighted,' admitted Frossard.

To his official duties, the Prince brought something of this same ardour. He had a warm and confident public manner, never imagining for a moment that the crowds wished him anything but well. He delighted in applause and loved driving through the streets, or better still, walking informally amongst the people, answering their salutes with his radiant smile. Once, at Bayonne, his tutor was astonished at the enthusiasm with which the young Prince was greeted; they could hardly get him away from the mob of excited women, some blowing kisses and others holding out their babies for him to touch. So fêted, so adored, it was no wonder that he lived in what Filon called 'a state of illusion', that his life had something of the unreal quality of a fairy-tale about it. The Empress used sometimes to worry about this cushioned existence. 'Has he any idea of wretchedness?' she once asked Filon. 'Does he even know what a poor man is?' *She* knew well enough, having been brought up in a somewhat Spartan fashion and having, throughout the reign, paid regular charitable visits—incognito—to the poor of the capital. She was all for taking Louis with her but the boy's governor whose word—where Louis's education was concerned —was law, decided otherwise.

It would have been impossible for Louis to live in France and have no idea whatsoever of the opposition to the Empire. On one occasion, when he was very young and was out driving with his governess, Madame de Brancion, he passed a group of workmen who did not raise their caps in answer to his friendly greeting. He was astonished. 'They are not very polite, those people,' he said. 'Why don't they salute me?'

Poor Madame de Brancion was at a loss. 'Those people,' she stammered, 'have their own preferences . . . they don't know you very well; they don't know your feelings . . .'

'Well,' answered the little boy earnestly, 'we must let them know that I love them dearly, that I love them all.'

It was a few years later that he came up against some more serious opposition. It had been decided that he would go to the Sorbonne one afternoon to present the prizes in the *Concours général*. As the Court was then in residence at Fontainebleau, Louis, accompanied by his governor and his tutor, travelled up to Paris by train for the ceremony. From the very moment of entering the hall, the two adults sensed a strain in the atmosphere, but the Prince himself seemed unaware that anything was wrong. He was politely if not enthusiastically applauded and for a while things went smoothly enough. His charm, or what Filon calls his 'simple, happy air' was having its usual effect. It was when he rose to present the second prize for Greek translation to a boy named Cavaignac that the trouble started. Young Cavaignac was the son of General Cavaignac, the Emperor's opponent in the presidential elections of 1848. A dedicated republican, Cavaignac had never forgiven Napoleon III for the *coup d'état* of 2 December 1851. The audience, alive to the drama of the moment, to the significance of a symbolic embrace between Empire and Republic, waited expectantly.

But as young Cavaignac rose to go towards the smiling Prince, his mother, Madame Cavaignac, motioned him to keep his seat. His refusal to receive his prize from the hands of Napoleon III's son was enthusiastically and aggressively applauded by his classmates. '*Vive Cavaignac!*' they shouted, and here and there was heard the dreaded cry, '*Vive la République!*'

Louis behaved admirably. It seemed as though he had noticed nothing amiss. Ignoring the incident, he went on presenting the prizes. But in the train home his two companions realized that he was keeping his head turned away from them and when he reached Fontainebleau he flung himself sobbing into his mother's arms. 'What can you expect?' remarked the Emperor quietly. 'Sooner or later Louis will have to face opposition.' The atmosphere at dinner that evening was very subdued. Louis's normally bright blue eyes were cloudy and the Emperor repeatedly stroked the back of his head. Later that night the Empress, always less adept than her husband at hiding her feelings, had an attack of hysterics: 'her cries and strident laugh which shook her body could be heard in all the *salons*', reported one of her ladies. The horrifying sound filled the entire Court with an unaccountable air of foreboding.

Such distressing incidents were very much the exception. In the ordinary way, Louis carried out his public duties in a glow of public approval. He accompanied the Empress to Nancy to celebrate the hundredth anniversary of the union of Lorraine with France. He went with his governor on a visit to the fleet. As official President of the *Exposition Universelle* he presented the awards; among the prizewinners was the Emperor himself and the public was enchanted by *le beau spectacle* of the alert young boy conferring an award on the adoring old man. However, the most memorable of his official journeys was to Corsica in 1869 to attend the centenary celebrations of the birth of the Great Napoleon.

The Corsicans adored him. 'The wild popular enthusiasm . . . leaped and gleamed about him like a fire,' says Filon, and wherever he went, the people crowded forward to get a glimpse of him. On the day that he visited the house in which Napoleon I had been born, the enthusiasm of the crowd was almost dangerous. When a futile attempt was made to keep them from surging into the house, the little Prince turned round and shouted in his young excited voice, 'Oh! Let them come in, they're part of the family!'

'No words,' says Filon, 'can describe the delirious joy of that mass of humanity, already vibrating with passion, on which that speech fell like a spark upon a heap of powder.' With one long, delighted cry, the Corsicans hurled themselves upon the flushed, bright-eyed youngster. 'I don't know how he got out alive!' one of his aides afterwards exclaimed.

How could one doubt, at times like this, that the 'little Prince', the 'Child of France' would one day sit upon the imperial throne? 'It is through this child,' the Empress claimed to have thought to herself at the Prince's christening, 'through *my son*, that the dynasty of the Napoleons will take final root in the soil of France . . . it is *he* who will put the final seal on the work of his father.'

4

Following the Prince Imperial in the line of succession was Napoleon III's cousin, Prince Jerome Napoleon, known irreverently as Plon-Plon. He was the only surviving son of Napoleon I's youngest brother Jerome, once King of Westphalia.

It was to the disagreeable Plon-Plon that Napoleon III had once quipped, on being accused of having nothing of the Great Napoleon about him, that he did, on the contrary, have his relations. The Second Empire was as replete with Bonapartes as the First Empire had been. And they were every bit as troublesome. Throughout his reign, Napoleon III was embarrassed by the behaviour of the various Bonapartes, Paterson Bonapartes, Bonaparte-Wyses, Murats, Bacchiochis and Cameratas who had come swarming to Paris on the establishment of the Second Empire. They quarrelled, they duelled, they ran up enormous debts; some of them even went so far as to oppose the Emperor's régime. In one important respect, however, these Second Empire Bonapartes were different from their First Empire predecessors: Napoleon III never repeated his uncle's mistake of entrusting the members of his family with positions of responsibility. The Second Empire was spared the rash of Bonaparte kings and sovereign princes which had, in no small measure, hastened the collapse of the First Empire.

Quite early in the reign, Napoleon III had divided his clamorous family into two distinct sections. One was known as the *famille civile* and the other as the *famille impériale*. The civil family, which had no rights to the succession, was made up of various female, disinherited or doubtfully legitimate branches. The imperial family proper consisted of the Emperor, the Empress, the Prince Imperial and the descendants of Napoleon I's brother, the late King Jerome. There were two of King Jerome's children living during this second decade of the Empire: one was Princess Mathilde and the other Plon-Plon.

Whatever characteristics Mathilde and Plon-Plon may have inherited from their father, his notorious frivolity was not one of them. They both took themselves very seriously indeed. Nor did they have anything of the submissiveness of their mother, Princess Catherine of Württemberg. They were both uncompromisingly independent. Mathilde was a plump, handsome, unconventional and outspoken princess, whose cultural enthusiasms had earned her the soubriquet of *Notre Dame des Arts*. Separated from her husband, the Russian Prince Demidoff, she lived quite openly with a painter by the name of Nieuwerkerque. Other than supplying the régime with an intellectual aura, so conspicuously lacking at the imperial Court, Princess Mathilde played no political role. Her brother, Plon-Plon, on the other hand, who at the age of thirty-seven had been married off to the sixteen-year-old Princess Clotilde, daughter of King Victor Emmanuel of Italy, considered himself to be one of the key figures of the Empire.

He looked like a somewhat bloated version of the Great Napoleon, or, as a visiting Austrian archduke once put it, like 'a worn-out *basso profundo* from some obscure Italian opera house'. But although Plon-Plon may have looked burlesque, he was no fool. He was intelligent, eloquent and idealistic; a dedicated liberal who was anxious to see a democratization of the imperial régime. A champion of those liberal and anti-clerical ideas which the Emperor Napoleon III himself was thought to favour, he was, in some ways, the Emperor's conscience. All this should have made Plon-Plon Napoleon III's right-hand man; instead, he remained a mere thorn in his side, the *enfant terrible* of the reign.

This was due to a certain perversity of temperament. Plon-Plon was never happier than when criticizing, attacking and undermining. His views might be sound but his manner of airing them was deplorable. Tactless, bad-tempered and erratic, he was incapable of inspiring trust or commanding sympathy. 'Prince Napoleon not very gracious,' was Queen Victoria's opinion of Plon-Plon; she found his manner 'rude and disagreeable in the highest degree'. He 'seems to take pleasure in saying something disagreeable and biting, particularly to the Emperor', she noted, 'and with a smile that is quite satanic'. Indeed, Plon-Plon was for ever bombarding the Emperor, both in private and in public, with advice. More than once his long-suffering cousin was obliged to rebuke him. 'From the day of my election as President of the Republic, during the Presidency and since the founding of the Empire, you have never failed to be hostile to my policy in speech and act. . . .' wrote the Emperor after a particularly critical outburst by Plon-Plon in the senate. 'I do not, of course, demand that your words should be a mere echo of my intentions and thoughts: but what I have a right to ask of a prince of my blood is that in speaking before the first body in the State he should at least clothe a difference of opinion, if such exists, in conventional language.'

If Plon-Plon was sometimes at loggerheads with the Emperor, he was always so with the Empress. There was very little love lost between him and Eugenie. He saw her as a reactionary ultramontane; she saw him as an ill-disciplined radical. He blamed all the more restrictive measures of the régime on her; she all its misdirected liberalism on him. To her, he was the Emperor's evil genius. As far as Napoleon was concerned, this sharp contrast between the political philosophies of his cousin and his consort was not unduly upsetting. Just as the Emperor was said to approve of the generally accepted notion that the Empress stood to the far right of him, so did he encourage the idea of Plon-Plon standing to the far left. This helped him maintain that middle position in the political line-up of the imperial family.

Plon-Plon's reasons for hating the Empress were not only ideological. Ambitious for power, he resented the fact that she was considered more important than he. On two occasions, during the Emperor's absence abroad, she had acted as Regent; he saw no reason why he should not have been entrusted with the task. 'The Empress is a fool,' he once exclaimed to Maxime du Camp, 'incapable of governing except among the dressmakers and yet she aspires to reign.' She could hardly wait, he claimed, for the death of the Emperor, so that she could rule France.

Nor did Plon-Plon leave Eugenie in any doubt about his feelings towards her. 'He loathed me . . .' the Empress remembered. 'At times he was positively carried away by fury; he raved, he foamed, he became demoniac!' Once, at a public dinner at Compiègne, when the Emperor turned to ask him to propose the health of the Empress, he refused. 'I wouldn't have stood such a performance,' claimed one of the guests, 'but you know the magnanimity of the Emperor, who regards him as a child and overlooks his tantrums.'

Plon-Plon despised the Prince Imperial almost as much as he did the Empress. He could never reconcile himself to the fact that Louis had a prior claim to the throne. Indeed, the birth of the Prince had so infuriated Plon-Plon that he had refused to sign the birth certificate. When finally prevailed upon to do so by his exasperated sister, Princess Mathilde, he signed with such a bad grace that he left a huge blot on the page. Since then he had always referred to Louis as 'that poor little brat' and was quite ready to assert that the boy was an imbecile.

He did nothing to hide his contempt for the Prince. Once, at Compiègne, Plon-Plon found himself alone with the boy in the *salon* in which the imperial princes assembled before dinner. Having nothing to say to each other, they moved forward to join the guests in another room. At the doorway Louis, from politeness and from fear of Plon-Plon, stood back to let him pass.

'Go on,' said Plon-Plon impatiently.

At the next door the same thing happened. Again the little Prince hung back, and again Plon-Plon, but even more gruffly this time, motioned him forward.

'Go on, then,' he barked.

At the third door, the last before the *salon* in which the rest of the company was assembled, little Louis made yet another attempt to let his cousin pass first. With a thrust of his great hand, Plon-Plon sent the boy hurtling through the doorway and into the room. Just managing to save himself from slithering full-length along the floor, Louis gave the company an embarrassed look and hurried to his father's side.

Although Louis might be put out by incidents such as this, he realized that they need not be taken too seriously. He knew that in his father's estimation Plon-Plon counted for very little.

As the Emperor's health deteriorated, so did Plon-Plon's hopes rise. He felt sure that he would soon be called upon to assume power. 'I am ready to act,' he once told his friends, 'and if any misfortune happened to the Emperor, it would certainly not be that simpleton of an Empress or that little brat of a Prince Imperial that they would fetch.'

By the year 1869 he was assuring Maxime du Camp that the Emperor was failing rapidly. Napoleon was more worn out than people realized, he said; there was no controlling hand any longer. 'The old man is worried,' claimed Plon-Plon. 'Recently he showed me a portrait of the Prince Imperial and remarked: "What will his destiny be?"' And, continued Plon-Plon, although France loved the Bonapartes ('of whom I am one, as you see if you look at me') she would never accept the rule 'of a woman and a minor'.

'If the Emperor dies, there will be a revolution,' he declared, 'and then my hour will come.'

CHAPTER TWO

The Liberal Empire

1

It was becoming increasingly clear, as the Empire neared the end of its second decade, that if Napoleon III wanted to remain on his throne, it would have to be by some way other than the pursuit of glory abroad. Almost every one of his foreign adventures had ended in disaster and his Empire, faced by a powerful and aggressive Prussia, was without a single European ally. Only by the consolidation of his position at home could Napoleon hope to secure the future of his dynasty.

Here the picture looked hardly more encouraging.

The régime which Napoleon III had established after his *coup d'état* of 1851 had been strictly authoritarian. All effective power had rested with the Head of State. His leading opponents had been ruthlessly imprisoned or exiled, the Press had been muzzled, political meetings banned and the *corps législatif* deprived of almost all its powers. Although the new constitution had allowed for elections, these were in the nature of window-dressing and the elected deputies were little more than puppets. The elections were significant only in that they acted as a barometer for measuring the amount of opposition to the government.

With the passing of the years, however, there had been a progressive, if sometimes barely perceptible, liberalizing of the régime. Whether the Emperor, whose motives were always obscure, was doing this for reasons of idealism or expediency was uncertain. There was a strong suspicion that these constitutional concessions were being forced on him and were not, as was claimed, being willingly granted in accordance with some grand design for the liberalization of the Empire. Nevertheless, in the ten years between 1860 and the end of 1869 the Emperor issued a series of decrees, each allowing the *corps législatif* more freedom of debate and question, and relaxing some of the more severe restrictions on the Press and public meetings. His aim, said Napoleon, after a further set of concessions in 1867, was 'to give to the institutions of the Empire their fullest possible development', but to many—the Empress Eugenie chief amongst them—the Emperor seemed to be not so much loosening his grip as losing it.

Yet side by side with this gradual relaxation of the imperial powers went a steady decrease in popular support. With each election the Opposition increased its vote. There were three main parties in opposition to the Emperor's régime: the Legitimists, the Orleanists and the Republicans. The Legitimists, who dreamed of a Bourbon restoration in the person of the Count de Chambord, drew their main support from the aristocracy, the clergy and the peasantry. The Orleanists, who planned to set up the Count de Paris as a constitutional monarch, were strong in financial and intellectual circles. The Republicans, ranging from moderate to radical, had a following amongst the industrial masses. Of these three parties, the Republicans were the most dynamic. Each election returned yet more Republican deputies to parliament.

However, it was not merely to appease this voluble Republican opposition that Napoleon was granting concessions. (Despite the increase in their representatives, there was never anything like a majority of Republican deputies in the *corps législatif*.) It was because of a new and progressive spirit amongst the Bonapartist deputies themselves that he contemplated reform. There was a gradual loosening of the once-unquestioned allegiance towards the régime; a shifting away from authoritarianism towards liberalism. A third force was emerging in the *corps législatif*: it was a force made up of government deputies favouring reform, and of opposition deputies willing to accept the dynasty, provided reforms were inaugurated. More than the increase in the number of opposition deputies, it was this regrouping in parliament which encouraged—or perhaps forced —the Emperor to grant further concessions. Once he had made the first move away from authoritarianism, he was compelled to keep going in the same direction. He had to move with the tide. 'March at the head of the ideas of your century, and these ideas follow you and support you,' he once declared. 'March behind them and they drag you after them. March against them, and they overthrow you.' He may not actually have been marching as boldly at the head of ideas as his maxim implied, but at least he was trying to keep up with them. In this gradual slackening of the reins of authoritarianism, the Emperor, said Adolphe Thiers, 'followed partly his own inclinations and partly the way things pointed'.

The general election of 1869 confirmed the trend of previous elections. The vote for the government, although still massive, had dwindled, while the opposition vote—mainly Republican—had risen by almost one and a half million. Not only Paris, but almost all the large cities of France had voted against the government. What made the results particularly disturbing was that the Republican votes were not merely—as in genuine democracies—against the governing party, but against the Empire itself. Then, in addition to the thirty Republican deputies, a great number of independents had been returned. Although these independents were not hostile to the dynasty, they were willing to support the Empire only on condition that it became more liberal. In their demand for reform, they were supported by a great many government deputies. This resulted in an entirely new situation in the *corps législatif*: on the right were the diehard Imperialists, on the left were the diehard Republicans, and in the centre a force composed of left-wing Bonapartist deputies and moderate independents. In other words, the old authoritarian régime had been undermined. The democratic sham had given birth to a democratic reality. The *corps législatif* was now a much more flexible body with a decidedly liberal tone which the Emperor could not afford to ignore. He must now choose between retaining what power he still held or granting a liberal constitution. The choice, of which he was perfectly aware, was outlined for him in a maddeningly smug but well-argued memorandum by his cousin Plon-Plon.

'The Emperor is therefore once more in a position to decide the destiny of France . . .' lectured Plon-Plon. 'If, by a change of policy and personnel, he enters on a course of constitutionalism and liberalism, if he agrees to sacrifice a part of his powers which is more apparent than real, there can be no doubt that he will be followed by the Chamber, and that his popularity in the country will be increased. Past mistakes will be excused; the Opposition, without being disarmed, will lose its influence over the masses; the Empire will strike its roots deeper than ever. If, on the other hand, the Emperor uses his influence to favour a reactionary clerical policy, if he continues to employ discredited and unpopular men like the present ministry, he may secure a passing success, he may dominate the country for a time, but he will be strengthening the republican, socialist, and revolutionary opposition of the future; and this new power given to it will be terribly dangerous when any crisis occurs at home or abroad . . .'

Plon-Plon was right. The Emperor must go the whole way and grant France a liberal constitution. Only by lifting the crown above party political strife would the Emperor be able to pass it on to his son. Liberty, it was now grandiloquently claimed, was to 'crown the edifice of Empire'. The once authoritarian Emperor was to become, if not exactly a constitutional monarch, at least a considerably less autocratic one and thus pave the way for an eventual parliamentary monarchy. Perhaps, in his heart of hearts, Napoleon would have preferred to remain what he was—an enlightened despot, a paternal autocrat, but by now he had very little option. In January 1870 he inaugurated the Liberal Empire. In some ways, Napoleon III's introduction of the Liberal Empire was in the nature of a gambler's last throw.

To head a new government formed by a coalition of a majority of Bonapartist deputies and the moderate independents, Napoleon III chose Emile Ollivier. Ollivier was a former anti-Bonapartist deputy who had gradually come to see eye-to-eye with the Emperor on the advantages of a democratic Empire. It had been Ollivier who, on the introduction of Napoleon's first concessions in 1860, had said, 'If this is the end of the road, you are lost, but if it is only a beginning, you are made.' The Emperor had kept an eye on Ollivier's career since those days and as early as 1865 he had been invited to the Tuileries for talks with the Emperor and Empress. He had come away enchanted. 'More than her beauty . . .' he had said of Eugenie,

'I was impressed by her ability to understand and discuss everything, by her resilient intelligence, her vivid talk animated by occasional flashes of wit and, occasionally, heated eloquence.' He found the Emperor, as did everyone, charming and well-intentioned.

But Ollivier had not been prepared, at that stage, to throw in his lot with the Emperor. Only now, in 1869, when he was quite certain that Napoleon honestly intended to abdicate personal power and to create a parliamentary democracy, did Ollivier consent to lead the government. There was one point on which he took a firm stand, however: for all his earlier admiration of Eugenie, he insisted that she be excluded from all ministerial and council meetings. With her reputation as a reactionary ultramontane, it would hardly do for her to be too closely identified with the new order of things. She complied, but with a bad grace. She was withdrawing, announced the official papers in somewhat defensive fashion, 'in order that opinions may not be attributed to her which she does not entertain and that she may not be suspected of an influence which she does not desire to exercise'. Yet once the Liberal Empire was an accomplished fact, it was she who encouraged her wavering husband to stick by it. She never pretended to approve of it but she realized, as Napoleon III never did, the advantage of sticking to something. 'I am deeply convinced that a consistent policy is the only real strength,' she wrote to him at this time.

The liberal government took office on 2 January 1870 and together Napoleon and Ollivier worked out a new constitution. That accomplished, the French nation was asked to vote on whether or not it approved of the new reforms. By the subtle phrasing of the proposition—did the electorate approve the liberalization of the Empire?—it was hoped to kill two birds with one stone: the liberals would vote approval of the new liberalism and the conservatives would vote for the continuation of the Empire. The question which was in fact being asked was whether or not the country still supported the Emperor Napoleon III. The date set for the plebiscite was 8 May 1870.

This was to be the third great plebiscite of Napoleon's reign. The first, held in 1851 to approve his assumption of supreme power after his *coup d'état*, had given him something like seven and a half out of eight million votes. The second, to pave the way for the establishment of the Empire the following year, had given almost an additional half million. In the eighteen years that had passed since that last plebiscite, however, much of the glory had rubbed off the imperial image. The Emperor had lost prestige abroad and confidence at home, and the Empire, for all the enduring glitter of its façade, was rocking on its foundations. Ollivier's so-called liberal government, claimed the fiery young Republican deputy, Léon Gambetta, was nothing more than 'a bridge between the Republic of 1848 and the Republic of the future; and it is a bridge which we intend to cross'. The plebiscite of 8 May would prove whether or not the eloquent Gambetta was right.

The results began to reach the Tuileries on the evening of 9 May. 'Those anxious hours will always remain in my memory,' wrote the Empress's *demoiselle d'honneur*, young Marie de Larminat. 'At first they were alarming, for the earliest results, those of Paris and the large towns, were decidedly unfavourable . . . the Empress became restless and easily upset, but the Emperor remained calm and smiling. As the night drew to a close, the provincial results began to drift in, and the early ones of the following morning brought only the triumphant ones. The final result was a massive vote of confidence in the Emperor. About seven and a half million votes were cast in favour of the Liberal Empire; not so many fewer than had been cast for the establishment of the Authoritarian Empire eighteen years before. The régime, quite suddenly, had taken on a new lease of life; 'confidence,' says Marie de Larminat, 'blazed like the dawn.' In England, *Punch* published a cartoon of France granting the Emperor and his son a new lease as tenants of the throne, and the Count de Paris, abandoning hope of an Orleanist restoration, made plans to settle in America. A crestfallen Gambetta admitted that the result had been a crushing defeat for the Republicans and that the Empire was stronger than ever, while his fellow Republican deputy, Jules Favre, advised a young friend to stay at the Bar, as 'there was nothing more to be done in politics'.

'The strength given to the government by this vote is such that the Emperor can with impunity commit every possible

47

mistake and remain unshaken on his throne,' claimed Ollivier. 'The fate of his dynasty is assured.'

The young Prince Imperial was with his tutor in the Pavillon de Flore, 'dreaming over a dictionary', when the final result of the plebiscite was brought to him. The sudden opening of the double doors was followed by the usher's cry of '*L'Empereur! L'Impératrice!*' and the sovereigns entered the schoolroom. Jumping to his feet, the Prince ran to meet them.

'Here, Louis,' said the Emperor quietly, 'is the final result of the plebiscite.'

Quickly the Prince read the figures and then looked, eyes radiant, at his father. To the watching tutor it seemed as if the Emperor was saying, 'It is you, my boy, whom they acclaim. It is your throne that is rising upon these seven and a half million votes. France is with us.'

2

The victory was celebrated in customary Second Empire fashion. There was a great ceremony in the Salle des États of the Louvre at which the results of the voting were formally presented to the Emperor, and there was a grand ball at the Tuileries. The scene in the Salle des États was as impressive as any of the many *spectacles* which had marked the past eighteen years of the reign. 'The Place du Carrousel,' says one observer, 'was ablaze with the trappings of war, the lace and stars of Imperial dignitaries, and all the brilliant uniforms of the military and civil servants of Imperial France. Never had the Empire looked more splendid or prosperous than when Napoleon III advanced, surrounded by his family, amid the acclamations. . . .' The Emperor, in his general's uniform, looked unusually animated. The Empress, in a dress of pale gold silk and a small hat of the same fabric trimmed with diamonds and osprey, looked radiant. The Prince Imperial was wearing, for the first time in public, his Guards uniform. Visibly moved, the Emperor spoke of his satisfaction at seeing the dynasty 'so firmly established' and assured his glittering audience that they would now be able 'to face the future without fear'.

The atmosphere at the *bal du plébiscite* was no less confident. The great rooms at the Tuileries were so dazzlingly illuminated and the gardens so aglow with coloured lights as to make the scene almost as bright as day. The Emperor and Empress circulated freely among the guests and, in answer to the thousands of congratulations, Napoleon, looking 'radiantly happy', murmured, *'Merci, je suis bien heureux.'*

But he was not as happy as all that. The results of the plebiscite, so seemingly gratifying to the uninitiated, were not entirely satisfactory. For one thing the Emperor's massive victory gave fresh heart—and voice—to the right-wing Bonapartists in the *corps législatif* which, in turn, caused some of the independent deputies to have second thoughts on the advisability of their recent close identification with them. Indeed, two of Ollivier's ministers resigned. For another, the results had revealed a disturbing trend. That the great industrial centres should vote against the Empire was to be expected, but that some 50,000 of the army should have voted *non* was more serious. To his old friend Lord Malmesbury, the Emperor confided his concern, but explained that the lack of support was due to the unpopularity of certain officers and to the profusion of new recruits. Over 300,000 soldiers, he added defensively, had voted for him. Lord Malmesbury, immediately alerted, answered that he had imagined the army to be 600,000, and not merely 350,000 strong. To this remark the Emperor 'gave no reply, but looked suddenly very grave and absent'.

With this observation, Lord Malmesbury had put his finger on a very sore point. The Emperor was deeply disturbed about the state of his army. A romantic in so many ways, the Emperor Napoleon III was a realist in military matters. It was, very largely, to the support of the army that he owed his position and it was to its reputation for invincibility that France still stood predominant in Europe. By no means exclusively a military man, Napoleon III had always made sure that his Empire remained unmistakably martial in tone. Under the Second Empire, the soldier was everywhere. Instead of *Liberté, Egalité, Fraternité*, grumbled Karl Marx, it was Cavalry, Infantry, Artillery. The *grands boulevards* resounded to the tramp of marching men, the Champs Elysées echoed to the clash of military bands, the Champ de Mars reverberated to the thunder of hoofs as the massed cavalry went charging past at imperial reviews. When the Emperor rode out, he was escorted by giant *Cent Gardes* in silver breastplates and horsehair streaming from their towering helmets. At the great camp at Châlons, while the cannon thudded out in honour of Napoleon's official birthday and thousands upon thousands of bayonets and lances glittered in the sun, the generals, 'gilded like archangels on the high altar', congratulated each other on the honours and awards gazetted in the latest *Moniteur*. On the colours, aflutter in the breeze and crowned by the Napoleonic eagle, were proudly emblazoned the new battle honours from the Crimea, Italy, Africa and the Far East. 'The varieties of cavalry uniform were innumerable,' wrote one observer, 'sky-blue lancers with Polish *tchapkas*, green hussars with fur busbies, helmeted blue dragoons and still more striking cuirassiers with breastplates well polished, towering plumes, and very big boots.'

It was all very splendid, but like so much else about the Second Empire, it was not quite as splendid as it seemed. For all the glamour of its uniforms, for all the panache of its bearing, for all the kaleidoscopic brilliance of its parades, the imperial army was not nearly as efficient a military machine as it should have been. It was neither as large, nor as well organized, nor as competently led as was generally supposed. It might have plenty of verve but it was sadly lacking in a great many more pedestrian but no less essential qualities. The campaigns in the Crimea and northern Italy had revealed an appalling lack of discipline and organization. The confusion had quickly been forgotten, however, in the self-congratulatory flush that had followed the two or three hardly-won victories. *On se débrouillera toujours* was the phrase that most aptly summed up the attitude of the imperial army and the fact that they had indeed always managed to improvise seemed to prove that the attitude was the right one.

Of the dangers of this outlook no one was more acutely aware than the Emperor himself. The Prussian victory over the Austrians at Sadowa in 1866 had brought home to him, more forcibly than ever before, the need to overhaul the French army. Unlike the majority of his countrymen, he did not attribute the Prussian victory solely to their possession of the new breech-loading rifle—the needle-gun—but realized that it was to their system of recruitment, their rapid mobilization and their orderly transportation that the Prussians owed their victory over the more cumbersome Austrian army. That France would be the next target of this formidable and well-disciplined force was becoming yearly more obvious. Bismarck, intent on welding the states of Germany into one unified nation under Prussia, had yet to bring the southern states—those lying nearest to France—under his control. The best way to accomplish this, other than by diplomatic coercion, would be by a successful war against the French Empire.

Thus, from the time of Sadowa, the Emperor began to concentrate his flagging energies on the problem of military reform. He could not have chosen a less opportune time. It would have been easy enough, in the days when he had held absolute power, to increase the size and strength of the army; now that he was liberalizing his régime, he was obliged to take notice of public opinion. And public opinion, for a variety of reasons, was dead against any change. It was feared that a more powerful army might be used as an instrument of oppression, that it would be squandered on the further pursuit of *la gloire*, that it would cost too much, that it would invite attack, that it would put paid to all hopes of disarmament and universal peace, that its formation would disrupt national life too drastically. The Left, growing yearly more powerful and more voluble, was firmly opposed to any further militarization of the régime. 'Do you want to turn France into a barracks?' cried the Republican deputy Jules Favre to Marshal Niel, the Minister of War. 'Take care,' countered Niel, 'that you don't turn it into a cemetery.'

Despite all opposition, Napoleon went ahead with his plans. France had hitherto relied on a relatively small army of professionals; therefore the Emperor's first task was to increase the number of recruits. Towards the end of 1866 he held a military conference at Compiègne. To achieve his target of a million armed men, he was anxious to replace the old system whereby a man could avoid military service by the buying of a less affluent substitute, with one of universal conscription on the Prussian model. With the conference considering this too drastic a change, he had to content himself with a reduction of the period of service of those men recruited under the old 'substitution' system (thus allowing for a speedier output of trained men) and with the formation of a force of part-time recruits known as the *Garde Mobile*. This way, he hoped to get an additional 500,000 men under arms. Even these watered-down proposals were considered too revolutionary when placed before the *corps législatif* and it was a very much emasculated version of the Emperor's original scheme that became law in January 1868. As it was, the formation of the *Garde Mobile* never really got under way. The government would vote only five million francs, instead of the fourteen considered essential to its effective implementation, and there was a reluctance on the part of the military authorities towards this arming of ordinary citizens. With republicanism widespread in all the great cities, it would be asking for trouble. 'To organize the *Garde Mobile*,' grumbled one imperial officer, 'will simply be to prepare an army for insurrection against the Government and society.'

If the army remained inferior in size to that of the Prussians, it was no better off in the quality of its commanders. The Emperor himself had almost nothing of the Great Napoleon's military genius. Except for the Italian War of 1859, he had precious little practical experience of warfare and his conduct during that campaign had not been such as to inspire confidence. Although never sparing himself, he had seemed to have only the vaguest idea of what he was about. Count Fleury, his *premier écuyer*, claimed that the Emperor could not master the movements of troops in the field nor even read a map intelligently. Aware of his shortcomings, the Emperor had had the good sense to have the records of his confused and contradictory orders destroyed at the end of the campaign. He was also far too sensitive to make a great commander. He had found the scenes of carnage of the battlefields of Magenta and Solferino extremely distressing. When the Swiss philanthropist, Henri Dunant, who had also been present at Solferino, inaugurated a campaign which resulted in the founding of the Red Cross, Napoleon III gave him every encouragement.

His generals were hardly more capable than he. The reputations of such men as Bazaine, Bourbaki, Canrobert and Mac-

Mahon rested on their achievements in Mexico and North Africa; not for a decade had they faced a European army and even then, when confronted by the equally inept Austrians, they had only just managed to snatch victory out of the general *mêlée*. Their experience was confined to the handling of small, swift-moving columns across arid plains and through rocky ravines; often little more than punitive raids, their campaigns had required more dash than organization. Administration was for the stolid Germans; the French commanders put their faith in *élan*.

To this business of organization the Emperor likewise turned his attention. A commission was set up to suggest ways in which the training, mobilization and concentration of troops could be improved upon but, as was the case for recruitment, the commission's proposals aroused so much opposition that they were gradually whittled away until they almost ceased to be of any value. Military expenditure was drastically cut by an unsympathetic *corps législatif* and with the inauguration of the Liberal Empire in 1870, all hopes of increased military spending faded. Emile Ollivier, embarking on an all-embracing scheme of social reform, needed all the money he could lay his hands on, and the Minister of War was forced to reduce his budget by thirteen million francs.

In the matter of weapons, the Emperor was somewhat more fortunate. The success of the Prussian needle-gun at Sadowa prompted him to put in hand the long-delayed production of the *chassepot*, a breech-loading rifle, superior in all respects to its Prussian counterpart. By the summer of 1870 there were a million *chassepots* available. Another highly regarded weapon was the *mitrailleuse*. This was an early version of the machine-gun: a bundle of twenty-five barrels, fired by the turning of a handle. Faced with the usual opposition, the Emperor was obliged to finance the *mitrailleuse* out of his own pocket. All his attempts to modernize the artillery, however, came to nothing. While the Prussians adopted Krupp's new steel breech-loading cannon, the French stuck to their old muzzle-loading pieces.

So all in all, in the four years between Sadowa and the plebiscite of 1870, the Emperor had accomplished very little in the way of army reform. He had the *chassepot*, he had the *mitrailleuse* and he had the beginnings of a *Garde Mobile*. How woefully inadequate these preparations were in the face of Prussian military efficiency, only he seemed to realize. By now, however, Napoleon III had lost both the ability and the inclination to force his will. Age and illness had sapped his resolve. It was so much easier to adopt a fatalistic attitude and to put one's trust, as did the rest of France, in the glorious traditions of the army. It must have been with considerable cynicism, nevertheless, that he listened, in the summer of 1870, to the boast of the new Minister of War, Marshal Leboeuf, that the imperial army was ready, come what may, 'to the last gaiter button'.

There was, of course, another method by which the French could equal Prussian military power: this was by the reduction of Prussian strength to something more in line with that of France. As is so often the case in periods preceding great wars, the air was thick with talk of disarmament, and the prospect of a general European disarmament provided Napoleon III with yet another straw to clutch at. The possibility of a reduction in arms spending would find great favour with the men of the Left whom the Emperor was trying so hard to woo; in fact, the irrepressible Jules Favre went so far as to put forward the somewhat tortuous argument that 'the strongest nation will be the one which disarms the most'.

Whether Prussia would be so enthusiastic about the idea was quite another matter. In January 1870 the British Foreign Secretary, Lord Clarendon, was asked by Emile Ollivier to broach the question of disarmament with the Prussians. He did so with faint hope of success. King Wilhelm of Prussia was far too proud of his armed forces to tolerate any change ('his army is his idol', wrote Clarendon to Queen Victoria), and Bismarck was far too astute to allow Napoleon this opportunity of achieving military parity. The Prussian Chancellor none the less allowed the disarmament negotiations to drag on for several months and it was not until April that year that the tireless Clarendon had to admit that it was 'useless to pursue the question further'.

The Emperor had once assured Clarendon that if 'anything like a challenge came from Prussia, it would be impossible for him to oppose the feeling of the army and the nation' and that he would be obliged, if he wanted to retain his throne, to make war. All that Napoleon could now hope for, was that no such challenge would be issued.

3

Unable to get the better of his prospective enemy, Napoleon III set about cultivating his friends. He did not, indeed, have a great many of these. In spite of the fact that for two decades he had dispensed hospitality on a scale unequalled by any other European sovereign, he had never managed to form any lasting friendships. Emperors and kings, princes and statesmen had flocked to Paris by the score, but with not one of them had Napoleon been able to establish an enduring alliance. For all the magnificence of his Court, his dynasty had never really been accepted into the charmed circle of European royalty and his diplomatic methods were such as to alienate any potential allies. No one seemed to trust him. His inscrutability of expression was thought to mask the most Machiavellian of schemes and his silence to hide the most sinister of intentions. Leopold I, the late King of the Belgians, had once complained that to live on the borders of Napoleon III's France was to be 'in the awkward position of persons in hot climates who find themselves in company, for instance in their beds, with a snake; they must *not move because that irritates* the creature, but they can hardly remain as they are, without a fair chance of being bitten. Heaven knows what dance our Emperor *Napoléon Troisième de nom* will lead us'.

Napoleon's most notable diplomatic triumph—the *entente* between France and Great Britain during the 1850s—was by now in ruins and Britain had once more withdrawn herself from European concerns. An alliance which, according to Queen Sophie of Holland, 'ought to have dominated the world, managed the affairs of the Continent and assured us an era of peace', had collapsed, and the British were once again firmly Gallophobe. Napoleon III had become far too aggressive for British liking. 'France,' wrote Queen Victoria in her emphatic fashion, 'must needs disturb every quarter of the Globe and try to make mischief and set everyone by the ears; and, of course, it will end some day in a *regular crusade* against the *universal disturber* of the *world*! It is really monstrous!' And when Carlyle contrasted 'noble, patient, deep, pious and solid Germany' with 'vapouring, vainglorious, gesticulating, quarrelsome, restless and over-sensitive France', he was merely expressing the sentiments of a great many of his countrymen.

With Russia, too, the Emperor's relations were distinctly cool. Napoleon III's championship of the Poles in their 1863 revolt against their Russian masters had not been forgotten by the Tsar Alexander II. Nor had a recent State Visit to Paris done anything to endear the Russian Emperor to Napoleon III's régime. His arrival had been greeted by shouts of 'Long live Poland!' and, on driving back one day with Napoleon from Longchamps, he had been shot at by a young Polish patriot. Napoleon's tactful observation that as the two of them had been under fire together they were now 'brothers-in-arms' was frigidly received by the outraged Tsar. He returned to Russia in a very bad humour. When, a couple of years later, Napoleon sent Count Fleury to St Petersburg to seek an alliance, the French approach was treated with disdain. Fleury was assured that the links between Russia and Prussia were far too close to allow for any Russian alliance with France.

From the Italians, Napoleon had more cause to expect gratitude. It was he, after all, who had made possible the establishment of the new Kingdom of Italy. Moreover, it was with the reigning House of Savoy that his dynasty had its sole royal link: the irascible Plon-Plon had married Princess Clotilde, daughter of King Victor Emmanuel II. But as long as French troops remained to protect the temporal power of the Papacy and thus prevent Rome from becoming the capital of the new kingdom, no Italian statesman was likely to sanction an alliance with France. Nor did certain recent French public statements do anything to improve relations between the two countries. A French minister of State had assured the *corps législatif* that Italy would *never* lay its hands on Rome ('You know in politics, one should never say "never",' had been the Emperor's comment) and General de Failly, reporting on a successful repulse of an attack by Garibaldi's men on Rome, announced that 'the *chassepots* had done wonders'. The unfortunate phrase led King Victor Emmanuel to reply that the *chassepot* had killed all hope of a Franco–Italian alliance.

There remained Austria. Here the Emperor had firmer grounds for hope of an alliance. With Austria having so recently been humbled by Prussia, she would be only too glad of an opportunity to reassert her position in Central Europe. In the summer of 1867 Napoleon and Eugenie went to Salzburg for an informal meeting with the Emperor Franz Josef and the Empress Elizabeth. They travelled by way of Karlsruhe, Stuttgart, Ulm and Munich, through the very South German states whose future hung in the balance. The warmth with which the French sovereigns were greeted along their route (there was a king to meet them at almost every station) seemed to indicate that these states were none too eager to be drawn into Bismarck's proposed Prussian-dominated Empire, and that they would welcome a Franco–Austrian alliance as a guarantee of their continued independence. The Salzburg meeting was marked by the utmost cordiality and was generally regarded as the first step towards a formal understanding between the two nations. The Empress Eugenie was particularly anxious for an alliance with Catholic and Legitimist Austria; the passion with which she argued in favour of it with the Austrian Ambassador, Prince Richard Metternich, was said to have left the Ambassador breathless. The Emperor relied on more oblique methods. Going behind the backs of his ministers and ambassadors, he sent secret emissaries to Vienna to open talks. By the beginning of 1870 he was assured that the Austrian army, which had recently been overhauled, was now ready for action and would be able, at six weeks' notice, to put 600,000 men in the field.

In March that year the Archduke Albrecht, nephew of the Emperor Franz Josef of Austria, paid an unofficial visit to the Tuileries. In the confidential negotiations which followed, the Archduke proposed a plan whereby Austria, Italy and France would send their armies into southern Germany, invite the uncommitted South German states to join them, and then march on Berlin. At the same time a powerful French fleet would sail for the Baltic sea. Although the Archduke stressed that the discussions were still at an academic stage, he promised, on his return to Vienna, to appeal to the Emperor Franz Josef to conclude a formal alliance.

When Napoleon, showing his hand at last, called together his generals to tell them of the Archduke's plan, he found them unenthusiastic. The Austrians were demanding six weeks after the declaration of war in which to get their army into the field; during that time France would have to face the Prussians alone. The generals suspected, not unreasonably, that by asking France for a six-week period of mobilization, the Austrians were merely playing for time. If the French were successful in the opening stages of the war, the Austrians would join them; if not, they would sit tight. Nor did the generals place much reliance on the South German states. They too, would be waiting for some sign of victory before committing themselves to France. The only possible way in which the Archduke's plan could be successful would be for all three armies—Austrian, Italian and French—to take the field simultaneously. The French army, the generals assured the Emperor, would not be strong enough to hold this particular position against the Prussians for six weeks.

In June, with his standing strengthened by the result of the plebiscite, Napoleon sent one of his aides-de-camp, General Lebrun, to Vienna to resume negotiations. As usual, the Emperor told his government nothing of his mission. In conversations with both the Austrian Emperor and the Archduke Albrecht, Lebrun was told that there was no possibility whatsoever of a concerted attack by the three armies. Austria still insisted on a delay of six weeks during which France would have to hold her own. However, if Napoleon turned up in South Germany, 'not as an enemy but as a liberator', said Franz Josef equivocally, 'I would on my part be compelled to make common cause with him'.

That was the best that Lebrun could get out of them. He returned to Paris late in June with the Franco–Austrian alliance no nearer realization. Napoleon III's Empire still stood alone.

4

Hardly less dangerous than the menace beyond the walls was the enemy within the gates. Napoleon III had as much to fear from the republicans as he did from the Prussians.

'France,' the writer Prévost-Paradol once said, 'is republican when she is under a monarchy, and she becomes royalist again when her Constitution is republican.' His maxim held good despite the Emperor's resounding victory in the plebiscite of 1870. The republicans might have been discouraged by the result but they had certainly not been defeated. After some initial despondency, they came to regard it as little more than a temporary setback. Gambetta could console himself with the thought that it would now rain so many liberties that the Empire would gradually drown. There seemed to be no reason why republicanism, which had been gathering momentum throughout the second decade of Napoleon III's reign, should not continue to do so. *Les Cinq*—the five Republican deputies who had been returned, in spite of all official pressure, in the elections of 1857—had swollen to thirty by the third election of the reign (the election preceding the 1870 plebiscite) and the government had lost almost a million votes. One of these new Republican deputies was confident that in the very near future, the *corps législatif* would be led 'inevitably, without disturbance, without rebellion, without use of the sword, without an appeal to subversive forces, and by the mere logic of events to inaugurate a new order of things'.

It was true that the republican strength was confined to the industrial areas (the countryside had always been conservative) but it was these areas, and Paris in particular, that tended to give the lead to the rest of France. It was in the capital, in unpredictable, fickle, explosive Paris, that régimes were made or destroyed. 'A shout from Paris,' it was said, 'and your crown flies off.' If Paris was not yet shouting, its voice (which, more than that of any other city in France, was the voice of republicanism) was certainly beginning to make itself heard.

French republicanism, during the Second Empire, embraced

an extraordinary diversity of peoples. They ranged from the most disinterested idealists to the most violent revolutionaries. There were politicians like Adolphe Thiers whose republicanism was scarcely distinguishable from Orleanism; there were the famous literary exiles like Victor Hugo and Louis Blanc; there were the habitués of the *salons* of Madame Juliette Adam and Madame d'Agout—deputies like the eloquent Jules Favre and the fiery Léon Gambetta; there were sharp-tongued critics like the lawyer Jules Ferry; there were journalists like Henri de Rochefort, in whose paper, *La Lanterne*, were published the most scurrilous attacks on the imperial family; there were dedicated revolutionaries like Auguste Blanqui, Charles Delescluze and Felix Pyat. Then there was the great mass of workers; for it was from *les ouvriers*, crowded into the slums of the great cities, that republicanism drew its popular support.

While the bourgeoisie of the Second Empire enriched itself to an almost incredible degree and France enjoyed such prosperity as never before, the workers in the cities remained underpaid, overworked and housed in the most sordid conditions. None of the gloss for which the Empire was so renowned had rubbed off on the poorer classes. It was said that over half the population of Paris lived 'in poverty bordering on destitution'.

That Napoleon III should be blamed for the state of affairs was both inevitable and justified. He had come to epitomize an economic system in which the rich became richer and the poor remained poor. Yet towards no section of the community did the Emperor have better intentions. He was determined, or, rather, he had been determined at the inauguration of the Empire, to use his power to improve the lot of all Frenchmen, regardless of class. His socialism was always of the Saint-Simonian type: he believed in a planned economy, an industrial society administered by men of science and industry for the benefit of the people as a whole. Poverty must be eradicated, not by charity, but by the provision of work. 'Nowadays,' he once wrote, 'the day of class-rule is over, the day of mass-rule has begun. The masses must be organized so that they can formulate their will, and disciplined so that they can be instructed and enlightened as to their own interests.' They must be given the opportunity, in fact, to help themselves. To this end, he embarked on a programme of social reform, introducing such things as old age pensions, provident societies and accident insurance. He legalized peaceful strikes and permitted the establishment of trade unions. He even planned a system of compulsory State insurance. No one was more generous than he in contributing to various philanthropic schemes.

Of Napoleon III's many sobriquets, perhaps the most apt was the one which took into account both the socialist and the despotic sides of his character—'Saint-Simon on horseback'.

Yet in this field of social reform, as in every other, the Emperor's achievements fell short of his intentions. His natural lethargy, the selfishness of the bourgeoisie, the conservatism of the peasants, the deep-rooted fear of working-class power, all combined to frustrate his efforts. The workers continued to be exploited. In their sullen dissatisfaction with the régime, they looked, in ever-increasing numbers, towards republicanism as the only sure way out of their misery.

As Napoleon III granted more liberties, so did republicanism become more voluble. The lifting of Press censorship and the relaxing of the laws on public meetings released a flood of invective against the régime. The shafts of Rochefort in *La Lanterne* became ever more deadly and the Emperor was openly slandered in public. The *Marseillaise*, forbidden for almost two decades, was once more sung in the streets. The elections of 1869 were accompanied by strikes and riots in almost all the large cities of France. At a gala soirée in honour of the Queen of Holland that year, the Place du Carrousel was filled with an angry crowd of rioters. 'Waldteufel's orchestra plays its most entrancing waltzes but only five or six couples venture on the floor,' noted a guest. 'When the music stops, one can hear the yells of the mob under the charges of the police.'

The *Affaire Baudin* of 1868 provided the republicans with an excellent platform from which to castigate the Empire. A recent book on the *coup d'état* had revived the memory of a minor revolutionary named Baudin who had been killed, in somewhat melodramatic circumstances, during the street fighting of December 1851. To provide 'the glorious martyr' with a more fitting monument than his present modest tomb, Delescluze, in his paper *Réveil*, opened a subscription fund. The unveiling of the monument was to coincide with the anniversary of the *coup d'état* and furnish the republicans of Paris with the chance of a demonstration against the Empire. Instead of ignoring the incident, the government brought Delescluze and his accomplices to trial. This gave Gambetta, who was defending Delescluze, the opportunity of delivering one of his most famous attacks on the régime. The Bonapartists, he said, claimed to have 'saved' France in 1851; why then had they never dared to celebrate the *coup d'état*? 'Well,' he cried, 'we will celebrate it every year till the country regains control and exacts expiation in the name of liberty, equality and fraternity.'

The accused were sentenced to pay various fines and serve various terms of imprisonment, but so elaborate were the precautions taken against a possible demonstration at Baudin's tomb that the government emerged from the affair covered with ridicule.

Affecting the Emperor more personally were the republican demonstrations against one of his cousins, Prince Pierre Bonaparte. Of all Napoleon III's embarrassing relations, Prince Pierre, a son of Napoleon I's wayward brother Lucien, was the most embarrassing. Early in 1870 he was involved in an incident which rocked the Second Empire to its foundations.

That January, Prince Pierre, whose perennially violent behaviour had debarred him from being received at his cousin's Court, wrote and published a political article. A certain journalist, a contributor to *La Marseillaise* (the notoriously anti-dynastic paper which Henri de Rochefort had founded in succession to his now banned *La Lanterne*) claimed to have been insulted by Prince Pierre's article. The journalist therefore challenged the Prince to a duel. The seconds who carried the challenge to Prince Pierre were two fellow-journalists named Ulrich de Fonvielle and Victor Noir.

When the two men arrived at Prince Pierre's home bearing the challenge, Pierre immediately lost his temper. He refused the challenge, claiming that his challenger was a mere tool of Henri de Rochefort, who, in his opinion, was the champion of '*la crapule*'. When the seconds insisted that they fulfil their mission, a scuffle broke out between the three men. Whether

Victor Noir did, as Pierre afterwards claimed, strike him across the face, is not certain; what is clear is that Pierre drew his revolver and shot Noir in the chest. Noir staggered out of the room, closely followed by Fonvielle. Pierre's bullet had struck Noir's heart. Within a few minutes he was dead.

The affair created an enormous furore. Prince Pierre was arrested that evening and imprisoned in the Conciergerie. The Republicans promptly turned the little-known Victor Noir (whose real name was Yvan Salmon) into a martyr. By that night his name was on everyone's lips. Over twenty thousand Parisians braved the five flights of stairs up to the little room where his body lay in state and on the day of his funeral, over a hundred thousand people crowded the streets leading to the cemetery. Enthusiasts unharnessed the horses and dragged the hearse themselves, while Noir's undoubtedly startled brother found himself carried shoulder-high along the route. As this singular cortège moved slowly through the dense, sullen crowd, there were cries of *'Vengeance!'*, *'Mort à Bonaparte!'* and *'Vive la République!'* By the time the bier reached the cemetery, the mob was in a dangerous mood and it was thought necessary to send a regiment of hussars cantering through the streets as a warning. A revolution was very narrowly averted that winter's afternoon.

When Prince Pierre faced trial, he pleaded not guilty, claiming that he had fired in self-defence. It was his word against Fonvielle's. Fonvielle swore that Pierre had flown into one of his well-known rages and had fired at Noir without any warning; Pierre claimed that Noir had struck him across the face and that Fonvielle had drawn a revolver on him. Nothing was proved and the Prince was acquitted of murder. He was sentenced, however, to pay compensation to Noir's parents. He went to Belgium, leaving the Emperor, who had made a point of having nothing to do with him all these years, to bear the full brunt of his recklessness.

Henri de Rochefort, in the meantime, was having a field-day. Were they living under the Bonapartes or the Borgias, he wanted to know. 'I was foolish enough to believe that a Bonaparte could be anything but an assassin,' he thundered. 'I thought an honest duel was possible in this family where murder and ambush are traditional. We weep for our dear friend Victor Noir, murdered by the bandit Pierre Napoleon Bonaparte. For eighteen years France has been in the bloody hands of these cut-throats, who, not content with shooting down Republicans in the streets, lay traps for them and murder them indoors. People of France! Have you not had enough?'

CHAPTER THREE

Summer

1

In spite of all the troubles crowding in on the Second Empire, one would have had to have been very perspicacious to appreciate that anything was seriously wrong with it during the summer of 1870. Superficially, things had seldom looked more promising. The Liberal Empire was well and truly launched; the prospects of peace had never, claimed Emile Ollivier, seemed better assured; the weather was perfect. Visitors flocked to Paris by the thousand. 'Good Americans, when they die, go to Paris,' quipped the Bostonian wit, Tom Appleton, but that summer the French capital was packed not only with live Americans, but with tourists from every quarter of the globe. To them, Paris was the most carefree city in the world, *en fête* from morning to night.

Something of this same air of joyous unconcern seemed to enfold the imperial Court. The result of the plebiscite had swept away almost all traces of tension and the members of the Household gave themselves over to the enjoyment of victory. 'After the trying year which had passed,' wrote young Marie de Larminat, 'the atmosphere seemed clearer, the intrigues of the Opposition to have simmered down, and a feeling of security reigned.' Augustin Filon, somewhat less naïve, reckoned that even if they dared not hope for permanent security, they could at least begin to believe 'in the possibility of a peaceful tomorrow'.

As soon as the plebiscite was over the Court moved from the Tuileries to the palace of Saint Cloud on the outskirts of the city. Among its many splendours—its opulent rooms, its balustraded terraces, its leafy park—they could forget the fears and uncertainties of the past year. A healing silence, broken only by the 'incessant whispering of the leaves and the distant murmur of the fountains' engulfed them. 'Saint Cloud had never seemed more beautiful . . .' remembered Filon, 'and never had I felt so intensely the atmosphere of majestic repose which, for me, belongs to this great residence.' Only twice a week would a line of carriages come bowling up the long avenue of chestnuts to deposit, in the palace forecourt, the ministers coming to attend the meeting of the council. For the rest, the Court amused itself with *char-à-banc* excursions into the near-by woods, with hilarious séances (spiritualism had always been popular with the imperial circle) or with endlesss talk beneath the trees. With the evenings so long and the weather so glorious, it seemed a shame to come indoors too soon.

The tone of the Court seems to have been particularly artless, almost juvenile, that year. It was as though the Emperor had already abdicated his position to the fourteen-year-old Prince Imperial. The palace seemed to be full of youngsters. Besides the Prince Imperial and his inseparable companion, Louis Conneau (the son of the Emperor's life-long friend, Dr Conneau), there were the Empress's two nieces (the children of her late sister Paca), the adolescent daughters of Madame Walewska, and the young maids of honour. 'This happy, playful, chattering world . . .' says Filon, himself still in his twenties, 'was indeed vastly different from the atmosphere of intrigue and plotting of a former day.' To the older, more sophisticated members of the Court, it was all too ingenuous by half. Those who remembered the great days of the Authoritarian Empire—the formality, the glitter, the licentiousness—were astonished by the transformation. 'It's like a boarding school!' grumbled one veteran. 'You mean a nursery!' muttered another. That archcynic, Prosper Mérimée, for many years mentor and confidant of the Empress, complained that he could not sleep for the peals of girlish laughter.

For the young people themselves, it was all enchantment. 'Nothing disturbed our serenity,' confessed Marie de Larminat, 'unless it were the melancholy face of the Emperor, which had never moved me more strongly.'

For the mood of euphoria which sustained the imperial circle did not extend to its two principal members. Both Napoleon and

Eugenie were feeling anything but serene. The Emperor, in addition to his worries about the army, the lack of foreign alliances and the future of the Liberal Empire, was becoming increasingly concerned about his health. He was by now in almost continuous pain. Madame Octave Feuillet, seeing him at a reception given by his cousin Princess Mathilde that year, was appalled by his appearance. 'He sat sombre and silent,' she noticed. 'His wan, expressionless eyes were fixed on the oriental carpet at his feet. The Empress appeared equally sombre. On the way out he whispered to her: "Quick. I am in horrible pain."'

On 3 July, the Emperor was finally induced to undergo a thorough medical examination. A secret consultation was organized by Dr Conneau. Five doctors, including a young surgeon by the name of Germain Sée, examined him and confirmed the nature of his illness. He had a stone in his bladder, the size, it was said, 'of a pigeon's egg'. Dr Sée, in his written report, advised an immediate operation, but the others disagreed. Marshal Niel, the Minister of War, had died in the course of this very operation the year before; the Emperor's life was too precious for the taking of any such risks. Dr Sée's report was shown to the Emperor who, in characteristic fashion, put it away in a drawer. It was never shown to the Empress. Had Eugenie realized the seriousness of her husband's condition, she might well have persuaded him to undergo the operation. She discovered the report among the Emperor's papers only after his death.

As for Eugenie, her depression stemmed from somewhat different sources. She was experiencing the chill wind of disillusion. Almost all the projects to which she had previously devoted herself with such single-mindedness of purpose had come to nothing. The Mexican Empire had collapsed, Napoleon was obviously about to abandon the Pope, the Austrian alliance was no nearer realization. The introduction of the Liberal Empire had clipped her wings in no uncertain fashion. Debarred from playing any part in affairs of State, she felt embittered and *de trop*. 'I would wish to put out of my memory everything in my life which has tarnished the bright colours of my illusions,' she had written to her husband from Egypt that winter. 'My life is over, but I can live again in my son, and I think the truest joys are those which come through his heart into my own. . . .'

Now when she was asked to assist in the furthering of some-one's career, she would promise to do what she could but would warn her applicant, with more than a touch of resentment, that he must never, for his own good, let it be known that she was interested in his career.

But Eugenie's spirit was too soaring (and her interest in pre-serving the dynasty too real) for her to withdraw herself, in a pet, from public life altogether. She still did what she could to help. Prévost-Paradol, for many years an enemy of the régime, had been won over to the Liberal Empire and accepted the post of Ambassador to the United States. Before leaving for Wash-ington that summer, he was advised to pay a courtesy call on the Empress Eugenie at Saint Cloud. He agreed, but with a bad grace. Eugenie went out of her way to make the call a success: she learnt as much about him as she could, she gave special instructions for his reception, she behaved in her most winning manner. All her efforts seem to have been in vain. She after-wards confessed to Filon that she had been disappointed at her visitor's 'chilling attitude'. As far as these new men were con-cerned, Eugenie had come to represent all the worst features of the old Empire—its authoritarianism, its clericalism, its belliger-ence, its theatricality—and they were not prepared to meet her half-way. It was no wonder that the Empress seemed quieter, and somehow disenchanted, that year.

There were times, however, during the course of this lovely summer, when even the Emperor and Empress seemed to have shaken themselves free of their preoccupations. Lillie Moulton, a young American whose beauty, vivacity and excellent singing voice had made her a popular guest at Court, tells of a picnic at the Grand Trianon in honour of the Archduke Albrecht. Preceded by outriders in green and accompanied by postilions in tricorne hats, the *char-à-bancs* went rolling through the forest of Marly and along the ruler-straight avenues at Versailles to the Petit Trianon. From there, in air 'deliciously balmy and warm', and 'filled with the perfume of lilacs and acacias', the imperial party strolled through the park to the Grand Trianon. With their surroundings recalling, so vividly, the mock-simplicities of the last days of Queen Marie Antoinette, Lillie Moulton found herself wondering 'if the same thought passed through the Empress's mind which passed through mine. Could history ever repeat this unfortunate queen's horrible fate?'

The thought had frequently passed through Eugenie's mind, for not only did she have a tendency towards self-dramatization, but she had a cult of Marie Antoinette. She had collected souvenirs of the ill-starred Queen throughout the reign and before many more months had passed, the 'horrible fate' of Queen Marie Antoinette was to be very much on her mind.

However, no such premonitions seemed to have marred the atmosphere as the party now sat down to a table spread beneath the *charmille* on the edge of the lake. The Emperor was in excellent spirits and the Empress showed concern only when, after the meal, the Prince Imperial went rowing on the lake. '*Prends garde, Louis! Ne te penches pas, Louis!*' she called out as the young Prince, in his usual exuberant way, went careering across the water.

It was well after nine that evening when they started back to Saint Cloud by a different route. A *piqueur*, finding a gate in the forest locked, had to wake the lodge-keeper. Wearing his night-shirt and muttering under his breath, the keeper fumbled sleepily with the locked gate. On realizing that it was the Emperor's carriage that was passing through, the poor man suddenly snapped to attention, waved his smoking candle and sang out a hoarse '*Vive l'Empereur!*'

'The Emperor,' says Lillie Moulton, 'was convulsed with laughter. I, who sat behind him, could see his shoulders shaking. . . .'

And so that brilliant June melted into July and the summer days grew warmer than ever. 'In this peaceful environment,' wrote Filon, 'it was easy to forget the existence of [Paris] ever seething with feverish agitation, but which was nevertheless still discernible, enveloped in its curtain of mist, from the highest windows of the eastern front of the palace.' But even in Paris the atmosphere seemed sanguine. At the end of June Emile Ollivier announced that in whatever direction he looked, he could see no thorny question being raised, and in England the Permanent Under-Secretary at the Foreign Office was able to claim that never, in all his long experience, had he ever known 'so great a lull in foreign affairs'.

2

Whatever similarities there might have been between the cities of Paris and Berlin, in atmosphere they were utterly unlike. If frivolity was the keynote of Second Empire Paris, sobriety was the chief characteristic of the Prussian capital. An earnestness pervaded every level of Prussian society, not only in Berlin, but throughout the country. From the King to the humblest peasant, the Prussians tended to take themselves very seriously indeed. 'Our poverty, our dull towns, our plodding, hardworking *serious life*, has made us strong and determined; is wholesome for us,' wrote the Prussian Crown Princess to her mother, Queen Victoria. 'I should grieve were we to imitate Paris and be so taken up with pleasure that no time was left for self-examination and serious thought!'

The Crown Princess need have had no fears on that particular score; her future subjects were hardly likely to imitate the Parisians. To the majority of Prussians, Paris—far from being the City of Light—was the City of Sin, the Modern Babylon, a latter-day Sodom and Gomorrah rolled into one. The average Prussian was much too pious, too stolid, too methodical for any such junketings. He was never one to give himself over to an unashamed pursuit of pleasure.

To this national serious-mindedness, however, there had been added, during the last few years, more than a touch of self-importance. This was due to an increasing awareness of Prussia's new standing in Europe. Under the skilled guidance of Bismarck, Chancellor since 1862, Prussia was being led to greatness. A successful war against Denmark in 1864 had gained her the Duchy of Schleswig; the defeat of Austria two years later had made her master of all northern Germany. It needed only the states of southern Germany to be stampeded into the fold for all Germany to be united under Prussia. Since her victory at Sadowa, Prussia, heading the North German Confederation, had become the second most powerful nation on the Continent, rivalled only by France. Thus, if the Prussians remained earnest, they were also becoming distinctly arrogant.

This blend of high-mindedness and high politics was not always a happy one. If one believed that might was right, that Bismarck's 'blood and iron' fashion of aggrandizing Prussia was the correct one, then well and good. It was those who were both earnest and altruistic who were caught in a dilemma. Prussian liberals, while approving of the unification of the German people, disapproved of the militant methods by which it was being achieved. Bismarck was fulfilling one of their most cherished ideals by the use of what they considered the most abhorrent of methods.

Nowhere was this uneasiness more apparent than at the Prussian Court. Seldom has greatness been thrust upon a less ambitious family. King Wilhelm was an austere, stubborn, simple-minded old man, utterly without pretensions to grandeur. Bismarck referred to him slightingly as 'an officer who does his duty, well-mannered with ladies'. However, King Wilhelm had two traits which were proving invaluable to his Chancellor: he was an unquestioning autocrat and a born soldier. The King's declaration, at his coronation in 1861, that 'I do not forget that the crown has come to me from God alone and that I have received it from His hands', showed that he was not one to be swayed by any new-fangled liberalism. This absolutism Bismarck put to good use. Equally useful to the Iron Chancellor was the King's pride in his army and his passion for soldiering. In fact, having once smelt powder, the King was likely to get carried away. Although he had had to be coerced into going to war against his fellow Germans in Austria in 1866, the Prussian victory at Sadowa had so excited him that it had been with the utmost difficulty that Bismarck (who always knew when to end a war) had been able to restrain him from pressing on to Vienna.

Thus, although there were frequent differences of opinion between the Chancellor and his master, Bismarck usually carried the day and could rely on King Wilhelm to sanction his schemes.

With Queen Augusta it was different. She hated Bismarck. A fussy, gregarious, frenetically-mannered old lady, with a head of old-fashioned ringlets and a leaning towards Catholicism, Queen Augusta did her utmost to counteract Bismarck's influence. She too, wanted German unification without Prussian aggrandizement. 'May Prussia be merged into Germany and not Germany into Prussia,' was her way of summing up her opposition to Bismarck's plans.

With these sentiments her eldest son, the Crown Prince Frederick, agreed. Tall and luxuriantly bearded, the Crown Prince was an intelligent, sensitive and liberally-minded prince but one who, as a dedicated soldier, found himself obliged to play a not altogether distasteful part in Bismarck's strong-arm methods. His wife, the Crown Princess Victoria, a more emotional character, found herself facing the same dilemma. She was torn between the liberalism imbibed, in such copious draughts, from her father, the late Prince Consort of England, and her pride in the military achievements of her husband's country. But to her, no less than to her husband and her mother-in-law, Bismarck was the villain of the piece.

This opposition within the royal family might annoy Bismarck but he never let it stand in his way. The support of the King was all he needed. With that, and with the enthusiastic help of Count Albrecht von Roon, the Minister of War, and Count Helmuth von Moltke, Chief of the General Staff, he was able to bring his schemes to fruition. Contrary to general belief, these schemes were never as methodically worked out as Bismarck afterwards pretended. The Prussian Chancellor, for all his celebrated shrewdness, was an opportunist; rather than issue challenges, he took advantage of them. 'Man cannot create the current of events,' he would say. 'He can only float with it and steer.'

He took care, however, to see that his boat was seaworthy. In the years between 1862 and 1870, in the teeth of the strongest opposition from the predominantly liberal Prussian parliament, the army had been sweepingly reformed. By the end of the decade, universal military service had ensured that the army was now a 'training school for the entire nation at war', and King Wilhelm, as Commander-in-Chief of the forces of the North German Confederation, had almost a million men at his command. It was the most formidable army that Europe had ever seen. Hand in hand with this building up of the armed forces went a perfecting of military organization. A highly efficient General Staff introduced new methods of mobilization, of railway communication and of deployment. The victory over Austria encouraged Moltke to think in offensive rather than defensive terms and by 1869 Prussian plans were ready. All that was needed was a war.

That this war would be against France there was very little doubt. War between the two countries seemed inevitable. To the majority of Prussians, France was the hereditary enemy. The conservatives were anxious to avenge themselves on the first Napoleon's victories (King Wilhelm had fought against France in 1814) and the liberals to forestall what they looked upon as French aggression. Europe was too small to contain two such aggressively patriotic nations—the one declining and the other burgeoning—as France and Prussia. Prussian nationalism was itching to assert, and French imperialism to reassert, itself. Mutually antipathetic, the two nations were bound to come to blows.

Bismarck, for all his ruthlessness (and as opposed to the Prussian General Staff) did not really want a war with France. For him, war was always a last resort. Commenting on the clash between Prussia and Austria, he once said, 'I had to try every way one after the other—the most dangerous last.' If the South German states could be brought into his proposed German Empire by any other way than war, then that was the way he would take. If not, then he would certainly not flinch from going to battle. By 1870, with the powerful Prussian army ready to act, it was simply a matter of waiting for some incident which could be used to complete German unification, either by diplomacy or war.

'A statesman cannot create anything himself,' he once said in sanctimonious fashion. 'He must wait and listen until he hears the steps of God sounding through events; then leap up and grasp the hem of his garment.'

His ear was cocked and he was crouched ready to spring.

Part Two

CHAPTER FOUR

The Hohenzollern Candidature

1

It was on Sunday, 3 July, that the bombshell burst. On that day the French Foreign Minister received a dispatch from the Ambassador in Madrid to say that Prince Leopold of Hohenzollern-Sigmaringen had accepted the offer of the crown of Spain.

The throne of Spain had been vacant for almost two years. In September 1868 Queen Isabel II, fat, oversexed and grossly incompetent, had been driven from her country by revolution. She had sought refuge in France and had since been living, with her children and her latest lover (her effeminate husband had taken advantage of this opportunity to set up a separate establishment) in a palatial home in the Avenue du Roi de Rome in Paris. Marshal Juan Prim, the statesman who had been largely responsible for her eviction and who was now Spain's Prime Minister, was anxious that the country remain a monarchy, provided that the monarch should not again be a Spanish Bourbon. To this end, Prim set about finding a new king for Spain. It was no easy task. The *Almanach de Gotha* was packed with possible candidates (there was always a Coburg to spare on these occasions), but not one of the many princes whom he approached was at all eager to exchange the security of his present position for the uncertainties of Spanish politics. Spain had always been a notoriously difficult country over which to reign. One after another Europe's reigning Catholic families declined the offer. By the summer of 1869 Prim had got round to the Hohenzollerns. He approached Prince Leopold, son of Prince Anton of Hohenzollern-Sigmaringen, a member of the Catholic branch of the Prussian royal family. He too, refused.

That Prince Leopold, a somewhat innocuous young man very much under the thumb of his father, did refuse was due not only to his own reluctance, but to the intervention of Napoleon III. For the Emperor of the French was very actively concerned in this matter of the vacant Spanish throne. As much as anyone, he wished to see Spain peaceful and prosperous, but he was determined that no prince in any way hostile to France should be allowed to mount the Spanish throne. If, at some future date, Napoleon were to find himself at war with Prussia, he could not afford to have an unfriendly Spain at his back. Nor would French pride, already smarting from a series of diplomatic defeats at the hands of Prussia, tolerate any further Prussian aggrandizement. Thus, when in 1869 the French Ambassador to Prussia, Count Vincent Benedetti, reported to the Emperor that the Spanish crown had been offered to Prince Leopold of Hohenzollern-Sigmaringen, Napoleon lost no time in instructing Benedetti to make it quite clear to Bismarck that France would never allow the Prince to accept. The candidature of Prince Leopold of Hohenzollern, he told Benedetti, 'is essentially anti-French; the country will not endure it and it must be pre-vented'. When Benedetti tackled Bismarck on the subject, the Prussian Chancellor was all affability. There was no question, he said, of Prince Leopold accepting the crown; France could rest assured on this point.

And so matters stood for the next few months. Not until February 1870, with all efforts at finding a monarch proving fruitless, did Prim again approach Prince Leopold. This time the affair was conducted in an altogether more resolute fashion. In the first place, Prim took the precaution of involving old King Wilhelm of Prussia in the matter; as good Hohenzollerns, Prince Leopold and his father Prince Anton were bound to abide by any decision made by the head of the family. Secondly, the negotiations were conducted in the utmost secrecy. Prim was making sure that Count Benedetti did not get wind of them this time. Thirdly, the redoubtable Count Bismarck began to interest himself in the matter.

Until this moment, Bismarck seems not to have been especi-ally concerned with the Hohenzollern candidature for the Spanish throne. He had tended to regard it as a family matter, pure and simple. By the beginning of 1870, however, he began to appreciate how very useful a weapon it might be in his task of unifying Germany. The task was proving more difficult than he had at one time anticipated. During the last few months the southern German kingdoms had shown an increased reluctance to be drawn into the Prussian orbit. Bavaria, Württemberg and Baden were becoming daily more hostile and within Prussia itself Catholic opposition to Bismarck was beginning to gather strength. Marshal Prim, moreover, had let it be known that if Prince Leopold did refuse the crown, it would be offered to one of the Bavarian princes. This would almost certainly put paid to Bismarck's plans for unification. A Bavarian dynasty on the throne of Spain would look to France and Rome, rather than to Prussia, for support and by maintaining contact with the 'anti-national' elements in Germany, would provide them with a rallying point. This was something which Bismarck could not risk.

What was needed to bring these reluctant kingdoms into the fold, reckoned Bismarck, was some issue—other than a religious one—which would lead to an upsurge of national feeling and the drawing together of the various states in a mood of defiant patriotism. An altercation with, or even a diplomatic triumph over, France, would be just the thing to create this mood. France must therefore be either provoked or humiliated. In the Hohenzollern candidature Bismarck saw his chance of doing just this.

He now threw himself heart and soul into the affair. In a long memorandum to King Wilhelm he urged the King to insist that Prince Leopold accept the offer of the crown. Here he came up against the first stumbling-block. Wilhelm was not at all agreeable. The whole project could lead to dangerous complications and humiliations and, as Prince Leopold himself was very much against the idea, the King had no intention of forcing his hand. Goaded on by Bismarck, however, King Wilhelm asked his daughter-in-law, the Crown Princess, to write to her mother, Queen Victoria, on the subject. The Queen, advised by Lord Clarendon, answered that she could give no opinion 'upon a matter in which no British interest is concerned, and which can only be decided according to the feelings and interests of the Hohenzollern family'. As this seemed tantamount to a promise that Britain would not intervene in the matter, Bismarck pushed ahead. A secret conference was held on 15 March attended not only by members of the Hohenzollern family, but, more significantly, by Bismarck, by Roon, the Minister of War and by Moltke, Chief of the General Staff. In spite of the pressure of this formidable triumvirate, Prince Leopold still refused. A relieved King Wilhelm was content to leave it at that.

But Bismarck was not. His agents were already flitting about Spain, doling out bribes to various Spanish deputies (once Leopold had accepted, his candidature would have to be put to the vote in the Spanish Cortes) and now the Chancellor himself tackled Leopold's father, Prince Anton, on the matter. By playing on Prince Anton's patriotism, his sense of duty and his vanity, the astute Chancellor wore down his resistance and got the Prince to accept the offer on behalf of his son. Prince Leopold, who throughout the negotiations had been little more than a cipher (although it was rumoured that his wife, a Portuguese infanta, was 'dying to be a queen'), agreed to the proposal. On 19 June he wrote to the King, telling him of his decision and requesting approval. With the gravest misgivings, King Wilhelm granted the request. 'I cannot but give my consent,' he wrote to Prince Leopold, 'though with a very heavy heart!'

Delighted, Bismarck had the news forwarded to Prim in Madrid. Prince Leopold's name could now go forward for his formal election by the Cortes. France would be confronted by a *fait accompli* and as she could hardly quarrel with the Cortes for choosing Leopold as their king, it would remain to be seen whether or not she swallowed the insult from Prussia.

The business concluded, Bismarck went to ground at once. He was thereafter blandly to assert that the question was one which concerned Spain and the Hohenzollern princes only and that he had had nothing to do with Prince Leopold's acceptance. But, by an extraordinary error in the decoding of the telegram from Berlin, Prim understood that Leopold's official acceptance could not be presented to the Cortes for a further three weeks; he therefore adjourned the Cortes until the autumn, intending to hold the election then. Any hope of keeping the news secret for several more months and of presenting France with a *fait accompli* was now gone. Within days the news was being whispered all over Madrid and Bismarck's machinations were obviously about to be exposed. In the circumstances, the best thing that Prim could do was to inform the French Ambassador that Prince Leopold had accepted the offer of the crown.

It was the Ambassador's telegram, carrying this momentous message, that reached the Quai d'Orsay on 3 July. The news was immediately recognized for what it was—a calculated slap in the face for France by Prussia. It set France aflame.

2

Almost the only person to keep his head during the following emotion-packed days was the Emperor Napoleon. He alone could appreciate how advantageous to France this premature uncovering of Bismarck's intrigues could be. Prussia was clearly in the wrong and if Prince Leopold could be induced to withdraw his candidature before his election by the reassembled Cortes, France would have scored a diplomatic victory.

But his was the voice of sanity in a wilderness of passion. Years of pent-up resentment against Prussia now burst forth and exploded heavenwards, carrying with it any such subtleties of diplomacy as might still have saved the situation. The Empress, echoing the nation-wide mood of belligerent outrage, was all for vigorous action; the possibility of 'a political triumph or war', reported Metternich, the Austrian Ambassador, 'has made her look ten years younger'. Nor was the Duke de Gramont, recently created Minister of Foreign Affairs, the man for circumspect measures. Vain, hot-headed and chauvinistic, he lost no time in announcing that 'France would go to war sooner than allow a Hohenzollern to rule at Madrid'. In a rousing speech to the *corps législatif* he declared that if Prussia did not back down and withdraw the candidature, the government would know how to fulfil their duty 'without hesitation or weakness'. The statement was greeted by fervent applause and much waving of hats on the part of the assembled deputies. Even the normally pacific Emile Ollivier was swept along with the tide. Not only was Ollivier anxious to prove that he could be every bit as firm as the diehard imperialists (he wanted to avoid the 'peace at any price' label) but, as a good democrat, he felt compelled to abide by the opinion of the majority of his countrymen. He made a public announcement to the effect that Prussia had slammed the door in his country's face and claimed that although his government wanted peace, it wanted it 'with honour'. Marshal Leboeuf, the Minister of War, stoutly declared that the army was ready to fight.

With all this bellicose talk ringing in his ears, Count Benedetti was now sent by the Duke de Gramont to Bad Ems, where King Wilhelm was taking the waters, to demand 'satisfaction' from Prussia. The King was to make a statement to the effect that not only did he disapprove of Prince Leopold's candidature but that he was commanding him to withdraw it. This King Wilhelm, politely but firmly, refused to do. But if Prince Leopold himself decided to withdraw, said the King to Benedetti, then he would do nothing to dissuade him. For the feverish Gramont, this was not nearly good enough. He bombarded poor Benedetti with telegrams, each more emphatic than the last, insisting that King Wilhelm issue a categorical renunciation of Leopold's candidature; otherwise, wired Gramont, 'it will be war'.

Then, quite suddenly, Prince Leopold withdrew. This, for the most part, had been Napoleon's doing. While his ministers were making inflammatory speeches and Gramont was demanding 'satisfaction' from the Prussian King, the Emperor had been resorting to less showy methods. He had asked the French Rothschilds to get the British Rothschilds to ask Gladstone to use his influence. He had approached King Leopold II of the Belgians (whose brother was married to Prince Leopold's sister) to write and tell Prince Leopold that 'the peace of the world' depended on his renunciation of the Spanish throne; the Belgian King, in turn, had asked his cousin, Queen Victoria, to urge Prince Leopold's withdrawal in order 'to avert the frightful storm which threatens the Continent'. He had sent a Rumanian agent (for the Emperor had been instrumental in placing Prince Leopold's brother Charles on the throne of Rumania) to talk to Prince Anton.

In the face of all this pressure, the Hohenzollern princes had capitulated. Prince Anton decided to renounce the throne on behalf of his son. The news reached Paris on 12 July, just nine days after the affair had first come to light. Napoleon, of course, was delighted, but hardly more so than King Wilhelm. 'A great weight has been lifted from my heart,' confessed the old King to his wife. The Emperor, appreciating how slight was the edge he had on Bismarck, urged Ollivier to make the most of the withdrawal in his announcement to the *corps législatif*. The news must be presented as a major diplomatic triumph and the matter then closed. '*C'est la paix!*' breathed the Emperor.

But France, by now, was in no mood for peace. Ollivier did the best he could but it was not good enough. 'Prussia is making a fool of you,' cried the excited deputies, and the Press dismissed the withdrawal as 'insufficient and derisory'. The truth was that instead of being relieved at the withdrawal of the candidature, a great many Frenchmen were disappointed. They had been left with a feeling of anticlimax, of having been cheated of their just revenge. General Bourbaki even went so far as to fling his sword to the floor in a fit of frustration and there were angry mutterings at Saint Cloud.

The cry now went up that a mere withdrawal of the candidature was not enough: Prussia, who had tried to humiliate France, must herself be humiliated. She must be forced to give a guarantee that the candidature of Prince Leopold would never again be raised. Only then would 'the honour of France' be satisfied. The idea of *garanties* was quickly taken up by the deputies, the Press and the crowd. Public opinion, dangerously inflamed, would be content with nothing less.

By few was the idea taken up more enthusiastically than by the Duke de Gramont. At five o'clock on the afternoon of 12 July he went to Saint Cloud for a meeting with the Emperor and Empress. Between the three of them (and without consulting Ollivier) they decided that Benedetti must be instructed to exact from King Wilhelm the promise that he would never again permit Prince Leopold to renew his candidature. The telegram was sent to Ems and the long-suffering Benedetti prepared once more to beard the Prussian King.

The stage was thus set for the famous interview at Bad Ems on 13 July 1870. Benedetti, anxious to get the matter settled as soon as possible, did not wait for the appointment which had been arranged for later that morning, but waylaid the King during his usual walk in the Kurgarten. As always, Wilhelm was the soul of courtesy and spoke to Benedetti of his satisfaction at Prince Leopold's withdrawal. When Benedetti raised the question of a guarantee, the King replied, with some coolness, that he was not prepared to commit himself any further. When Benedetti persisted, Wilhelm raised his hat and walked on.

Arriving to keep his original appointment later in the morning, Benedetti was told that King Wilhelm had nothing further to discuss with him. A telegram was then sent from the King to Bismarck, giving him an account of the interview.

Bismarck was at dinner with Moltke and Roon when the telegram arrived. He at once recognized its potential. By a little sharpening of its already sharp tone, it could be made to seem positively insulting. It would provide him with exactly that 'red rag to the Gallic bull' for which he was searching. By some slight but skilful editing, the King's treatment of Benedetti was made to appear distinctly high-handed. That the French Ambassador had suffered a polite but firm rebuff there could be no doubt whatsoever. The editing completed, the telegram (known, to history, as the 'Ems telegram') was released to the Press. Copies of it were also sent to all Prussian representatives abroad.

Its publication had precisely the effect that Bismarck had intended.

'You see before you,' cried the impassioned Gramont on receipt of the news, 'a man whose face has been slapped.'

'They are confronting us with war,' agreed Ollivier.

Yet the irony of it was that during the last few hours there had been a slight shift of opinion in favour of a peaceful solution among the council of ministers. Some of them were beginning to get cold feet. It had by now been decided that 'any honourable transaction' would be acceptable and a note to delay an earlier order for mobilization was drafted. When someone suggested the convening of an international conference to settle the matter, the idea was enthusiastically taken up and greeted, on the part of the exhausted Emperor, by floods of tears.

But there was by now little hope of getting the fevered deputies to agree to any such back-tracking measures. 'If we took the proposal to the Chamber,' declared Ollivier, 'they would throw mud at our carriages and hiss us.' As the day wore on (it was Bastille Day, 14 July) and one council meeting followed another, so did any way in which an 'honourable solution' might be achieved seem more and more difficult to find. In the face of Bismarck's calculated insult (by now the Ems telegram had been circulated to all the governments of Europe) France had one choice only: she must either swallow her pride or give it full rein. By nightfall the war party—always the more voluble—had once more achieved the upper hand, and shortly before midnight the majority of the council was persuaded into voting in favour of war.

On the following day, 15 July, Gramont in the senate and Ollivier in the *corps législatif* asked the members to vote the necessary war credits. The senate was enthusiastic but the *corps législatif*, with its dynamic Republican opposition, debated the matter for eleven hours. Not until Marshal Leboeuf had assured them that the army was ready, and Gramont had hinted that Austria and Italy were backing him up, and Ollivier had declared that he was accepting responsibility for war '*d'un coeur léger*' (he had to spend the rest of his long life explaining that what he had meant was a *confident* rather than a *light* heart) did the *corps législatif* pass the credits. But then they passed them almost unanimously.

The certainty of war was greeted with a roar of approval by the Paris crowd. For a week the city was in a state of delirium. To one observer it seemed as if the capital had suddenly been transformed into a vast lunatic asylum whose keepers had gone on holiday; or rather, whose keepers, almost without exception, were as mad as their patients. The population could hardly wait for nightfall on that fateful 15 July to start their illuminations: 'In the streets,' says a visiting Englishman, 'there was one closely wedged-in, seething mass, and the noise was deafening.' The summer night was filled with shouts of '*A bas la Prusse!*' and '*A Berlin!*'. Raggedly formed processions marched along the boulevards waving banners and singing the no longer banned *Marseillaise* and *Champs de la Patrie* at the tops of their voices. Troops of dragoons, cantering through the frenzied mob, were greeted with shouts of *'Vivent les Cuirassiers!'*, to which the men cried back, *'A Berlin!'* and *'Vive la France!'* A cabman, having driven a Prussian attaché to the station to join his regiment, refused to accept the proffered fare. A man did not pay for being driven to his own funeral, said the cabman. An equally droll bookseller rigged up a huge strip of calico on which had been scrawled the words, *'Dictionnaire Française-Allemand à l'usage des Français à Berlin.'*

At the Opera, Madame Marie Sass appeared on the stage in a white tunic and blue cloak figured with Napoleonic bees, holding in her hand a huge tricolour flag. Adopting her 'best dramatic attitude' and amid scenes of 'indescribable emotion', she burst into a spirited rendering of the *Marseillaise*. The Duchess de Mouchy who, by lucky chance, was wearing a white dress trimmed with red bows and a wreath of bluebells in her hair, rose to her feet and led the audience in singing the chorus. The spectacle ended with heartfelt cries of *'Vive la France!'*

'The really fine thing,' declared one naïve witness, 'is that there are no longer any party distinctions in Paris: there are neither Republicans nor Bonapartists: at the moment there are only Frenchmen . . . in the Place de la Concorde there were more than three thousand people who danced around the column, crying *'Vive l'Empereur!'*

In this uproarious fashion did France prepare to go to war. Anyone who mentioned caution was simply shouted down. When Thiers castigated the government for declaring war 'over a mere matter of form' when the Hohenzollern candidature had already been withdrawn, no one was prepared to listen. Friendless, unprepared and for the flimsiest of reasons, the Second Empire launched its attack on the most efficient military power of the day. Yet the theory that a headstrong France had been trapped into war to suit Bismarck's deep-laid plans for the unification of Germany is not quite accurate. Bismarck had indeed made use of the Hohenzollern candidature to provoke her but by then war between the two nations had become inevitable. Had they not gone to war over the Hohenzollern candidature in 1870, they would have gone to war over some other issue the following year. The military leaders in both countries were convinced that the sooner this happened, the better would be their chances of success. Both Leboeuf and Moltke felt sure that they were going to war at the best possible time. 'The moment is so well chosen,' wrote a member of the imperial Household, 'that it is said to be providential.'

Of the outcome of the war, the French had no doubts whatsoever. It was to be a swift and glorious campaign culminating in the most resounding of victories. When Ollivier declared that he was accepting responsibility for the war with a light heart, his slip did not sound nearly so terrible in July 1870 as it was to do in later years. It very neatly summed up the mood of the moment. So confident were the French generals that the campaign would be waged deep in the heart of the enemy's territory that they did not even bother to prepare or issue any maps of the French countryside; all the maps were of Germany. The Prussian army was dismissed, in the Military Almanac, as 'a magnificent organization, on paper, but a doubtful instrument for the defensive, and which would be highly imperfect during the first phase of an offensive war'. At Saint Cloud they were saying that the declaration of war had 'plunged the whole of Prussia into stupefaction; that neither the King nor his ministers were desirous of war'. Bismarck was said to be in a state of anguish lest all his work for Prussia be destroyed; 'he has everything to lose and nothing to gain; that is why he never wanted war.'

When Marie de Larminat wrote to her mother from Saint Cloud to tell her that she could not possibly take her holiday at the moment, her tone was sanguine. 'If the war lasts two months,' she wrote, 'I hope that the Empress will give me a little holiday this autumn. . . .'

On 18 July—the day of the formal declaration of war—the senators and deputies, all aglow with optimism, crowded into the Galerie de Diane at the Tuileries to deliver a loyal address to the Emperor. Eugène Rouher, heading the deputation from the senate, spoke for all France when he declared, in his expansive fashion, that Germany would 'soon be freed from the [Prussian] domination that oppresses her, and peace restored to Europe by the glory of our arms'.

The Emperor, in thanking him, spoke the first sensible words that had been heard during the whole of that flushed and boisterous week.

'Gentlemen,' he said quietly, 'we are entering upon a long and arduous war.'

3

On the evening of 17 July, Charles and Lillie Moulton, having been invited to dine at Saint Cloud, arrived at the château to find it strangely silent. As they stood in the echoing vestibule, a member of the Household came hurrying out of one of the *salons* towards them.

'Did you not receive my letter countermanding the dinner?' he asked.

When they assured him that they had not, he explained that, because of the imminent declaration of war, the dinner had been cancelled. The Moultons at once sent for their carriage, but as they stood waiting for it, a message arrived from the Empress to say that as they had already arrived, they had better stay.

'And stay we did,' says Lillie Moulton, 'and I never regretted anything so much in my life.'

To the two embarrassed guests, the evening had all the quality of a nightmare. As they entered the drawing-room, Eugenie came forward to greet them very briefly, but the Emperor, who had always been so attentive, said nothing. His guests had never seen him appear so old and ashen-faced before. Beside him stood the Prince Imperial, looking serious and preoccupied. When dinner was announced, Napoleon gave his arm to the Empress and led the Household into a small dining-room. Throughout the meal neither the Emperor nor the Empress spoke one word. The food was eaten in silence, with no sound other than the clink of cutlery to break the unnerving stillness. Telegram after telegram arrived for the Emperor; each would be opened by an aide-de-camp and placed before him. Every so often the Emperor would look across the table to the Empress with a 'distressed look' that tore at the heartstrings. It was no wonder that Lillie Moulton wished herself a hundred miles away.

After dinner they all returned to the drawing-room. Here things were no better. Both the Empress and the Prince

Imperial stood staring at the Emperor and the Emperor stood staring at the floor. The rest of the company remained as silent and as motionless as statues. Finally Eugenie moved forward and took her husband's arm. At the door she paused to say *bonsoir* to the Moultons. The Emperor stood a moment as though dazed and then, nodding his head, left the room. The Moultons said a hurried good night to the *dames d'honneur* and fled.

If France was indeed going to war with a light heart, its Emperor was doing so with an extremely heavy one. He understood only too well how pitifully unprepared was France for the coming struggle. He realized, better than anyone, that defeat would mean the downfall of his dynasty. He knew, as only he could know, what utter madness it was for him to take command of the army. For it had been decided that the Emperor must go to war. Despite the fact that he had only the slightest grasp of military strategy, that he was almost too ill to stand, that he was pessimistic, vacillating and exhausted, it was taken for granted that, as a Napoleon, he would lead his army.

'Is it true,' asked his cousin, the forthright Princess Mathilde, when she visited him at Saint Cloud on the day after the declaration of war, 'that you are taking command of the army?'

'Yes,' he replied.

'But you are in no state to do so!' she cried. 'You can't ride a horse any longer or even endure the jolting of a carriage. How will you manage on the day of battle?'

'You exaggerate, my dear . . . you exaggerate,' he murmured, but, admitting that he did not look too good, he made a characteristic gesture of fatalism with his hands.

With old Marshal Randon he was more frank. '*Je suis bien âgé, bien peu valide, bien peu apte à faire campagne,*' he sighed.

But now that war had been declared, Napoleon simply resigned himself to whatever might happen. He had always been a fatalist. He had always believed that what was written was written. Nothing that he could do would now change the course of events. The Countess de Mercy Argenteau, in her somewhat fanciful book of memoirs, tells of how the Emperor once visited her during this period and showed her his horoscope. In it was predicted the fall of the Empire. 'What is written in this paper has always proved true,' he is supposed to have said to her, 'and I have not the slightest doubt but that it will prove true to the end. Perhaps I ought not to have read it, though I am convinced that this would not have changed the course of destiny. . . .'

Perhaps he never said any such thing, but far more reliable witnesses have testified to Napoleon III's fatalism. Queen Victoria spoke of his reliance 'on what he calls his *star*, and a belief in omens and incidents as connected with his future destiny'. Lord Malmesbury, too, mentioned that extraordinary resignation which, he imagined, could come from no creed other than fatalism.

It was to this creed that the Emperor now submitted himself. 'In the passive strength of his philosophy,' says one of his biographers, 'he prepared to drag himself through whatever ordeal might be set down for him; he could not will, he could not direct, but he could endure. It was the mood of a stoic. . . .'

But, of course, it was not very reassuring for those around him. Discomfited by that lugubrious expression, that lethargic behaviour, that utter lack of enthusiasm, they consoled themselves with the thought that the Emperor had always been a man of few words. 'His thoughts were a complete mystery to us all,' says Filon. It was probably just as well that the Emperor never voiced them.

For inspiration, however, they could always turn to the Empress. Eugenie's mood, unlike that of the Emperor, was in complete accord with public feeling; 'everyone here, and the Empress most of all,' wrote Marie de Larminat to her mother, 'desires war so intensely that it seems to me that it must be a foregone conclusion. . . .' The young *demoiselle d'honneur* might have been allowing her own ardour to get the better of her judgement but there is no doubt that Eugenie had been caught up in the blaze of patriotism that now swept through France. War, she believed, was preferable to any further humiliation from Prussia. As Eugenie was never one for keeping her opinions to herself, she spoke out in favour of the war with all the vehemence of her nature. Here was an opportunity of avenging Sadowa, of blotting out the disgrace of Mexico, of consolidating the dynasty. Here was the chance for the Second Empire to regain its prestige. 'She seemed to live in a state of enthusiastic excitement from the moment war was declared,' says Marie de Larminat, 'an enthusiasm which she passed on to us, and which gained all the youth to her side.' The Empress at this time was much closer in spirit to the youngsters at Court—the boys who could hardly wait to get into uniform and the girls who went dashing off to pray at Notre-Dame des Victoires—than she was to the Emperor. And this difference between them, between the negative, pessimistic, apathetic Emperor and the positive, optimistic and vigorous Empress was to be emphasized during the coming weeks until, like a band drawn taut, it reached snapping-point.

At the moment, it was the Emperor's attitude that seemed odd, not hers. 'Like almost all the world,' wrote Ernest Lavisse, 'the Empress believed that victory was certain and would be swift.'

In the widely believed accusation that it was the Empress Eugénie who plunged France into war with Prussia in 1870, there is very little substance. For just as Napoleon III was to be blamed for losing the war, so, in later years, would the Empress Eugénie be blamed for starting it. She is said to have seen the war in the light of a crusade of Catholic France against Protestant Prussia, as a means of re-establishing the Caesarism of the early days of the Empire, as a way of regaining the personal authority (for she was to be Regent in her husband's absence) which she had lost with the introduction of the Liberal Empire. She was even charged with having purposely sent the Emperor to his death, knowing full well how ill he was, so that she might rule France until her son's coming of age. She was accused of having given the lead to the war party in the council chamber, of having overridden all arguments in favour of peace, of having forced the Emperor's hand when he seemed to be wavering. She is said to have cried out, in an impassioned moment, 'This is *my* war!' It was a phrase that was to follow her to the grave.

'She and she alone has been the cause of all France's misfortunes,' exclaimed Princess Mathilde when it was all over, 'this woman has ruined the best and most generous of men and with him our poor country.'

But all this was hindsight. Eugenie was never allowed to wield as much influence as that. With or without her encouragement France would have declared war on Prussia in July 1870. The Empress was undoubtedly in sympathy with the war party but she did not control it. There was nothing extraordinary about her enthusiasm at the time; she was no more belligerent, nor more blind, than the rest of them. She was certainly never the warmongering virago that her enemies have made her out to be. In fact, for as many instances as there were of her enthusiasm, there are proofs of her uncertainties.

Marie de Larminat spoke of periods when the Empress's 'extraordinary strength of mind' gave way and she fell prey to the most agonizing attacks of nerves. Parieu, the President of the Council of State, always claimed that it was quite untrue that the Empress exerted her influence for war. 'What do you think of all this, M. de Parieu?' she asked him one day during the crisis.

'Madam, I think that if England were to offer her mediation, we should be very wrong not to accept.'

'I think so, too,' answered Eugenie.

This was hardly the attitude of a fire-eating amazon.

On the night that the war credits were voted, a courtier, finding the Empress pacing the pathways at Saint Cloud, remarked on her sombre mood.

'How can I feel anything but concern on the eve of great events?' she answered. 'Here is a great country like France, peaceable, prosperous, and now engaged in a conflict from which, even if all goes well, so much destruction, so much sorrow will come. The honour of France is engaged: but what disaster if fortune should go against her! We have only one card to play. If we are not victorious, France will not only be diminished and robbed, but swallowed up by the most frightful revolution ever seen.'

4

Of the Prince Imperial's attitude towards the war, there were no doubts whatsoever. It was one of joy unsurpassed. These were to be the happiest weeks of his life. For the causes of the war he cared not one jot. His only anxiety during the days that preceded the declaration of war was that the war might be avoided; when it was declared, he was ecstatic. And when he was told that he was to accompany the Emperor to the front, there was simply no containing him. He could hardly eat, he could hardly sleep, he could hardly keep still. He was in a state bordering on delirium.

His fervour was given every encouragement. No one could resist that shining face and that effervescent manner. He was surrounded, moreover, by people every bit as exhilarated and optimistic as himself. If there were one or two who seemed just a shade less certain that it was all going to be such a glorious adventure (and Filon, the boy's tutor, was one of them) Louis simply avoided their company. There were plenty of others to back up his enthusiasms. Saint Cloud was full of self-appointed prophets ('sensible people . . . able to view things impartially', as Marie de Larminat put it) who were able to assure their listeners that the war 'was in accordance with all France's aspirations' and that the hour could not have been better chosen. 'Even if this war is unsuccessful, a most unlikely contingency,' pronounced one of the seers, 'it will establish France and the *Emperor* in a better situation than if peace had been concluded. . . .'

The Prince's German master was particularly zealous in his encouragement of Louis's illusions. His parents lived at Mayence, and as Louis would obviously be making a speedy and triumphant entry into that German city, the master would be very grateful if the Prince would afford them his protection.

Such requests would be treated by the Prince with the utmost gravity. He might be beside himself with excitement at the prospect of going to war but he never for a moment doubted that he was to be seriously employed as a soldier. There was to be no make-believe this time. His childhood curls had been cut off and his showy grenadier's uniform exchanged for the practical dress of a *sous-lieutenant d'infantrie*. One day a small black box, a trunk similar to that of any sub-lieutenant, was brought into his room. 'There's my box,' explained the boy to Filon, 'all my things must go into that.' A wink from Uhlmann, the

Prince's valet, told Filon that Louis's baggage would certainly be taking up more room than that.

If the Prince found his father's attitude a little puzzling (he had been momentarily disconcerted by the Emperor's restrained speech to the senators and deputies), he found himself in full accord with his mother. And she with him. The two of them, in fact, had never been closer than now. To Eugenie, no less than to Louis, his going to war was a serious business. The Emperor might claim that his son was joining the army not 'to play at soldiers, but to learn his *métier de souverain*', but Eugenie believed that he was going away to fight. That his life was to be in danger, she was quite certain. 'Louis,' wrote Eugenie to her mother, the Countess de Montijo, 'is full of spirit and courage, and so am I. Certain names carry obligations, and his are heavy, so he must do his duty as I am sure he will. You are very fortunate to have had only *daughters*, for at times I feel like a wild animal; I could take my little one and carry him away to the wilderness and tear everyone who tried to lay hands on him. Then I reflect and tell myself that I would rather see him dead than dishonoured. In short, I feel myself a prey to so many contrary ideas that I dare not think of them. And meanwhile I encourage Louis—not that he needs it. . . .'

He certainly did not need it. With each fresh departure of the officers from Saint Cloud for the front he became more and more impatient to be off himself. The date was finally set for 28 July. Before they could leave, however, there was to be a great farewell dinner, attended by the whole Court and the officers of the garrison, in the Galerie de Diane. It turned out to be one of the most exhilarating occasions of Louis's young life. The atmosphere was said to have been 'electric with warlike excitement'; the diners, flushed with martial ardour and enlivened by champagne, became more and more exultant. Normally phlegmatic men, says Filon, seemed about to burst out shouting. As the clamour reached its height, the band of the Guards suddenly struck up the *Marseillaise*.

The effect was indescribable. The eighteen-year-long ban had only just been lifted and although the battle song had been played *ad nauseam* in the streets of Paris during the last week, this was the first time that it had been heard at Court. 'A thrill

94

ran through the room,' says Filon, and as its triumphant notes clashed out, even the most cynical were carried away on a tide of emotion. 'You may imagine the effect on an impressionable, nervous boy,' says Filon of the Prince Imperial. 'He was electrified. . . .'

Later that night, in the company of the faithful Louis Conneau and the girl cousins, the Prince tramped about the lawns of Saint Cloud, singing the tune at the top of his voice. The tutor could not understand how the boy had come to know it. Until a fortnight before, even the humming of the tune would have meant imprisonment; who could possibly have taught the Prince the words? Yet there they all were singing lustily, while above them the sky—as though to match their mood—was aglow with shooting stars. One of the girls assured M. Filon that if he were to cry '*Victoire!*' before the shimmering tail of the star faded, France would be sure to win the war.

There was to be one last excursion before the Emperor and his son left for the front. The Court paid a pilgrimage to Malmaison. It was strangely appropriate that their last visit should be to the house that had been so closely associated with the dawn of the Napoleonic saga. The rooms, with their furnishings looking so sparse to the eyes of a later generation, were full of memories of the optimistic days of the Consulate and the First Empire. Here was the Great Napoleon's study, decorated like a tent; there was the work-basket, spilling over with the embroidery threads of the soignée Josephine; across the lawns young Hortense de Beauharnais—the mother of Napoleon III—had trailed her muslin skirts. And it was from here, on a summer's day over half a century before, that the first Napoleon had set out on the road to exile that ended on Saint Helena.

The house, so damp and musty now, struck a curious chill in the hearts of the visitors; 'even on this bright summer day,' says Filon, 'the house and gardens had a melancholy and deserted appearance. . . .'

The Emperor left Saint Cloud on the morning of 28 July. He was headed for Metz, near the frontier. Unable to face any public demonstrations, Napoleon had decided not to leave from Paris. The imperial train was drawn up at a little station by the Orleans gate of the park; from here it would join the main line from

Versailles and then travel to Metz without touching the capital. The weather, which until then had been perfect, turned suddenly gloomy that morning; the sky clouded over and a chill wind swirled the first leaves from the trees. In the pale light of the platform were assembled the imperial family, the members of the Household and a handful of ministers and officials. It was a doleful scene. The Emperor shifted slowly from group to group, muttering his farewells in that kind and abstracted fashion. It was rumoured that he had lost his nerve a little while before; that the full horror of the situation had suddenly been brought home to him; that he had talked incoherently of treating with the King of Prussia before it was too late. But it *was* too late, and by now he had regained his habitual calm.

The Empress too, was calm and, fully alive to the drama of the occasion, was at her most heroic. The Prince Imperial, of course, was highly excited, but his eyes were red and he clutched the Empress's hand tightly. As he was about to clamber aboard the train, the Empress marked the sign of the cross on his forehead. Her last words to him were very much in character. 'Louis, do your duty,' she commanded.

Napoleon's last words were no less typical. As the train began to pull out, with the faces of the Emperor and his son framed in the wide window of the imperial saloon, Napoleon suddenly remembered something.

'Dumanoir,' he called to one of his chamberlains, 'I did not say good-bye to you.'

A strange hush spread along the platform at the sound of these touching words. Then the train, gathering speed, disappeared from sight and a heartfelt cry of '*Vive l'Empereur!*' went up and was carried away by the fitful wind.

'This was the last time that I heard this loyal cry in France,' says Filon.

CHAPTER FIVE

Metz

1

'All hope is now at an end,' wrote the Prussian Crown Princess to her mother, Queen Victoria, 'and we have the horrible prospect of the most terrible war Europe has yet known before us, bringing desolation and ruin, perhaps annihilation. . . . We have been shamefully forced into this war, and the feeling of indignation against an act of such crying injustice has risen in two days here to such a pitch that you will hardly believe it; there is a universal cry "To arms", to resist an enemy who so wantonly assaults us.'

The Queen was all sympathy. Her whole heart and fervent prayers, she assured her distraught daughter, were with her 'beloved Germany'.

'Words are too weak to say *all* I feel for you or what I think of my neighbours!' wrote the Queen. 'We must be neutral *as long as* we can, but no one here conceals their opinion as to the extreme *iniquity* of the war, and the unjustifiable conduct of the French! Still, *more publicly*, we cannot say; but the feeling of the people and the country is *all* with you, which it was not *before*. And need I say what I *feel*? . . .'

That the sympathy of a great number of the British people was with Prussia was due, in no small measure, to yet another of Bismarck's astute moves. Four years before, in 1866, when Napoleon III had been fumbling about in an effort to obtain some sort of compensation from Bismarck for French neutrality during Prussia's war with Austria, the Emperor had proposed a secret treaty between Bismarck and himself. By the terms of this treaty, Prussia would—at some future date—help France annex Belgium. 'Should the Emperor be forced by circumstances to send his troops into Belgium or to conquer her, Prussia will provide armed assistance,' read the most crucial sentence. Count Benedetti had made a copy of the draft treaty in his own handwriting and had handed it to Bismarck. The Prussian Chancellor, while taking care not to commit himself to the proposal, had led the Emperor to believe that he approved of it and had put Benedetti's copy safely away in a drawer. It lay there for four years.

A soon as France declared war on Prussia, Bismarck instructed Count von Bernstorff, the Prussian Ambassador in London, to show Benedetti's explosive document to Gladstone, the British Prime Minister. A few days later the text of the treaty was released to the London *Times*. This timely publication of Napoleon III's designs on Belgium—Britain's godchild—appalled public opinion. 'Your Majesty will, in common with the world,' wrote Gladstone to Queen Victoria, 'be shocked and startled.' A treaty was hastily drawn up in which Britain, in the event of either France or Prussia violating Belgian territory, promised to help the opposing side to expel the intruder. Thoroughly alarmed, the Queen asked her Prime Minister for an immediate assurance that Great Britain's defences were on a satisfactory footing, as the country 'may be exposed to a sudden and unexpected attack at any moment'.

But Prussia was hoping for more than sympathy from Britain. The Crown Princess, growing more feverish by the day, claimed that the feeling in her country was that the British, together with the Russians, the Austrians and the Italians, should have threatened to take up arms against the French; as it was, Britain's strict neutrality was proving of inestimable value to 'the aggressor'.

The Crown Princess's father-in-law, King Wilhelm, expressed himself in similar, if less frenetic, terms. 'In consequence of the universal indignation against the disturber of the peace,' he wrote to Queen Victoria on 26 July, 'I was led to hope, I may candidly confess, that, after your mediation was rejected by France, some common action of the European Powers might result in favour of our just cause, and either prevent war, or at any rate hasten its favourable conclusion.' The results of a French victory, of the establishment of a 'Napoleonic dynastic power' in the centre of Europe, were too appalling to contemplate, he declared. What the old King was hoping for, of course, was armed support from Britain. He reminded the Queen, a shade querulously, that her 'excellent husband', the late Prince Albert and her 'dear uncle', the late King Leopold of the Belgians, had both considered Germany's cause 'worthy of support. . . .'

Victoria needed no reminding. With every passing day she became more and more agitated. 'The Queen,' she blurted out to her Foreign Secretary, Lord Granville, 'is overwhelmed with letter-writing, telegrams and the terrible anxiety and sorrow which this horrible war will bring with it. The Queen hardly knows how she will bear it! Her children's home threatened, their husbands' lives in danger, and the country she loves best next to her own—as it is her second home, being her beloved husband's, and one to which she and all her family are bound by the closest ties—in peril of the gravest kind, insulted and attacked, and *she* unable to help them or to come to their assistance . . .'

Not all the Queen's relations shared her anguish at the plight of her beloved Germany. At a dinner at the French Embassy on the evening before the declaration of war, the Prince of Wales is claimed to have expressed to Count Apponyi, the Austrian Ambassador, the hope that Austria might join France in defeating Prussia. The Prince of Wales, staunchly Francophile, had the highest regard for Napoleon and Eugenie and had never forgiven Prussia for her brutal attack on his wife's country—Denmark—half a dozen years before. The Prince's partisan remarks were repeated to the Prussian Ambassador in London who promptly forwarded them to Berlin. The Prince's sister, the Prussian Crown Princess, was furious and lost no time in dashing off a letter to their mother. 'The King and everyone are horrified at Bertie's speech which is quoted everywhere,' she reported. When confronted with his indiscretion, Bertie, in best royal fashion, denied ever having made it.

In spite of these conflicting and heatedly expressed royal preferences, Britain remained firmly uncommitted. She was determined to hold aloof from any Continental entanglements. Gladstone had done everything possible to keep France and Prussia from going to war and although he blamed France for its 'feverish determination to force a quarrel', he thought that Bismarck was just as much to blame as Napoleon III. 'Six of one and half a dozen of the other', was how *Punch* captioned its cartoon of Napoleon III and King Wilhelm both protesting their innocence before a judicial John Bull. The London *Times* was not prepared to be nearly so impartial. It had no doubt that France was the aggressor. The French attack on Prussia was 'the greatest national crime that we have had the pain of recording in these columns since the days of the First Empire'. It was an 'unjust, but premeditated war', and 'the act of France —of one man in France'. There could be no doubt, continued *The Times*, 'as to the side on which the world's sympathies will be enlisted'.

But wherever the fault might lie, Gladstone claimed that it was better for Britain 'to promise too little than too much' when it came to the question of giving support to its European neighbours. British sympathy might be with worthy Prussia rather than with frivolous France but she was not prepared to go to war for the sake of what Lord Granville called 'a point limited to a matter of etiquette'.

As for the outcome of the struggle, most Englishmen assumed that, after a 'bloody business', the French 'Red-breeches' would beat the 'Sauerkrauts'. 'Nothing shall ever persuade me,' wrote Delane, the editor of the London *Times*, to one of his correspondents, 'that the Prussians will withstand the French, and I would lay my last shilling upon Casquette against Pumpernickel.'

In Prussia itself there were no divided loyalties. Princess Alice, Grand Duchess of Hesse, assured her mother that 'there is a feeling of unity and standing by each other, forgetting all party squabbles, which makes one proud of the name of German!' If the Prussians were less frenzied than the French in their reaction to the declaration of war, they were no less enthusiastic. Huge crowds gathered outside the Neues Palais at Potsdam and their old King, with 'a quiet dignity about him which could only increase one's love and respect' was obliged to show himself time and again on the balcony. That they were embarking on a just, indeed, an almost holy war, the Prussians had no doubts whatsoever. God, they believed with a somewhat chilling self-righteousness, was firmly on their side. Lutheran hymns were sung as often as *Die Wacht am Rhein*. 'The enthusiasm is grand and imposing,' wrote one enraptured observer. 'There is something so pure and elevated about it—so sacred and calm and serious—and when I see our finest and noblest men all joining and collecting round their aged Sovereign, they seem to me to be indeed "the noble army of martyrs".' To a British war correspondent, these 'masterful, fighting, praying people' seemed not unlike the Ironsides whom Cromwell had once led to victory.

In the South German states there was rather less enthusiasm. There was no question, however, of their not joining Prussia. They were bound by treaty to come to Prussia's aid if she were attacked. Within a few days of the declaration of war, the gratified Crown Prince was able to claim that 'most of the German Princes are arriving to offer their services to the King and express their devotion to the common good of the Fatherland'. Even if the feelings of the various South German governments towards Prussia were lukewarm, their populations, said the Crown Prince, were 'fired with a unanimous zeal'. Bismarck's plan was working.

On the last day of July, King Wilhelm, as nominal Commander-in-Chief, left Berlin for Mainz, near the French frontier. With him, as effective head of the German forces, was the brilliant General von Moltke. With mobilization going like clockwork, three German armies were soon ready to move towards France. The First Army was commanded by the aged General von Steinmetz; the Second Army by the King's nephew, the circumspect Prince Frederick-Charles; and the Third Army by the virtuous Crown Prince.

'The King embraced me with the deepest emotion,' wrote the Crown Prince in his diary before leaving to take command of his men. 'We both felt that we must prepare ourselves for a contest involving the most sacred rights and privileges, perhaps the very existence, of the Fatherland, a battle that must be fought out with streams of the noblest blood of our People!'

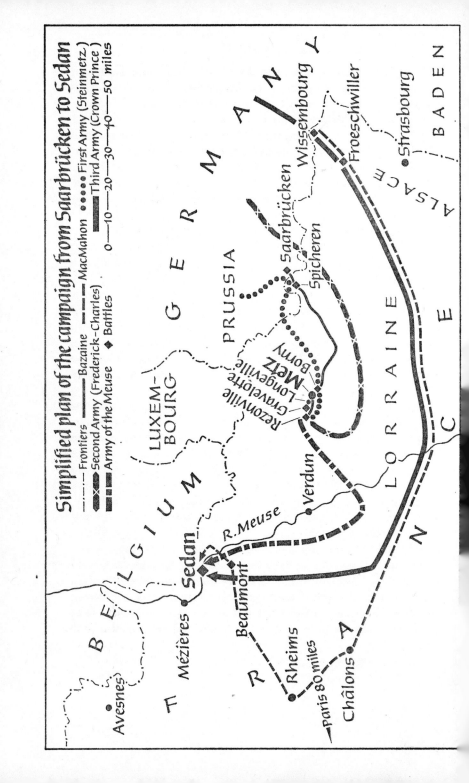

Simplified plan of the campaign from Saarbrücken to Sedan

--- Frontiers   —— Bazaine   ——— MacMahon   •••• First Army (Steinmetz)
××× Second Army (Frederick-Charles)   ——— Third Army (Crown Prince)
▬▬ Army of the Meuse   ◆ Battles

0 — 10 — 20 — 30 — 40 — 50 miles

GERMANY

BADEN

ALSACE

PRUSSIA

LORRAINE

LUXEM-
BOURG

BELGIUM

FRANCE

Wissembourg

Froeschwiller

Strasbourg

Saarbrücken

Spicheren

Metz
Borny
Longeville
Gravelotte
Rezonville

Verdun

R. Meuse

Sedan

Mézières

Beaumont

Rheims

Châlons

Avesnes

Paris 80 miles

2

The Emperor Napoleon reached Metz at six o'clock on the evening of 28 July. This ancient fortified city, straddling the Moselle River, lay in gently undulating country some thirty miles from the German frontier. The fact that the city's new fortifications had not yet been completed did not bother the French unduly; it seemed unlikely that Metz would ever have to be defended. The Emperor's resounding Order of the Day, issued soon after his arrival, echoed this optimism. 'Whatever may be the road we take beyond our frontiers,' he wrote, 'we shall come across the glorious traces of our fathers. We shall prove worthy of them. All France follows you with its fervent prayers, and the eyes of the world are upon you. On our success hangs the fate of liberty and civilization.'

That the French army would indeed be taking the road into the enemy's territory was a foregone conclusion. Not only would an offensive be in accordance with French military tradition but it would mean the only possible hope of victory. Between Luxembourg on the one side and Switzerland on the other, the French frontier jutted like a half-bent elbow into Germany. To the north lay Prussia, to the east Baden and the other South German kingdoms. If the French could cross the frontier near the bend of the elbow and score a decisive victory, they might well be able to separate northern from southern Germany, win the South German kingdoms to their side and encourage Austria and Italy to join in. To this end there was concentrated, in the provinces of Lorraine and Alsace (the one to the north-west and the other to the south-east, together forming that jutting elbow) the entire French army under the personal command of the Emperor. Under him were the three most illustrious marshals of the Second Empire: Marshal Bazaine at Metz, Marshal MacMahon at Strasbourg and Marshal Canrobert in the rear, at the great military camp of Châlons. With Napoleon now having joined Bazaine at Metz, the French thrust into Germany was expected at any moment.

It did not come. And why it could not possibly come was only too apparent to the newly-arrived Emperor. The success, indeed the very possibility, of a French offensive depended entirely on the speed of mobilization; if the French could launch their attack before the ponderous Prussians had time to mobilize, they might well carry the day. But there was by now little chance of that. The French mobilization had been chaotic. The confusion throughout north-eastern France was indescribable. Reservists, having to report first to their regimental depots and then to their regiments, found themselves wandering all over the country. Zouaves might have to travel from the north of France to a depot in Algeria before being dispatched to join their regiment in Alsace. A band of reservists from Lille spent over six weeks in search of their regiment, only to find that it had been destroyed in battle a mere eighty miles from where they had originally set out. Nor was the fact that reservists did reach the depot any guarantee that they would be fully equipped once they arrived there; harassed commanders simply fitted them out as best they could and then sent them packing. They might then spend days, or even weeks, on trains that were continually being shunted off on to sidings, and even when they did finally reach their regiments, it was to find things in an even worse muddle there. The railway lines were in so clogged a state that very few supplies (always supposing that they had been dispatched in the first place) could get through. When they did, they often lay neglected for lack of unloading facilities or unclaimed for want of an order. There was a shortage of everything: of arms, ammunition, tents, blankets, cooking utensils, horses, transport, medical supplies, ambulances, maps, money and especially food. Headquarters were inundated with frantic telegrams. 'Have arrived at Belfort,' read a typical one, from General Micheler. 'Cannot find my brigade. Cannot find the divisional commander. What shall I do? Do not know where my regiments are.' '*Débrouillez-vous*' became the stock instruction; they were to improvise for the time being. Everyone must wait for the arrival of the Emperor. Once he reached Metz, things would surely get moving.

It was the vainest of vain hopes. Napoleon III was no longer the man to bring order out of chaos, nor to provide the spark necessary to inspire men to superhuman efforts. Of that resolute figure who, by his *coup d'état* of 1851 had made himself master of France, hardly a shadow remained. The confusion at headquarters simply plunged him into an even deeper despair. It was all so much worse than even he had anticipated. Instead of finding the 385,000 fully armed men that he had been led to expect, he was met by fewer than 200,000, many of them ill-equipped, ill-disciplined and poorly trained. In an anguished letter to Eugenie, written soon after his arrival, the Emperor explained that as there were too few men and nothing ready, all chance of a speedy offensive had been lost. '*Je nous considère d'avance comme perdus.*' The one hope of victory, in fact, was gone. With each day that passed (and they had already entered the third week of mobilization) their chances of success diminished. Slowly and methodically, the Prussians were building up their strength. By the beginning of August, to the delighted astonishment of General von Moltke, the French army had still made no move.

But by now it had been decided that they must do *something*. France, and particularly Paris, must be given proof that the army had launched its promised drive into enemy territory. Paris wanted a victory and a victory she must have. It was agreed that they would attack Saarbrücken.

That Saarbrücken was a little town of doubtful strategic importance, defended by one infantry regiment, was neither here nor there. It was enough that it was across the frontier and that its capture would mark the first advance into Prussia. Thus, on the morning of 2 August, a French force of no fewer than 60,000 men, moving forward with all the precision and glamour of an army on review, bore down on Saarbrücken. They were briskly received by the Prussians who, having held them at bay for a few hours, slipped away in good order. By noon the French were in command of the heights above the town and the skirmish was over. But the town was not occupied, the enemy was not pursued, the telegraph station was not destroyed. For two days the French remained on the heights and then struck camp and marched back into France.

For all its insignificance, the action achieved the desired result: by the time the news reached Paris, the pointless skirmish had become the triumphant 'Battle of Saarbruck'. It was confidently assumed that the celebrated advance *à Berlin* was under way.

Present on the battlefield that day were the Emperor and the Prince Imperial. A consummate showman, Napoleon III was quite ready to make use of his son to add lustre to the somewhat faded imperial image. As Louis was the heir, not only to the Empire, but to the Napoleonic military tradition (of which the Emperor himself was such an inadequate representative) it was necessary that the Prince be closely associated with any French victories. It was an obligation which Louis was only too ready to fulfil. Saarbrücken was his first taste of real war and he was savouring every morsel to the full. Of the confusion at headquarters which had so depressed the Emperor, he knew nothing; to his inexperienced and optimistic eyes, everything looked splendid. At one stage during the morning father and son rode up to the firing line and Louis experienced the bliss of hearing the whizz of bullets and the crash of shells about him. He afterwards told his friend Tristan Lambert that his first thoughts had been of God but then 'the noise, the excitement of the soldiers and the smell of powder began to thrill me, and I felt as though it were a review'.

'The Prince,' wrote one of the officers to his wife that evening, 'was admirably cool and natural in his behaviour.' He thought that this little display of imperial pluck at the beginning of the campaign was an 'excellent omen' and that it would be bound to give the men confidence.

The Emperor was tremendously proud of the boy's behaviour. He could hardly wait to tell Eugenie all about it. His telegram to her that afternoon was supposed to announce the capture of Saarbrücken but in fact, it was almost all about their son. 'Louis has just received his baptism of fire. His coolness was admirable. He was as unconcerned as if he had been strolling in the Bois de Boulogne. . . . Louis has kept a bullet which fell close to where he was standing. Some of the soldiers wept when they saw him so cool.'

Of one of his own experiences during that day Napoleon told Eugenie nothing. The action was drawing to a close and the last of the firing dying away when the Emperor, who had been on his horse for most of the morning, suddenly dismounted. He collapsed into the arms of one of his aides.

'Your Majesty is in pain?' whispered the astonished officer.

'I am suffering horribly,' gasped Napoleon. 'I would prefer to walk a little. That relieves me.'

With the slightest jolting moving the stone in his bladder, riding had become a torture for him these days. But he refused to send for a carriage. All that he could do was to assume that impassive expression and hope that the excruciating pain would pass off. It would not do for Louis, so flushed and so confident, to see his father in such a humiliating predicament. After all, he was a Napoleon, and he had just won the first battle of the war.

3

The Empress Eugenie's Regency, which was to end so tumultuously, began quietly enough. For one thing the government, headed by Ollivier, was determined to keep her in her place. Give her an inch, they reckoned, and she would take a yard. Augustin Filon, assuming the duties of secretary to the Regent, was amazed by how little contact there was between Eugenie and the ministers. They never consulted her and barely informed her of their decisions. While they deliberated in Paris, she remained at Saint Cloud. 'She was Regent in name only,' says Filon, 'and she wielded no power as Regent.'

But then Eugenie had never been one for the tedious, day-to-day business of government. She had no patience with red tape, paper-work, detailed discussion or routine. She saw her duties in a completely different—and far more theatrical—light; she had never intended wasting her time on what she considered to be trivialities. She must exploit the drama of her position to the full. As a beautiful woman and a valiant mother, she would be able to accomplish far more than any fusty politician. When the writer Octave Feuillet paid her one of his flowery compliments ('You are at this moment, Madame, the living image of the motherland. On your noble forehead we can read all the sentiments which animate you, all that you suffer, all that you hope,

all your anguish, all your pride, your enthusiasm, your faith . . .')
it is unlikely that Eugenie considered the picture overdrawn.
She had never been one to underrate herself.

Her present ambition was twofold. First, she must rally the
entire country to one cause, and second, she must win allies for
France.

One of her earliest duties gave her an opportunity of furthering her first aim: she paid an official visit to the fleet at Cherbourg. By the dispatching of a squadron to the North Sea,
Napoleon III hoped to rally the Danes to his side. Denmark
had been the first country to suffer defeat at the hands of
Bismarck's Prussia and now, six years after that defeat, would
be only too glad of an opportunity of revenge. In unofficial talks
with the Danes, France had agreed to land a force of some
30,000 men on Germany's North Sea coast. This would be
augmented by a Danish force of equal size and together they
would march into Holstein or Hanover. Like the Austrians,
however, the Danes were waiting for some signs of a French
victory before committing themselves. In anticipation of this,
Admiral Bouet-Willaumez was preparing to sail a French
squadron into the North Sea. It was the Empress Eugenie who
travelled to Cherbourg to see it off.

She received a vociferous welcome. The Empress had always
loved the sea ('all the palaces in the world are not worth a ship's
deck,' she used to say) and she felt eminently at home amongst
sailors. She now made an inspiring speech to the officers, ending
it with the reading out of the Emperor's proclamation to the
army. After hearing Mass aboard the flagship, she toured the
arsenal. For an hour she followed the departing fleet out to
sea and then returned, through acclaiming crowds, to the
station.

No less valuable than such successful public appearances were
her private manœuvrings. To quieten the dangerous rivalry
between various sections of the Press, and to give at least some
semblance of unity in the face of national danger, she tried
to get the opposing newspapers to moderate their tone. On
the one hand she asked the journalist Paul de Cassagnac to
play down his dogmatically expressed imperialist views and
on the other she appealed to Adelon, Emile Ollivier's secretary,

not to force the closing down of two virulent opposition papers, *La Presse* and *Le Rappel*, because of their inability to pay a certain fine. This was no time, she realized, for the government to be making enemies. Eugenie's plea for leniency bewildered Adelon. Expecting her to insist on measures of the utmost severity against the opposition Press, he was surprised to find that the reputedly reactionary Empress 'was more liberal in her ideas than he was himself'.

To the question of foreign alliances she devoted herself with rather more zest. She had always considered foreign affairs to be her forte. There was nothing to be looked for from Britain or Russia, who were determined to remain neutral, or from the United States, who had never forgiven Napoleon III for his intervention in Mexico. It was on the Ambassadors of Italy and Austria that the Empress was pinning her hopes. Although Eugenie had never really come to terms with the new kingdom of Italy and had never hesitated to voice her opinions on the rapacity of the Italian nationalists and the brigandry of King Victor Emmanuel, she had gradually come to accept Count Constantine Nigra, the Italian Ambassador. A man of considerable charm and culture, he seems, says Marie de Larminat, to have been 'captivated' by Eugenie. Not all the fascination in the world, however, was going to get Italy to side with France while Napoleon III refused to evacuate his troops from Rome.

With Prince Richard Metternich, the Austrian Ambassador, the Empress was on closer terms still. Not only was Austria the one country with which Eugenie most fervently desired an alliance, but the intelligent and well-mannered Metternich was very much a man after her own heart. His wife, the pert and lively Pauline, was her particular friend. In the racier days of the Second Empire it was Pauline Metternich, *l'ambassadrice des plaisirs*, who set the pace. It was this intimacy with the Metternichs that led Eugenie to believe that an alliance with Austria was more likely than it in fact was. The Emperor Franz Josef was not nearly as amenable as his Ambassador's behaviour seemed to indicate. None the less, a lengthy conversation with Metternich seems to have convinced Eugenie that the hoped-for alliance was about to be concluded, and so important did she consider the talk that she decided to travel to Metz to report it in person to the Emperor.

Before she could get away, she was overtaken by events. On the last day of July she received Napoleon's first letter, telling her that the state of unpreparedness at the front had put paid to all hopes of an offensive. The news, she afterwards said, 'broke her arms and legs'. In her distress she repeated the highly confidential tidings to—of all people—Richard Metternich. She was confiding in him, she said, not as the Austrian Ambassador but as a friend, and begged him to tell the news to no one other than his wife Pauline. '*Nous avons fidèlement gardé le terrible secret*,' claims Pauline; perhaps so, but Eugenie's indiscretion was hardly calculated to foster a Franco–Austrian alliance.

On the day that the Empress received the news, she sat at luncheon with the tears streaming down her cheeks. When the Duchess de Malakoff tried to console her, Eugenie, wiping her eyes with her napkin, refused to be comforted. 'I must not weaken,' she announced.

The news of Saarbrücken, following soon after, was much more cheering. Like the rest of Paris, the Empress believed that a significant battle had been fought and won, and she could hardly contain herself. There were no tears at table now. With her red-gold hair gleaming and her sea-green eyes a-sparkle, she sat at dinner that evening, holding forth at great length about the day's events. She was especially proud of Louis. It was only right, she explained to the delighted company, that he had come under fire in the month of August; everyone knew that August was a lucky month for the Bonapartes. And then he had emerged from the battle unscathed! She was quite sure that he had a charmed life.

When, in the full flush of her maternal pride, she showed the Emperor's telegram about Louis's behaviour at Saarbrücken to Ollivier, he decided to publish it. All that confidential information about the Prince—about his coolness, about the men having wept, about the way he had kept a bullet as a souvenir—could do nothing but good. In fact, once published, the telegram did nothing but harm. Meant to arouse a wave of admiration for the brave young Prince, it released a flood of derisive laughter. The opposition Press seized upon the Emperor's doting phrases and heaped pitiless ridicule on the head of the Prince. Louis became, instead of the hero of his parents' imagination, *l'enfant de la balle*, a Napoleon who picked up spent bullets to keep as souvenirs.

The opposition never let Louis forget 'the bullet of Saarbrücken'. Nor, for his part, did Louis ever forget their taunts. Amongst the papers found in his wallet after his tragic death in Zululand at the age of twenty-three was a little piece of paper, rolled up like a cigarette. It was an article from a recent Parisian newspaper, ridiculing him by reviving the story of 'the bullet of Saarbrücken'.

4

The fourth of August marked the beginning of the disasters. On that morning the German Third Army, commanded by Crown Prince Frederick, crossed the frontier into Alsace. With the Emperor, Leboeuf, Bazaine and the Army of the Rhine in Lorraine, it was MacMahon who commanded in Alsace. It was thus a division of MacMahon's army, stationed at the little border town of Wissembourg, that met the advancing Germans. Fighting broke out soon after eight. All morning, and with great courage, the small French force resisted the vastly superior German one, but by three in the afternoon the battle was over and the remnants of the division came stumbling through the trampled vineyards in full retreat.

MacMahon himself (having moved up from Strasbourg) was a few miles farther south at Froeschwiller. The defeat of his isolated division at Wissembourg did not worry him unduly. The Germans had outnumbered his men by eight to one and the main body of his army was now established in an excellent position on the Froeschwiller ridge. He doubted that the Germans would attack him at all. Indeed, the battle which developed a day later, on 6 August, was the result of an early morning skirmish between the outposts of the rival armies. Neither the Crown Prince nor MacMahon had ordered the battle. The skirmish developed, the fighting gained momentum and by noon a full-scale battle was under way. Outnumbered and out-gunned, the French fought with customary persistence and *élan*, but it was hopeless. Not all the bravery on earth could halt the enemy. As a last resort, MacMahon ordered a cavalry charge and the gallant *cuirassiers*, with helmets flashing and horsehair flying, went thundering down the slopes, simply to be checked by walls and hedges and shot down by well-placed Prussian infantrymen. By half past four it was all over. While the Prussians and Bavarians (united now in victory) cheered the Crown Prince as he came riding his horse through the drifts of smoke, the dispirited remains of MacMahon's army fled westwards into the setting sun. French killed and wounded totalled 11,000, almost half the force. The Germans had suffered nearly as heavily but there was no doubt that they had won a resounding victory. All Alsace lay open at their feet.

That night MacMahon sent the Emperor a telegram. 'I have lost a battle; we have suffered great losses in men and material. The retreat is at present in progress. . . .'

The news could hardly have come at a worse time. On the very day that MacMahon and the Army of Alsace lost the battle of Froeschwiller, Bazaine's force—the Army of the Rhine—was beaten at Spicheren. It was General Frossard, previously military governor to the Prince Imperial and now in command of the 2nd Corps, who sustained the defeat. Like MacMahon at Froeschwiller, he was established in a seemingly impregnable position: the Spicheren heights to which he had withdrawn a few days after the pointless advance on, and retreat from, Saarbrücken. On the morning of 6 August—again as at Froeschwiller—the opposing sides simply blundered into battle. Moltke had never ordered it. It was the German First and Second Armies, commanded respectively by General von Steinmetz and Prince Frederick-Charles, that now attacked Frossard. By all the rules, Frossard should have carried the day. A fatal underestimation of the enemy's forces, however, stopped him from sending for the three French divisions that were lying in idleness less than ten miles from the battle; he remained sanguine until it was too late. Not until seven that evening, having held firm all day, did he appreciate that he should have asked for reinforcements earlier; as the Prussians moved up through the charred and shattered woods to threaten his flank, he had to abandon his position and fall back. When reinforcements finally came hurrying up, they were met by Frossard's columns in full and bitter retreat. The Prussians, having fought doggedly but unimaginatively (they had suffered even more casualties than the French) came swarming over the darkening hills to claim another victory.

Throughout this disastrous day, the unsuspecting Emperor, now back at his headquarters in Metz after that ephemeral victory at Saarbrücken, was making yet one more effort to get his bemused army to take the offensive. One of the many differences between the French and Prussian armies was that whereas the Prussian generals, from Moltke down, were only too eager to give commands, no one on the French side was at all anxious to do so—the Emperor least of all. What was needed at the front was one firm hand, not, as was the case, several flabby ones. But on this morning of 6 August, Napoleon finally bestirred himself to instigate some plan of action. It was decided that four army corps would be assembled close to the frontier and from there they would launch an all-out attack on the advancing enemy. It was, in fact, an excellent plan. Put into effect a couple of days before, it might have stood a chance of success. But all through that long summer afternoon Napoleon received reports of the battle that was being fought by Frossard at Spicheren and that evening he was handed Mac-Mahon's telegram telling him of the disaster at Froeschwiller. Still later he heard that Frossard had fallen back, abandoning Spicheren heights to the enemy. By the following morning it was clear that Frossard was in full retreat (his exact whereabouts were unknown) and that Bazaine, just south of Spicheren, was in danger. All hope of an offensive was now gone. Napoleon, his nerve shattered, ordered the entire imperial army to fall back on Châlons.

These twin battles of 6 August were probably the most decisive of the war. From that moment on the Emperor's defeatism spread like a cancer throughout the army. Not only was there now no likelihood of a French invasion of Germany, but France herself lay at the mercy of the invader. The French had never had much taste for a defensive campaign. The defeats dealt a death-blow too, to any hopes of a foreign alliance. Austria gave up all pretence of future military aid and King Victor Emmanuel, ignoring the Duke de Gramont's hint that it might be fitting for the Italians to march to France's aid by the very route which she had once marched to theirs, exclaimed, 'Poor Emperor! I pity him, but I have had a lucky escape.' The Danes, too, could now find no good reason for abandoning their neutrality and the French squadron was left to sail, rather forlornly, around the North Sea.

Had France been able to score two resounding victories on that day and follow them with a resolute invasion of Prussia, she might well have been joined by Austria, Italy, Denmark and the South German kingdoms, and the history of Europe during the following half-century would have been very different.

On the night of the catastrophe, Napoleon sent a telegram to Eugenie. 'Our troops are in full retreat,' he wired. 'Nothing must be thought of now beyond the defence of the capital.'

CHAPTER SIX

The Change of Crew

1

Things in Paris had been hardly less chaotic. To Parisians, celebrating the victory of Saarbrücken with a fervour that had not abated since the declaration of war, the news of the defeat of MacMahon's division during that first skirmish with the Crown Prince's army at Wissembourg on 4 August, came as a distinct shock. Its effect was not so much deflating as enraging. Overnight, the mood of the crowd turned ugly. Having no other outlet for its fury, a mob attacked and wrecked the premises of any shopkeepers with German-sounding names. Towards noon on that fatal 6 August, however, rumours of a great victory spread through the city. It was claimed that the Crown Prince's army had been defeated and that twenty-five thousand Germans had been taken prisoner. At this unconfirmed report (everyone claiming that someone else had actually seen the dispatch) Paris again gave itself over to an orgy of rejoicing. 'I have never seen such an outburst of enthusiasm,' reported Edmond de Goncourt. 'One kept running into men pale with emotion, children hopping about in excitement and women making drunken gestures.' In the Place de la Bourse, the celebrated Capoul was singing the *Marseillaise* from the top of an omnibus and the indefatigable Marie Sass was singing it standing up in her carriage, 'practically carried along by the delirium of the mob'. A crowd surged into the Place Vendôme to demand more news of Emile Ollivier; he had none to give them.

When, later that day, the rumours of victory were officially denied, the reaction of the disappointed crowd was violent. Angry groups ranged the still-decorated streets, demanding that the flags be hauled down and the Chief of Police gave warning that his force was 'in for a warm time' that night. Ollivier, taking fright, issued a proclamation asking Parisians to remain calm and then drew up a decree putting Paris under martial law. This he sent to the Empress at Saint Cloud for her signature. With it he sent a letter asking her to return to Paris immediately. The revolution, thought Ollivier, would not be long in starting.

Eugenie kept her head. She signed the decree and promised to return to Paris the following day, bringing with her what Ollivier had described as 'all the troops at her disposal'. These numbered no more than 160 light-infantrymen. She then retired to bed.

The rest of the company, however, remained up. Alarmed by the reports from Paris, the members of the Court moved uneasily about the drawing-rooms. It was a hot night, made doubly uncomfortable, says Marie de Larminat, by 'an indefinable presage of evil in the air'. At eleven a telegram arrived from the Emperor's headquarters. Filon, who had been entrusted with the code used by the Sovereigns, set about deciphering it. He was helped by the Marquis de Piennes and M. de Cossé-Brissac. The message which the three men now decoded was the news of the twin defeats of Froeschwiller and Spicheren. 'We were stunned and almost stupefied,' says Filon, 'with the horror which overwhelms the first recipients of bad news whose unpleasant duty it is to announce it to the world.'

For a moment the three men looked at each other in silence. It was Piennes who spoke first.

'Who is going to tell the Empress?' he asked.

Filon and Brissac said nothing.

'Very well,' said Piennes, 'I will go myself.'

He returned to the room a few minutes later. 'Do you know what she said?' he asked. '"The dynasty is lost; we must think only of France".'

Within fifteen minutes the Empress was dressed and ready to leave for Paris. Wearing a dark dress and looking very pale, she entered the drawing-room in which the entire Court was now assembled. At the sight of her, Madame d'Essling, weeping bitterly, rushed forward.

'Ah, Madame!' she sobbed.

Eugenie cut her short. 'No sentiment, please,' she said. 'I need all my courage.'

Having called a meeting of the ministers for that very night, the Empress set off for the Tuileries. There, at three in the morning, amongst the dust-sheeted furniture of the empty palace, she presided over the council. She found the ministry divided. Alarmed by the revolutionary tumult in the streets and apprehensive of opinion in the Chambers, certain members of the ministry—Ollivier amongst them—were all for staging a *coup d'état*. The leading deputies of the Left would be arrested, Parliament would be prorogued and the Press silenced. To these reactionary suggestions from the leading figures of the Liberal Empire, the Empress refused to listen. She insisted on strict constitutionalism and, in her stand, carried the majority of the members with her. Her refusal to comply with Ollivier's demand for Napoleon's immediate return to Paris was equally adamant. The Emperor could not return to the capital 'under the shadow of a defeat'. They all agreed, however, that the army should not retire on Châlons. So massive a retreat would have disastrous political consequences; Napoleon must remain at Metz and the army could fall back from the frontier to join him there. Ollivier lost no time in sending the Emperor a telegram to inform him of the decision. Eugenie then backed up Ollivier's message with a rousing telegram of her own. She was quite certain, she assured her husband, that by standing firm they would soon drive the Prussians clear across the frontier. 'Courage then; with energy we will get the better of the situation. I will answer for Paris.'

At noon on 7 August the Empress's proclamation, announcing the defeats and calling upon all Frenchmen to work together, was placarded throughout the capital.

'Let there be but one party among you, that of France; one single flag, that of national honour. I am here in your midst. Faithful to my mission and to my duty, you will see me in the forefront of danger to defend the flag of France.'

She was coming, well and truly, into her own.

The disasters of 6 August had stirred the men of the Left, too, into action. For years they had been attacking the régime for its excessive militarism; now, casting aside all traces of pacifism, they attacked it for its military ineptitude. Memories of the stirring days of the Revolutionary Wars, of the time when all

117

Frenchmen had fought together to save the motherland, came flooding back. What was needed now was a *levée en masse*. Jules Favre cried out for the arming of the citizens of Paris and Léon Gambetta demanded that the Prussian menace be met by 'a nation in arms'.

Nor were the Republicans the only ones clamouring for a change. The great majority of senators and deputies, echoing the mood of the crowds in the streets, were demanding more vigorous action. The hunt for scapegoats was on. The cry now went up that Ollivier's ministry must go. The Empress, who had no power to dismiss the ministry, none the less agreed to the summoning of the Chambers. If they voted the ministry out of power, she could then appoint a new one.

If, in these moves, the Empress was exceeding her powers as Regent (it was for the Emperor, not her, to convoke Parliament and form ministries) she felt that she was more than justified. She could not, at a time like this, refer everything to the Emperor. Her 'usurpation of power,' says Filon, 'infringed only the prerogative of the Emperor', and not the national will. But he remained uneasy about it. 'Your Majesty is acting in a revolutionary manner,' he warned her. 'I must,' was the Empress's peremptory reply.

She thereupon recalled the Chambers for 9 August. It turned out to be the most momentous sitting in the short history of the Liberal Empire. That one day saw the introduction of sweeping changes. Ollivier, in a last-minute show of resolution, tried to save his ministry, but it was impossible. He was attacked by both the Republican Left and the Imperialist Right. Inflamed by war fever, the moderate Bonapartist deputies who had hitherto supported him swung inevitably to the right, and Ollivier lost his always shaky majority. His ministry fell and the old Imperialists, who again held the majority, hurried to the Tuileries to consult the Empress on the formation of a new government. Relieved to be rid of Ollivier's liberals, Eugenie lost no time. To head the new ministry she chose General Cousin de Montauban. Decorated with the exotic title of Count de Palikao since his leadership of the expedition to Peking in 1860, he had been stationed, half-forgotten, at Lyons for the last few years. Palikao who, according to Filon, 'enjoyed a semi-popularity on account of his being in semi-disgrace', came hurrying to Paris to lead what the *corps législatif* had demanded—'a Cabinet capable of providing for the defence of the country'. The ministry (one historian has called it 'the familiar war-time masquerade of reaction in the bright clothes of patriotism') proved themselves to be very capable indeed and within hours of taking office had introduced several energetic measures. Money was raised, Paris was provisioned and fortified, a second government—to sit at Tours—was organized, all men from twenty-five to thirty-five were drafted into the *Garde Mobile* and two new army corps were raised. 'Wonderful activity reigned,' writes one witness, 'confidence reviving everywhere.'

The Emperor himself was not nearly so sanguine. 'I don't know what they are doing in Paris,' he complained. 'They have lost their heads. They have overthrown the ministry. It is not in the midst of the storm that one changes one's pilots and crew.' By now there was nothing that he could do about it, but he did find time to write a touching letter to Ollivier, telling him how much he regretted his departure. Had it not been for the Franco–Prussian War, Emile Ollivier might have gone down in history as one of the greatest statesmen of nineteenth-century France. As it was, he retired to Switzerland and faded from the political scene.

It was not only in Paris that things were to be changed. The new ministry now turned its attention to the front. Leboeuf, the Minister of War, who had given the jaunty assurance that the army was ready to the last gaiter button, had already been dismissed by the new Council of Regency and the War ministry taken on by Palikao. But, of course, everyone knew where the real fault lay: it lay with the Emperor Napoleon. While he remained in command, the French could never hope to win a battle. When Jules Favre demanded that 'the army be concentrated in the hands of one man—but not the Emperor', he was merely expressing what a great many people, including Eugenie and her ministers, were thinking.

Indeed, the Emperor himself was beginning to think along these lines. On the morning after the disasters, one of his staff had tactfully suggested that the Emperor's physical condition was making it impossible for him to be in personal command of the army. With this, the Emperor was inclined to agree. Might it not be possible for him to assume a status similar to that of his rival, the King of Prussia? He would remain constitutional head of the army while a new Commander-in-Chief, corresponding to General von Moltke, could conduct the campaign. There would be nothing degrading about that.

But where to find such a man? Leboeuf was in disgrace. MacMahon had lost his reputation at Froeschwiller. Canrobert, recently arrived at Metz from Châlons, was too conscious of his own shortcomings to accept. There remained Bazaine.

As a soldier who had risen from the ranks to the heights of Marshal, François Achille Bazaine had always been popular with the man in the street. Although physically unattractive (he was squat and pudding-faced) he was known to be personally brave and socially unpretentious. Knowing little of his limitations—his hesitation, his timorousness in command, his tendency to sulk—the public began to urge his appointment as supreme commander. Almost overnight this no more than competent regimental officer, whose main recommendation was that he had not yet been defeated, was transformed into a hero; a man of the people who was going to lead France to victory. Incited by the Press, all Paris set up a clamour for *notre glorieux Bazaine*. As Napoleon seemed quite prepared to accept the choice, Bazaine was duly appointed and the appointment approved by the Empress. On 12 August, just over a fortnight after joining his army at Metz, the Emperor handed over supreme command. It must have been a bitter gesture for a Napoleon.

What was he to do now? While he remained at Metz, Bazaine, who at the best of times lacked initiative, would continue to defer to him. The Emperor's suggestions, however tentatively put, would still be treated as commands. In any case, the army seemed none too eager for him to remain. The obvious course of action would be for him to return to Paris and there take up the reins of government once more. But would it be wise, or even safe, for him to return to the capital at this stage? The Empress certainly did not think so. 'Have you considered,' she asked him in one of her dogmatic telegrams, 'all the consequences which would follow from your return to Paris under the shadow of two reverses?' Napoleon was inclined to agree with her and indeed, if he did have any desire at this time, it was simply to remain with the army. Unwanted in Paris and un-wanted at the front, he decided on a compromise. He would go to Châlons. There, in the great military camp that had known him at the zenith of his power, he might be able to help organize a new army. Before he left, however, it was decided that Bazaine, too, would withdraw from Metz. Unless the Army of the Rhine fell back within the next few days, their line of retreat would be cut off. The German Second Army was already thrust-ing into France south of Metz, driving a wedge between Metz and Paris. Bazaine would make for the fortress of Verdun, half-way to Châlons. This would not upset Paris quite so much as a retreat all the way to Châlons and, once at Verdun, Bazaine might be able to link up with the elusive MacMahon. Mac-Mahon, deaf to all orders to fall back on Metz after his defeat at Froeschwiller, was now known to be somewhere in that vicinity.

Thus, on the morning of 14 August, both Napoleon and Bazaine set out from Metz. Neither was very convinced that he was doing the right thing. The new Commander-in-Chief regretted leaving so well fortified and amply provisioned a base and the Emperor saw his own departure as the irrefutable proof of his rejection by the army. As a result, Bazaine was to move with what looked like almost deliberate slowness and the Emperor to remain as close to the retreating troops as possible.

It was Napoleon who started out first. Leaving Bazaine to cope with the monumental task of getting the dispirited army out of the city, he climbed heavily into his waiting coach. Then, escorted by a troop of glittering *Cent Gardes* and trailing a long line of carriages and *fourgons*, the grey-faced Emperor went trundling down the hot, dusty road towards Châlons.

2

In all that sea of confusion that was the French front line, no one was more confused than Louis, the Prince Imperial. He simply could not understand what was happening. Ever since that glorious day when he had ridden his horse along the ridge above Saarbrücken and had listened, enchanted, to the noise of battle, things had gone wrong. Instead of advancing—flags streaming, eagles flashing and bands blaring—from Saarbrücken to Berlin, they had, for some unaccountable reason, withdrawn. And not only had they withdrawn but they had then given themselves over to a bewildering succession of marches and counter-marches until the news of the defeats of Froeschwiller and Spicheren had come in. At this, Louis could hardly believe his ears. Was it really possible that the great Marshal MacMahon, the hero of Magenta, had been defeated and was fleeing from the enemy? Or that General Frossard, his own military governor whom he had always 'revered as an oracle in the art of war', had been similarly routed? It must have been incomprehensible. And what must have been more incomprehensible still was the fact that instead of launching into an instant and glorious revenge, the army, after a further period of agonizing irresolution, was now retreating. His adored father—a Napoleon and an Emperor—had not only been cast aside but was being bundled off, like a piece of excess baggage, on the road to Châlons. The two of them were now travelling, not towards the sound of the guns, but away from it and with an urgency that looked very much like flight. To the youngster sitting in the jolting carriage beside the tired old man, it must have been scarcely believable.

But Louis, like his mother, had immense reserves of confidence. He was an unquenchable optimist. Too young, moreover, to appreciate the full extent of the disaster, he imagined that things would soon right themselves again, that there would be a halt to this endless retreating and that the army would make a stand and deliver its smashing counter-blow. Although no one tried to keep the truth from him, he would not admit it to himself. This flight, this humiliation, these long faces would not last for long. The nightmare, like all nightmares, would soon be over and the morning would reveal things to be as joyous as they had been before.

Indeed, by the end of that first day's travelling, his optimism seemed to have been justified: the news was slightly better. While the Emperor's cortège had been rumbling down the road out of Metz, Bazaine's retreating troops had been engaged in battle. The advancing Prussians (it was their First Army, under Steinmetz) had stumbled upon the French at the hamlet of Borny, just beyond Metz, and, determined that the French should not slip away unhampered, the Prussians had opened fire. In the muddled fighting that followed, the French more than held their own, but Bazaine, dead set on carrying out what he still regarded as the Emperor's 'commands' to retreat, refused to take advantage of the situation. 'I gave orders that no one should accept battle today,' he ranted. 'I absolutely forbid anyone to advance a yard.' It was an inconclusive fight with both sides claiming victory, but for once the French had not actually been driven back. When Bazaine arrived at Longeville, at the villa in which the Emperor was spending the night, to report on the day's fighting, he was met by smiling faces. 'You have broken the spell,' exclaimed Napoleon and everyone agreed that the engagement had marked the turn of the tide. The universal faith in Bazaine's qualities as a commander had obviously been justified.

The general satisfaction did not, however, prevent the Emperor from giving Bazaine one of those inhibiting pieces of advice which merely encouraged the Commander-in-Chief's habitual irresolution. With a slender chance that Austria and Italy might yet join France, Bazaine was 'to risk nothing by too precipitate action, and above all avoid any further reverses'. The army, in others words, must be kept intact.

An aspect of the engagement at Borny which seems to have escaped the self-congratulatory group at the Emperor's villa that evening was that the fighting had delayed the withdrawal by something like twelve hours. For there could be no question of the retreat not continuing; the need to get away was as imperative as ever. In fact, now that the enemy was so close, it was more imperative than ever.

But nothing seemed able to hurry Bazaine. Not until ten the following morning did he order the withdrawal to continue. Having given that order, he gave no more. At snail's pace, along congested roads, in conditions of the utmost disorder, the Army of the Rhine stumbled along the highway towards Verdun, leaving a cloud of dust to mark its passing. All the while the Prussians moved nearer. The First Army, commanded by

Steinmetz, followed close behind. The Second Army, commanded by Prince Frederick-Charles, was to the south, moving parallel to the French. Having already out-distanced them, however, its tip was beginning to curl northwards. It would soon be astride the Metz–Verdun road, cutting off the French line of retreat.

That day was 15 August, Napoleon's fête day and one of the great anniversaries of the Empire. At dawn Marshal Canrobert found the Emperor sitting at a table at Longeville, silent and immobile, his head resting in his hands. In front of him was a cup of muddy-looking coffee.

'Ah! It's you, Marshal,' murmured the Emperor. 'What is the matter? Any news?'

'No, Sire,' replied Canrobert, 'but today is the fifteenth of August, your Majesty's birthday, and as I have done for many years, I bring you my best wishes.'

'Yes, so it is,' replied the Emperor, shaking his head sadly. 'But I had not thought about it. It is very kind of you to have remembered it, Marshal.'

With that he lapsed back into silence.

His reverie was shattered by the sudden crash of shells. He hurried to the bedside of the still sleeping Prince Imperial.

'Up, Louis!' cried Napoleon. 'Up and dress! The Prussians are shelling the villa.'

As the boy scrambled into his clothes, he looked out of the window to see a shell bursting in the garden below. A group of officers had been sitting there drinking their coffee; the explosion killed three of them.

The imperial caravan got under way as quickly as its bulk would allow and by the afternoon it was at the village of Gravelotte. Here the Emperor put up at an *auberge* which stood beside the road. Wrapped in a long cloak and wearing his *képi*, Napoleon sat in the sunshine to watch the retreating troops file by. There was no cheering. The troops were sullen, and the sight of the imperial carriages, the liveried servants and the brilliantly uniformed escort, made them more sullen still. Late that afternoon Bazaine came riding up. He had brought the Emperor a bunch of flowers to mark the imperial fête. Between them they decided that the Emperor would take final leave of the army the following day. By now it was known that MacMahon was falling back on Châlons; Napoleon would join him there.

He was ready at dawn. Bazaine, only too thankful to be rid of his depressing presence, came to wish him godspeed. Napoleon again spoke of the necessity to get the men to Verdun as quickly as possible. 'To your charge I commit the last army of France,' he muttered. 'Think of the Prince Imperial.' With that he set off.

All his energies were now concentrated on getting to Chalons. It was not that he was going to be of any more use at Chalons than he had been at Metz, but at least the journey gave him an illusion of purpose. It became an end in itself. He decided that the escort of heavy dragoons was too slow; not far out of Gravelotte he changed them for a more swift-moving escort. In some ways it was just as well. Reconnoitring bands of Prussian Uhlans were already cantering across the countryside through which he must pass. In fact, just before reaching Etain, the convoy came across an Uhlan patrol, but the Prussian horsemen turned tail and disappeared over the brow of the hill. The fleeting encounter fired Louis's imagination. First the breaking of the spell of bad luck at Borny and now the headlong flight of an Uhlan patrol! At Etain he wired the good news to the Empress. 'I am very well, and so is Papa. Everything is going better and better. . . .'

By one o'clock they were at Verdun. The townspeople watched the arrival of the imperial party in bemused silence. An obliging *sous-préfet* wanted to know whether or not he should tell them to cheer. The Emperor's only thought was to get on to Châlons. As the railway ran from Verdun, Napoleon decided to abandon his cumbersome caravan and take a train. This was easier said than done. It took several hours for the railway authorities to scrape together a locomotive, a third-class carriage and a collection of cattle-trucks. Some cushions were laid across the wooden seats and the Emperor and his son clambered aboard. Not until almost midnight were they able to get away.

By then Bazaine had lost another battle. While the Emperor had been racing towards Verdun, Bazaine's army had been attacked near Rezonville. As usual, the fighting started in the most haphazard fashion; neither side had meant to give battle that day. Bazaine had been concentrating on keeping his forces out of trouble and Moltke, assuming the apparent confusion of the enemy to be a blind for some deep-laid plan, was moving with caution. But as the French lay encamped near Rezonville (Bazaine had again been slow in getting them started) a Prussian corps, not realizing that what they were about to tackle was in fact the entire Army of the Rhine, opened fire. The battle quickly developed and if the French had fought with more resolution and the Prussians with less, Bazaine could easily have carried the day. He was obsessed, however, with safeguarding his communications with Metz and his hesitation seemed to permeate the entire French army. The day's fighting was characterized by the usual smoke-dimmed confusion, the usual thunderous noise, and the usual suicidal and spectacular cavalry charges.

By nightfall the fighting had died down and both French and Germans were claiming victory. But there was no doubt that, strategically, it was the French who had suffered the more severe blow. The enemy had cut their road to Verdun. With his army in a state of complete disarray, Bazaine decided that he would have to fall back in order to reorganize his forces before continuing the retreat. It was to be, in fact, a withdrawal within a withdrawal. Thus, on the morning of 17 August, the exasperated French army found itself once more on the march; only now it was marching, not towards Verdun, but back towards Metz.

While the Emperor's makeshift train went rattling through the night towards Châlons, Bazaine's army went trudging in the opposite direction towards Metz. From this time on a belief was to take root that Bazaine's withdrawal back to Metz had been intentional. He had waited until he was rid of the Emperor before scurrying back to the safety of the fortress in which he was to be besieged and which he would eventually surrender to the enemy. What other reason could there be for his agonizing slowness, for his lack of firm directions, for his refusal to fight back? It was all part of a treasonable and long-premeditated plan. No one could believe that such gross incompetence could be anything but deliberate.

But that time had not yet come. Bazaine had still one more battle to lose.

CHAPTER SEVEN

The Crisis

1

Châlons was barely recognizable. The camp which had once been a show-place of the Empire was now a shambles. It looked as though it had been sacked by an invading army. Indeed, the remnants of MacMahon's defeated troops that now poured into the camp behaved exactly like invaders: they looted, they destroyed, they drank themselves into a state of insensibility. 'Instead of the fine regiments of other days,' noted one shocked staff officer, 'there was a mass of beings without discipline, cohesion, or rank, a swarm of dirty, unarmed soldiers. . . .' From the east rattled the trains bringing in the survivors of Froeschwiller: 'soldiers of the line without rifles or ammunition pouches, Zouaves in drawers, Turcos without turbans, dragoons without helmets, cuirassiers without cuirassiers, hussars without sabretaches.' Yelling obscenities and ripping off what remained of their sun-bleached uniforms, they staggered off the trains, often to fall asleep wherever they happened to fall, 'scarcely moving even if you kicked them'.

'The officers,' said one observer, 'dared not say a word, or if they did open their mouths, they gave the word of command with that timidity which is so sure a sign of a defeated and demoralized army.'

Almost worse than this disorderly jetsam of Froeschwiller, were the eighteen battalions of the *Garde Mobile de la Seine*. Young, truculent and afire with republican ideas, they bitterly resented being brought from Paris and never hesitated to voice their dissatisfaction. They too, treated their officers with contempt and were likely to burst into spirited renderings of the *Marseillaise* at the slightest provocation.

Finally there were the new recruits—country boys with

127

neither the inclination nor the experience to fight. They could not even keep step, let alone handle a rifle.

It was out of this unpromising material that MacMahon had to forge a new army. That he managed to create a not inconsiderable one of some 130,000 men was a tribute to the resolution with which both the new government and the army were facing the crisis.

The arrival of the Emperor did little to improve matters. In fact, his presence merely antagonized the already surly troops. The sight of the imperial lackeys, splendid in green and gold, hurrying about with steaming cups of chocolate on silver salvers was hardly calculated to placate the hungry men. Nor was the sight of the Emperor himself one to inspire any feelings of loyalty. With those hooded eyes and that flaccid manner, he looked unconcerned, almost callous. He appeared to be interested in nothing other than his own comfort. He commanded no respect whatsoever. Whenever the *mobiles* went tramping past the magnificent imperial tents, one of their number would call out: '*Vive l'Empereur!*'

As one, the others would bellow the response.

'*Un! Deux! Trois! . . . Merde!*'

And the officers pretended not to hear.

It did not need this ribald salutation to bring home the fact of his unpopularity to Napoleon. He knew only too well that he was redundant. It was left to his cousin, Plon-Plon, recently arrived at Châlons, to emphasize it fully.

Until this moment, the capricious Plon-Plon had played almost no part in the conduct of the war. Military strategy was not his *métier*. As the situation worsened, however, so, in his perverse way, did he begin to take an interest. Within the last few days the problem of the Empire had become a political rather than a military one (Paris was seething with revolution) and as politics were something about which Plon-Plon imagined he knew a great deal, he now plunged into the *mêlée*.

On the morning after Napoleon's arrival at Châlons, Plon-Plon conferred in private with Generals Trochu, Schmitz and Berthaut. Of the three, General Louis Jules Trochu was the most notable. Now fifty-five years of age, he was an erect, handsome and fiery-eyed soldier with a distinguished military record. However, for all his talents, he had somehow never made his mark. As an Orleanist he was not popular at Court, and a certain independence of outlook set him apart from his fellow officers. He was talkative to a fault. For the past three years, moreover, he had been in semi-disgrace: in a published pamphlet entitled *L'Armée française en 1867* he had made use of secret military information to draw attention to the inadequacies of the French army. For this breach of confidence and outspoken criticism Trochu had never been forgiven by his colleagues. He was a man, they said, who was not to be trusted. With the opposition, however, he enjoyed immense popularity; General Trochu was the darling of the Paris mob. Fully alive to this fact, Palikao's government had already tried to turn his popularity to good account. On the formation of the new cabinet, they had offered him the Ministry of War. Trochu, who could never resist the opportunity of making a speech, had made his acceptance conditional on his being allowed to expose all the errors of the imperial régime since 1866. This he intended to do from the tribune of the *corps législatif*. As the time was clearly inopportune for any such washing of dirty linen in public Trochu had not been appointed. Now, in the confusion of these August days at Châlons, he was about to be given another chance.

In Plon-Plon's tent that morning, a plan was worked out whereby some order would be brought out of the present chaos. That the implementation of the plan would put an end to what Plon-Plon regarded as the Empress's overbearing behaviour in Paris would be all to the good. Agreed on their scheme, the four men sallied forth to attend the conference which the Emperor had called for that morning.

Napoleon was feeling very ill that day. The breakneck journey from Gravelotte to Châlons (it had taken almost twenty-four hours) had been too much for him. The jolting of the carriage and the lurching of the train had been a continuous torture. The most that his doctor could do was to try and deaden the pain. As a result, Napoleon faced the conference in his usual state of drugged apathy. For the most part the talk between Plon-Plon, MacMahon, Trochu and the others flowed on without any contribution from the Emperor. He sat silent, staring vacantly at the ground.

The only point on which all were agreed at these opening stages was that the army could not remain at Châlons. It was indefensible. But where were they to go? The eighteen battalions of the *mobiles de la Seine*, growing more churlish by the day, would not hear of going anywhere other than back to Paris. In truth, said General Berthaut, having so little equipment and even less experience, they would be better off behind fortifications than in the open. 'Why not send these *mobiles* back to Paris where they can be made use of?' urged Trochu. 'To my mind, those young men will fight much better if they are stimulated by the thought that they are defending their homes. This is their right and duty.' His arguments carried the day and it was decided to send the *mobiles* back that evening.

Then what of Napoleon himself? Was he to remain with the rest of MacMahon's army? Plucking up courage, one of his officers suggested that the Emperor's present position was unworthy of him. 'A Sovereign of France must either be at the head of his troops, or at the head of his government; and at a time like this . . .'

'It's quite true,' muttered the Emperor. 'I seem to have abdicated.'

This was Plon-Plon's cue. The Emperor, he announced in his didactic fashion, had already abdicated twice: once from the government in Paris and a second time from the command of the army at Metz. It was essential that he reassert himself. The only way to do this would be to return to Paris and head the government once more. It would be a risky step; 'But, what the devil,' declared Plon-Plon, 'if we must fall, let us at least fall like men.' To render the defeated Emperor's return more palatable to the Parisians, General Trochu must be appointed governor of the city. That way some of Trochu's popularity might brush off on the discredited Emperor. The governor would act as the Emperor's shield against the revolutionary fervour of the crowd. A single proclamation would announce the return of both Emperor and governor; Trochu would go ahead to soften public opinion and Napoleon would follow a few hours later. 'You will find,' promised Plon-Plon, 'that all will go well.'

1 Napoleon III, Emperor of the
French 1852–70

2 Eugenie, Empress of the French;
during the early years of the Second
Empire

3 Eugenie, Empress of the French.
Painted by Winterhalter towards the
end of the Second Empire

4 Louis, the Prince Imperial of
France, photographed at the age of
thirteen, in 1869

5 'The Four Napoleons'. A Second Empire print showing Napoleon I and his son (afterwards Duke of Reichstadt) and Napoleon III with the Prince Imperial

6 Prince Napoleon (Plon-Plon), irascible cousin of the Emperor Napoleon III

7 The Emperor and the Prince Imperial leaving for the front from station at Saint Cloud

8 'Six of one and half a dozen of the other'. A *Punch* cartoon of Napoleon III and King Wilhelm, each protesting his innocence before John Bull

9 'A vision on the way – "BEWARE!"' A cartoon, published soon after the outbreak of the Franco–Prussian War, showing the ghost of the Great Napoleon cautioning the Emperor Napoleon III and the Prince Imperial

10 Count Otto von Bismarck. His ambition
to unite all Germany under Prussia led to
the outbreak of the Franco–Prussian War

11 King Wilhelm of Prussia, the courteous
and autocratic old monarch who was
proclaimed Emperor of Germany in 1871

12 Crown Prince Frederick of
Prussia, intelligent, sensitive and
liberally-minded heir of King
Wilhelm

13 Uniforms of the Prussian Infantry during the Franco–Prussian war

14 Uniforms of the French Infantry during the Franco–Prussian war

15 Napoleon III and his generals. From contemporary photograph. Front row only from the left: Bourbaki (seated), Trochu (arms folded), MacMahon, Bazaine (hand in tunic), Canrobert (arms folded), Plon-Plon (bare-headed), Leboeuf (behind the Emperor), Napoleon III (seated), the Prince Imperial

16 Marshal Bazaine, Commander-in-Chief of the French Army, whose military ineptitude contributed to the collapse of the Second Empire

17 The Paris crowd in the Place Vendôme, demanding news of the war from Emile Ollivier

18 'Two Mothers'. A cartoon from *Punch* showing the Empress Eugenie hugging the Prince Imperial while a sorrowing *France* says: 'Ah, Madame, a sure happiness for *you*, sooner or later; but here are dear sons of *mine* whom I shall never see again.'

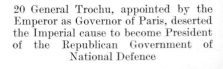

19 Marshal MacMahon. His march to relieve Bazaine ended in the disaster at Sedan

20 General Trochu, appointed by the Emperor as Governor of Paris, deserted the Imperial cause to become President of the Republican Government of National Defence

21 Panic-stricken French troops trying to force their way into the town of Sedan

22 The white flag being waved above the walls of Sedan on the afternoon 1 September 1870

23 General Reille delivering Napoleon III's letter to King Wilhelm of
Prussia on the hilltop above Frénois

24 Napoleon III and
Bismarck outside Madame
Fournaise's cottage on the
morning after the Battle of
Sedan. From a painting by
Camphausen

25 Napoleon III, escorted by Bismarck, on the morning after the Battle of Sedan. From a painting by Camphausen

26 The Republican leader, Jules Favre, proposing the deposition of the Emperor Napoleon III in the *corps légistatif*

27 '*La fin de la légende*'. A caricature of Napoleon III after the fall of the Second Empire

28 Napoleon III and the Prince Imperial. Photographed in England in 1871

29 Camden Place, Chislehurst, Kent. Exile
home of the Imperial family after the fall of
the Second Empire. Napoleon III died in a
room at the back of the house

30 The Emperor Napoleon III photographed on his death-bed

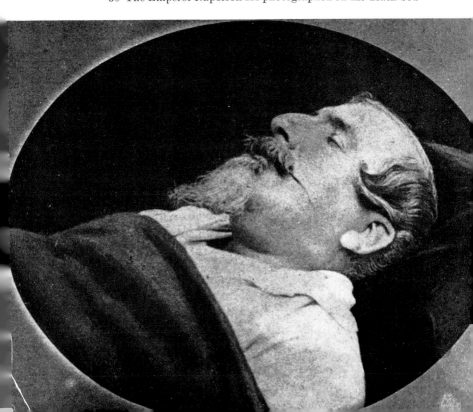

Napoleon was not so sure. Had he sunk so low that he must crawl back to his capital behind Trochu? Was Trochu to be trusted? What would Eugenie say? Eventually, after yet more discussion, Napoleon suggested that he consult the Regent. At this Plon-Plon lost his temper.

'Consult the Regent,' he exclaimed. 'Aren't *you* the Sovereign? This has got to be decided at once!'

As Trochu so admiringly noted, Plon-Plon was now the only Napoleon that counted.

A further suggestion, that the entire army of Châlons retire on Paris as well, helped make up Napoleon's mind. MacMahon agreed that this would be the best possible course. Beneath the walls of the capital, he would be able to manœuvre with much more confidence. This way, the Emperor would be returning to his capital at the head of an army. Napoleon was still not completely convinced, however, that he could trust Trochu. Drawing MacMahon to one side, the Emperor asked whether Trochu was likely to remain loyal to the dynasty. When the Marshal had reassured him on this point, Napoleon agreed to the plan. General Trochu was to take the *mobiles* back that very evening and Napoleon would follow with the Army of Châlons within a day or two. That settled, Trochu was appointed governor.

The new governor was not one to let the occasion pass without a few appropriate words.

'A grave injustice has been done to me by throwing doubt on my loyalty,' he complained. 'I deserve the trust which Your Majesty is putting in me, and I promise Your Majesty that as governor of Paris, I will furnish convincing proofs of my devotion to the cause.'

'Trochu,' Napoleon was to say long after the General had deserted the cause, 'was always fond of phrases.'

2

The new plan had been made on the assumption that Bazaine was still coming on towards Verdun. The news of his reverse at Rezonville the day before had not yet reached Châlons. When it did arrive, the confident tone of Bazaine's telegram implied that his withdrawal had suffered a temporary setback only and that he would soon be on his way again. But the battle of Gravelotte, fought by Bazaine on 18 August—the day after the conference at Châlons—was to put an end to any such hopes.

Gravelotte was the first deliberate and full-scale battle of the war. Until then all the fighting had developed haphazardly; it had never been the result of carefully laid plans on the part of the respective commanders-in-chief. But at ten-thirty on the morning of 18 August, General von Moltke himself commanded both the First and Second armies to attack Bazaine, and Bazaine, for once, was ready to meet them.

The French were drawn up along an undulating plateau from just outside Gravelotte in the south to the village of St Privat in the north. Opposite them at Gravelotte, and separated from them by a deep ravine, were Moltke, Steinmetz and the First Army. In the north, opposite St Privat, was Prince Frederick-Charles with the Second Army.

The battle opened towards noon. At Gravelotte, the Prussian First Army fought with suicidal determination. Time and again they flung themselves against the French defences and time and again they were driven back. By sunset the valley between the two armies was filled with Prussian dead. 'All day long,' wrote Archibald Forbes of the *Daily News* in best Victorian war correspondent fashion, 'from noon until nearly the going down of the sun, the roar of cannon and the roll of musketry has been incessant. The deep ravine . . . was a horrible pandemonium wherein seethed masses of German soldiery, torn by the shell-fire of the French batteries, writhing under the stings of the *mitrailleuses*, bewildered between inevitable death in front and no less inevitable disgrace behind. Again and again frantic efforts were being made to force up out of the hell of the ravine and gain foothold on the edge of the plateau beyond; and ever the cruel sheet of lead beat them back and crushed them down. . . .'

The French held firm. If ever the imperial army should have won a battle, that battle was Gravelotte. The Prussians fought rashly and wastefully and by nightfall their First Army was in a state of panic-stricken confusion. Having suffered almost twice as many casualties as the French, they were all but ready to concede victory. But the French did nothing to claim it. Never once did they exploit the opportunities offered them; never once did they take the offensive; never once did they pursue their faltering enemy. Throughout the day their fighting remained passive. This was due, almost entirely, to the attitude of Bazaine. Having stationed himself well behind the lines, he concerned himself with the battle as little as possible. He issued almost no orders and such as he did issue simply encouraged the negative quality of the French resistance. 'Not everyone,' said Marshal Canrobert afterwards, 'can command an army of a hundred and forty-thousand strong: it is difficult to manage when one isn't used to it.' As Bazaine was certainly not used to it, he played for safety. Saddled with too much responsibility, he abdicated all.

Inevitably, the French line weakened. Marshal Canrobert, commanding the right wing at St Privat, was outflanked by the Second Army and had to fall back. With no reinforcements being ordered up by the listless Commander-in-Chief, the retreat developed into a rout. Thus, while the Prussian First Army, before Gravelotte, was assuming that they had lost the battle, the Second Army was forcing the French right wing to retreat helter-skelter towards Metz. Not until after midnight did the despondent Moltke realize that the French were falling back. By morning the enemy had disappeared altogether. The Prussians had been handed yet another victory.

On 19 August Bazaine withdrew to Metz. 'The troops are tired out with these endless battles . . .' he reported to the Emperor, 'they must be allowed to rest for two or three days.' They rested, in fact, for two or three months. Henceforth the Army of the Rhine, a fully armed and well organized force of over 150,000 men, remained inactive around the great fortress of Metz. *Notre glorieux Bazaine*, having once burnt his fingers, was not going to risk stretching out his hand a second time. From now on he was prepared to do no more than sit tight and hope for the best.

3

The Empress Eugenie had never doubted that she would one day be called upon to hold, for a brief space of time, the centre of the world's stage. As Empress of the French, she had always been fully alive to the dramatic potential of her position. The history of France was full of examples of the behaviour of queens in times of danger and the tragic fate of Eugenie's particular heroine, Marie Antoinette, was never far from her mind. There were even more apposite examples than this. Over ten years before, when Eugenie had been acting as Regent during Napoleon III's absence in Italy, she had been quick to compare herself with that earlier Napoleonic Empress, Marie Louise, at the fall of the First Empire. Eugenie knew how severely that bewildered girl had been criticized for her behaviour in those tumultuous days; *she* would certainly never be guilty of such timidity in the face of disaster. Born during an earthquake, on the fifth aniversary of the death of the Great Napoleon, Eugenie felt sure that fate had some great moment of crisis in store for her.

The moment had now arrived. The crisis had come and Eugenie had risen equal to it. In the last act of the gaslit tragedy of the Second Empire, the Empress Eugenie stood revealed as its undoubted heroine.

'From the very first hour . . .' says the admiring young Filon, 'the Empress had become the centre of everything, the soul of the defence and the real head of the government.' In all the confusion and disintegration of those August days in Paris, she remained at her post—determined, defiant, energetic. She was the driving force behind every important decision taken by the Regency; she was the rallying point for the Imperialists.

And, of course, she was in her element. The Empress may not actually have been enjoying herself but there is no doubt that she was playing her part with a tremendous sense of fulfilment.

With the new ministry, headed by Palikao, she worked in perfect harmony. Unlike the liberals who had made up Ollivier's cabinet, these were men after her own heart—patriotic, uncomplicated, uncompromising. They all had something of her own single-mindedness of purpose. She conducted cabinet meetings with great skill, she initiated many of the measures taken for the defence and provisioning of the capital, she arranged for the national art collections to be moved to places of safety, she saw to the safekeeping of the crown jewels, she organized two hospitals in the Tuileries and visited them daily. 'We shall dispute every foot of the ground,' she said one day. 'The Prussians don't know what they are in for. Rather than accept humiliating terms, we will keep up the fight for ten years.'

But, as with the hammer-blow of each new defeat, morale deteriorated and the revolutionary clamour increased, so did her confident bearing become more and more difficult to maintain. In private, amongst the little band of faithfuls now encamped in the echoing, dust-sheeted apartments of the Tuileries, she occasionally revealed something of her anguish. Wearing always the same beige woollen dress and little black shawl, she moved restlessly from room to room, hardly eating, sleeping only with the help of large doses of chloral. 'Her face was torn with anxiety and mortification . . .' says the unhappy Marie de Larminat. 'All traces of beauty had disappeared from the pale face which seemed graven in sorrow; I thought that she would never, never smile again.' When the news of yet another disaster reached the Tuileries, she would send her young *demoiselles d'honneur* scurrying off to Notre Dame des Victoires. 'I am unable to go myself,' she would say, 'but you go and pray, pray.'

Yet her courage never failed her. One had only to spend a few minutes in her company to come away with confidence restored. So overcome by her example was Henri Chevreau, the Minister of the Interior, that he one day burst into tears. 'She is as firm as a rock!' exclaimed an admirer, and even one of her critics had to admit that she was behaving like 'a Roman'. 'I begin to believe that the Salic Law is quite wrong,' confessed Filon to her one day, 'because men will do more for you than they would for the Emperor.' If everyone had her courage, claimed a friend, 'the country would be saved'.

It was an opinion that Eugenie herself would have heartily endorsed. She was quite sure that a show of resolution could

135

work miracles. That by her own attitude she would be able to arouse and hold the admiration and loyalty of the Parisians, she had no doubts whatsoever. '*Je réponds de Paris*', she had told the Emperor; in other words, she could manage Paris perfectly well without any help from him.

Her only ambition, she declared time and again, was to save France. 'The dynasty is lost . . .' she had cried out on hearing the news of those twin defeats of 6 August, and since then she claimed to be working only for the sake of her country. She wanted Frenchmen of all parties to come together in a great *Union Sacrée*. She longed for the deputies of the Left to forget, as she had done, all about the future of the dynasty and to concentrate on the national danger. There was one honour which she would not forgo, she said when it was all over, 'that of having only one thought, the preservation of the country, and throughout, to have sacrificed to the country's welfare all thought of our dynasty'. She may well have been sincere in this, but she would have had to have been less than human had she not harboured a secret hope that she might yet save the Empire for her son. Surely she was living proof of the vigour and disinterestedness of the dynasty? Surely her heroism would not go unrewarded.

There was another way in which the dynasty could prove its worth. Now that all chance of a brilliant victory seemed lost, there was still one way in which the Emperor could make his mark. Defeated, he could never hope to save his Empire, or even his name, but if he were to be killed in some heroic action, the glory of his death might yet reflect favourably on his dynasty. 'The Emperor's death at the head of his troops seemed to her desirable. . . .' wrote one witness of the Empress, and amongst that distraught company that roamed the Tuileries, the conviction grew that the most valuable service that the Emperor could render them would be to get himself killed in battle. In that moment of high and glorious emotion all France would surely rally to the brave widow and her bright-eyed son. And even if it did not, what more stirring end to this latest Napoleonic saga?

The advent of General Trochu brought such grandiose speculations to an abrupt halt. At midnight on 17 August he

arrived with the news that he had been appointed governor of
Paris and that the Emperor would be returning to the capital
within a few hours. His listeners could hardly believe their ears.
Trochu might be the darling of the Paris mob, but he was the
bête noir of the right-wing Imperialists. To have to hand Paris
over to Trochu was bad enough but for the Emperor to come
crawling back with his tail between his legs was unthinkable.

The Empress gave Trochu a very cool reception. She had
never liked him. His slight squint, she felt sure, was a sign that
he was not to be trusted. However, with extreme reluctance, she
accepted him as governor. Palikao was no more welcoming. 'I
can't imagine why the Emperor sent you,' he grumbled. 'You'll
only add to my difficulties.' It was no wonder that Trochu
went off to seek more congenial company elsewhere.

The proposed return of the Emperor neither Eugenie nor
Palikao would countenance. Under no circumstances must
Napoleon come back to Paris. During the course of a discussion
which the watching Filon called 'long, agitated and more or less
incoherent', the Empress made clear her views. The decision
for the Emperor to return had been inspired, she said pointedly
to Trochu, by his enemies. He would never enter Paris alive.
'Do you know, General,' she argued, 'that fifty armed men could
walk straight into this room and murder me without any
difficulty? But they do not attack me. Why? Simply because I
do not defend myself, and because they know that if I disappeared the Empire would still remain. But imagine the
Emperor in this palace, which is a trap for Sovereigns. What
would happen to him? Imagine the onslaught of all the bitter
enemies who are now combined against him. There would be a
choice: either the army would side with him, and then there
would be civil war between the army and the people of Paris;
or else the troops would desert him, and revolution and massacre
would follow. In either case who would profit? The Prussians.'

Nor would the Empress and Palikao hear of MacMahon's
army retiring on the capital. Paris was quite able to defend itself.
For MacMahon to fall back would look like a desertion of
Bazaine. As far as Eugenie and her ministers knew, *notre
glorieux Bazaine* was still battling valiantly to get his troops
to Verdun. How could MacMahon think of leaving him in the

lurch and retiring to the safety of Paris? No, the thing to do would be for MacMahon to march resolutely to the assistance of Bazaine and for the two marshals together to 'strike a great blow'.

The Empress's vigorous arguments carried the day and a telegram was sent off to Châlons advising both Napoleon and MacMahon to stay where they were.

It has since been claimed that, strategically, the return of the Emperor and the Army of Châlons to the capital would have been the best possible course of action. The Germans, with lines of communication dangerously stretched, would have had to have faced a still powerful army in a well-fortified position. But to Paris, in those feverish August days, things looked very different. The government lived in daily expectation of revolution. Only three days before there had been an abortive attempt at rebellion at La Vilette. 'What letters of blood would have covered that unwritten page of our history which described, under the date 17 August, the return of the Sovereign into the midst of a people maddened with exasperation and bitterness and athirst for vengeance?' asked Filon. What would have been the reaction of the populace to the desertion of their latest hero—Bazaine? If Bazaine, the one-time private soldier, were abandoned to his fate while Napoleon and MacMahon scurried into the safety of Paris, could the government and dynasty hope to survive? They had no idea that Bazaine was himself busily scurrying into the safety of Metz. It was an 'imperative duty for us to avoid any act which might bring about a revolutionary movement', declared one of the ministers. And, besides all this, Palikao's newly-organized and complicated system of supply and reinforcements was not geared to any such sudden change of plan.

Lest her husband should still entertain any ideas of returning to Paris, Eugenie backed up her original telegram with an explanatory letter. She handed a rough draft of the letter to Filon for copying and he, appalled at its harsh and commanding tone, entreated her to rewrite it. He would have preferred it to have been a simple dispatch, giving an account of the situation and the views of the different ministers, while leaving the Sovereign to make up his own mind about a possible course of action. Had the once-mighty Emperor Napoleon really fallen so low?

'Do you think,' answered Eugenie, 'that I am not the first to feel all that is horrible in his position? But the message that you propose to send would not stop him, and he is lost if we do not stop him.'

So the letter went off.

That it was due to the Empress Eugenie's uncompromising stand that Napoleon and MacMahon did not fall back on Paris on 18 August there is no question. To her credit, she never pretended otherwise. 'For myself,' she afterwards said, 'I deliberately accept *the whole of the responsibility* for those political events in which I was concerned as Regent.' However, for the rumour that she kept Napoleon at bay in order that she might continue wielding power in Paris, there is very little justification. She was merely acting, as always, from what she considered to be the highest motives: she sincerely imagined that what she was doing was in the best interests of France. Her motto, she always declared in that robust fashion, was 'Do what you must, come what may'. She was doing, she had no doubt, what she must.

It was in this spirit then that Eugenie sent off the letter that brought home to Napoleon, perhaps as never before, 'all that was horrible in his position'. One of her favourite traits in a man, she used to say, was 'to do right, even if it involves personal sacrifice'. Well, if Napoleon did not know what was right, it was up to her to tell him. She always knew.

4

So now he had nowhere to go. Bazaine had not wanted him at Metz; MacMahon had not wanted him at Châlons; and Eugenie did not want him in Paris. His very last attempt to assert his will had ended in this humiliating rebuff. He, who a mere three weeks ago had still been looked upon as the dominant sovereign on the Continent of Europe, was now nothing more than an encumbrance to his government and his army; an embarrassment to be kept well away from both the council chamber and the battlefield. Eugenie's uncompromising letter probably crushed what little remained of his spirit. He at this stage decided, he afterwards said, 'to give himself up to the course of events'. In fact, he had very little choice.

There was one thing that he could do, however, and that was to get rid of Plon-Plon. It would be an infinite relief to be free of that nagging, reproaching, grumbling presence, particularly now that Eugenie had so obviously had her way and the Emperor stood revealed as little better than a hen-pecked husband. So Plon-Plon was sent to Italy. He was to see if he could persuade his father-in-law, King Victor Emmanuel, to enter the war. It was a hopeless mission, but he went. With him went the last chance of Napoleon ever being spurred on to independent action.

Marshal MacMahon was in a hardly less bemused state than his master. He, too, did not know what to do with himself and his army. The government would not allow him to fall back on Paris and with the Prussian Third Army, under the Crown Prince, drawing nearer to unfortified Châlons every day, he could not possibly remain where he was. Nor was his army anything like strong enough to take the field on its own. What was he to do? A born second-in-command, he longed for someone to give him an order. In desperation he sent a wire to Bazaine. Bazaine was, after all, his Commander-in-Chief. MacMahon should have known better. Bazaine's answer, richly typical, merely mirrored MacMahon's own irresolution. 'I presume that the minister would have given you orders,' he wired blandly, 'your operations being at the moment entirely outside my zone of action.' This was no help at all and a subsequent message from Bazaine, informing MacMahon that he hoped to resume his chequered retreat in a day or two, merely increased MacMahon's confusion. Should he presume that Bazaine was again setting out from Metz or should he accept the far more likely possibility that there was no hope of Bazaine ever breaking out? If Bazaine were still coming on, then should he advance to meet him? Or if Bazaine were indeed besieged, would it not be better for him to fall back on Paris in spite of all orders to the contrary?

At this point the telegraph line between Metz and Châlons

was cut. Another appeal for orders from MacMahon to Bazaine, smuggled through the enemy lines by a messenger, brought no reply whatsoever. Nor did frantic telegrams to neighbouring commanders bring any clarification of the situation. Bazaine was obviously trapped and MacMahon was left feeling more uncertain than ever.

On the afternoon of 20 August his mind was made up for him. The enemy cavalry was reported to be jogging boldly across the countryside less than twenty-five miles from Châlons. Moving with an urgency notably lacking from recent manoeuvres, the army—and with it the Emperor—cleared out of Châlons. In pouring rain the troops trudged out, leaving the once-proud military camp in a state of utter desolation. They were headed, this time, for Rheims. MacMahon, forced into making a move of some sort, had decided on a compromise. As Rheims lay to the north of Châlons, he would be neither retreating west towards Paris nor advancing east towards Bazaine. That way he could still retire on Paris at some future date without actually seeming to desert Bazaine at present. He was settling, in fact, for the worst of all possible worlds. The only result of this compromise was that he lost still more valuable time.

Paris was suffering no such agonies of irresolution. Palikao knew exactly what MacMahon must do. He must march boldly to the rescue of Bazaine. Any other possibility was unthinkable. With *notre glorieux Bazaine* in danger of being besieged in Metz, it would be political suicide to abandon him. That it might mean military suicide to try and rescue him was something which Palikao was not prepared to admit. Having convinced his fellow ministers of both the advisability and the feasibility of his plan, Palikao dispatched Eugène Rouher, the president of the senate whose political standing had at one time earned him the sobriquet of *vice-empereur*, to Rheims to give MacMahon his new orders. Anxious though MacMahon might be for orders, these he was not prepared to carry out. It was madness. Rouher, who had arrived primed with all Palikao's arguments in favour of a march to relieve Bazaine, was soon made to appreciate just how mad it was. Faced with the military realities of the situation, Rouher gave way. Between them he and MacMahon drafted a proclamation in which it was announced that the Emperor and MacMahon would return to Paris after all and that once there, the Army of Châlons would form the nucleus of a great new force—that Nation in Arms for which the men of the Left were crying out with such vehemence. The proclamation drawn up, Rouher returned to Paris. The Army of Châlons was expected to follow him within a few hours.

It never did. Not only was the project anathema to the government, but that night a message reached Châlons from Bazaine. It was the dispatch which had been sent off three days before, after the battle of Gravelotte. In it Bazaine had announced that he was withdrawing to Metz to rest his men for two or three days only, and that he would then be breaking out to the north. This meant that he was probably already on his way. MacMahon could hardly ignore this latest development. If Bazaine were indeed on the move, then MacMahon would not be embarking on a foredoomed march to relieve him; he would be going to join him. United, the two armies would be able to strike that eagerly anticipated 'great blow'. MacMahon dare not fall back on Paris now; he must try and form a junction with Bazaine. The retreat on Paris was cancelled and on 23 August, the Army of Châlons set out in a north-easterly direction towards the River Meuse, close to the Belgian border. In the phrase that seemed to inject new confidence into the Parisians, MacMahon and Bazaine were about 'to join hands'.

And in the dust of MacMahon's disgruntled army, passive, unprotesting and of no more use than one of his own cumbersome *fourgons*, travelled the Emperor Napoleon III.

Part Three

CHAPTER EIGHT

The Road to Sedan

1

All Europe stood amazed at the string of French reverses. It seemed barely conceivable that the once-mighty Empire should have been brought to its knees so rapidly. The various Continental countries, instead of waiting to see whether or not they should join France in crushing upstart Prussia, now began regarding the victors more seriously. 'The attitude of the Great Powers, now that our successes are more and more conspicuous, grows more favourable to us,' noted the Crown Prince Frederick. 'This is certainly encouraging, but no less certainly significant for, if things had gone the other way, they would with one accord have fallen on us.'

The British Foreign Minister, Lord Granville, claimed that any possibility of the neutral powers trying to stop the war was by now quite out of the question. Neither the sensitive French nor the triumphant Prussians would welcome it. Granville blamed the rapid French disintegration on 'a loose, unprincipled Government, and to everything having become so corrupt'. With Lord Lyons, the British Ambassador in Paris, reporting that the dynasty was falling 'lower and lower' and that the Empress 'has much pluck, but little hope', Gladstone was already preparing for the fall of the Empire. It might be the best thing for Europe, he assured Queen Victoria. Although the Prime Minister was 'always very fond of the French', noted the Queen in her Journal, 'he thought a Bonaparte on the throne had always an element of uncertainty and danger. . . .'

Victoria was inclined to agree with him. She felt sorry for the Emperor in his present predicament, but she had never forgiven him for his Italian campaign of 1859. Since then, there had been very little contact, or sympathy, between the two sovereigns.

The Prince Consort, she told her daughter, the Prussian Crown Princess, 'had the worst opinion of him, which was never removed'.

The Crown Princess needed no reminding. But, as the Prussian victories mounted, so did her previously outraged tone become more patronizing. 'I am very glad I am not in the Empress's position'; she assured her mother, 'the Emperor's, too, must be a dreadful one. . . . Ever since the Emperor's health has been failing, the prestige of his genius has been waning and he has made one blunder after another. It is a melancholy history.'

'May we all learn what frivolity, conceit and immorality lead to!' she wrote on a later occasion, in that same sanctimonious fashion. 'The French people have trusted in their own excellence, and have completely deceived themselves.'

Nor, in her exultation, could the Crown Princess resist having a dig at her brother, the Francophile Prince of Wales, by comparing his inactivity with the achievements of her husband, Crown Prince Frederick. 'I am sure dear Bertie must envy Fritz who has such a trying, but such a useful life. I had rather see him serve his country than sit by my side. . . .'

At that very time Fritz, the Crown Prince, was marching his victorious Third Army towards Paris. He still had no idea that MacMahon had set out to relieve Bazaine. Nor had Moltke. It never occurred to the Prussian High Command that the French would do anything so foolish. So, leaving the First Army under Prince Frederick-Charles to see that Bazaine did not escape from Metz, Moltke continued to march his other two armies (the Crown Prince's Army and the newly constituted Army of the Meuse) towards Paris. When his cavalry patrols, scouting ahead, found that Châlons had been deserted, Moltke very naturally assumed that the French were falling back on Paris. This would be their only sensible course of action. For MacMahon to march to the aid of Bazaine, thereby exposing his flank to not only one, but two, enemy armies, would be the height of folly. 'I could not myself think it possible that an adversary of Marshal MacMahon's standing would commit such gross blunders,' said the Crown Prince afterwards.

Not until the evening of 25 August did Moltke realize that

MacMahon was doing precisely that. He obtained his information, ironically enough, from a copy of the Parisian newspaper, *Le Temps*. In it was a report that MacMahon had set out from Rheims in a north-easterly direction. At this Moltke made a snap decision: he ordered both the Crown Prince's Army and the Army of the Meuse to halt their march towards Paris and to swing northwards instead. They were to head towards the doggedly marching MacMahon. The trap was being set.

2

When the Army of Châlons set out from Rheims, the Prince Imperial was still with it. Although the boy had no real conception of the desperateness of the situation, he was aware that something had gone very wrong. These humiliating retreats, these endless debates, these constant changes of plan were bringing home to him, ever more distinctly, the unheard-of possibility that France might be beaten. What he probably appreciated better than the series of strategic blunders which had led the army to this present impasse, was that the troops themselves had lost faith. There was more than a hint of disloyalty in the air. His appearance among them might still raise a cheer but for the most part they were sullen and, at times, downright hostile. They were no longer that proud and enthusiastic body of men whose martial boasts had once been like music to his young ears. And what had happened to his father? It must have been obvious, even to the devoted Louis, that the Emperor had been cast to one side and that his opinion now counted for very little.

Unlike Napoleon, however, the Prince Imperial was incapable of resigning himself to the hopelessness of the situation. He fretted continuously. He was always asking for news and suspected that it was being kept from him. He sought reassurance everywhere. He lived in daily expectation of a turn of the tide, of a glorious *ravanche*, of a resounding victory that would send the enemy reeling back over the frontier. With each new reverse he bit back his disappointment and began to hope afresh. It would not do for a soldier to show discouragement.

L
147

Ever the Prince, he presented a brave face in public, while looking, all the time, for some reflection of his own—simulated—confidence in the faces of those around him.

In time, the strain began to tell. He had always been highly strung and, living as he now was—in a state of permanent tension, of hope deferred and disappointment suppressed—his health began to give way. He became restless and feverish; his sleep was fitful and he lost his appetite. He suffered from the most violent headaches. He should, of course, have been sent back to Paris, but Eugenie was adamant that his place was with the army. Obsessed with the parallels between the lives of Marie Antoinette and herself, she did not want Louis to suffer the fate of the little Dauphin. Louis must not, like his predecessor, become a prisoner of the revolutionaries. 'I would rather see my son killed by the enemy,' she is said to have cried out, 'than become another Louis XVII.' She still dreamed, moreover, that Louis would in some way cover himself with honour. Were he to return meekly to Paris, all hope of her dream coming true would be dashed. In nothing was the Empress more of a Roman mother than in her attitude towards her son.

Of all the desperate marches which the French army had been forced to make during the past month, this march from Rheims towards the River Meuse was probably the worst. At snail's pace, in streaming rain and squelching mud, hungry, demoralized and convinced that they were heading towards their doom, the men trudged on. Almost all discipline had gone by the board. When the troops wanted to eat they simply broke rank and pillaged the countryside with ruthless disregard of the local peasants. At night they fought each other over half a loaf of bread or a relatively dry patch of earth on which to sleep. When the villagers called out to ask where they were going, they yelled back, '*A la boucherie! A la boucherie!*' What infuriated them as much as the rain and the lack of supplies and the general muddle-headedness which had brought them to their present pass, was the presence of the Emperor. Muttering curses, they would have to move to one side while the seemingly endless train of imperial carriages came splashing past, and, in the evenings, while the rain extinguished their own camp fires, they

would see the Emperor's comfortable tents and smell the food
which was being prepared in his well-equipped field kitchens.
With each day they resented his presence more and more. Even
the officers began to complain about him. 'We are dragging our
golden ball and chain,' they would mutter, as his *fourgons*
held up their line of march. One day an officer had to grab
a rifle from a soldier who had positioned himself in a hedge;
the man had been taking careful aim at Napoleon's passing
carriage.

'*Misérable!* What are you doing here?' cried the officer.

'Oh,' replied the man airily, 'I was just going to pick off the
cochon who brought all this on us.'

But no one, not even Louis, knew what Napoleon was suffering. By now he was very ill indeed. With his lack-lustre eyes, his
grey complexion and his whitening hair, he already looked like
a corpse. Every lurch of the carriage was agony for him. Once
he had to get it to stop so that he could clamber out and rest his
head against a tree. 'Ah,' he whispered one day to an aide-de-
camp, 'if I were only able to die.' He was no less tormented
by the sufferings of his men. They imagined that he cared nothing for them but, in fact, their discomforts, their privations, the
hopelessness of their position were constantly on his mind.
Even better than they he realized that this insane manœuvre
could lead only to their destruction.

In all the blackness of his despair, there was one flicker of
light—the presence of his son. No matter how deep the humiliation or how desperate the foreboding or how frightful the pain,
he could still put out his hand and feel beside him the reassuring
presence of Louis. In the heart-rending chaos of the last few
weeks, one thing had remained unaltered: the love between
father and son. This alone had made the Emperor's days
endurable.

Now he would have to sacrifice even this solace. By the end
of the third day's march it had become clear to the Emperor
that the end could not be far off. As the Army of Châlons crawled
north-east towards the Meuse, the Prussians were swinging in a
great arc to the south of them, cutting them off from Paris.
Within a few days the French would be trapped with their backs
to the Belgian border. Napoleon, determined that his son should

not be exposed to the coming disaster, arranged for the boy to leave the army. In the care of three aides-de-camp and a detachment of *Cent Gardes*, he was to be sent to some frontier town from which he would be able to slip into Belgium if necessary. This time Napoleon made the decision without referring to Eugenie; he probably guessed what her answer would be.

At dawn on 27 August, father and son parted company. Louis, for all his apprehensions, was dry-eyed. He knew that as a soldier it was not for him to question or disobey commands. The Emperor, as always, looked calm, almost detached, but his heart must have been breaking. Would he ever see Louis again? So certain was he that his own death could not be long in coming, that it must have seemed unlikely. Was this to be their last embrace?

They parted, and under a grey sky, the Prince Imperial's little cortège went clattering away in the direction of Mézières.

3

Having dispatched MacMahon to effect his celebrated junction with Bazaine, Palikao's government prepared itself for what it assumed would be a siege of Paris. As far as they knew, the Prussian Third Army, under the Crown Prince, was still heading towards the capital. They had no idea that it was swinging northwards—away from Paris—in order to trap MacMahon on the Meuse. Almost all the energies of Palikao's ministry, therefore, were directed towards equipping the capital for a prolonged investment. In less than three weeks eighty new battalions of the National Guard were recruited and armed, bringing the defenders of Paris to a total of 270,000 men. The outer forts and inner ring of defences were equipped with heavy guns, a great many of which (on Eugenie's suggestion) were borrowed from the navy. To delay the approach of the Prussian siege artillery, bridges and locks were destroyed and tunnels blocked. Over 300,000 head of sheep and cattle were brought into the capital and pastured in the Bois de Boulogne and the Luxembourg Gardens. By the beginning of the last week of

August, Paris felt that she was ready to hold out against the enemy for as long as was necessary.

'I think,' wrote the Empress Eugenie to her nieces on 26 August, 'that the Prussians will be before Paris in a few days and that the siege will begin. . . . I view the situation calmly. Maybe this is because of tiredness and uncertainty, but I regard this development as good and I have hope. . . .' Indeed, one suspects that she may have been looking forward to an investment; her particular talents would be very suited to the role which she would then be called upon to play. Defiant, valiant and unyielding, she would come to symbolize the spirit of France unvanquished. What Joan of Arc and La Grande Mademoiselle had been to other centuries, she would be to this. 'We shall hold out in Paris if we are besieged, or if we are out of Paris we shall still hold out to the end,' she one day declared. 'There can be no question of peace.' She is said to have toyed with the idea of riding her horse through the streets of the capital in an effort to inspire the populace to greater heights of patriotism, and in another, less triumphant, mood, she claimed that even if she were not wanted as Empress, she would like to be allowed to remain as a simple hospital nurse. She would be content with any residence, with any rank, just as long as she was able 'to experience all the sufferings, the perils, the anguish of the besieged capital'.

'Believe me,' she wrote to her mother in a less exultant moment, 'I am not defending the throne, but *honour*, and if after the war, when not a single Prussian will be left on French soil, the country does not want us, then perhaps, far from noise and people, I may forget. . . .'

Of considerable comfort to the Empress during this agonizing period was the presence of her old friend, the writer Prosper Mérimée. Mérimée had known Eugenie since her childhood (as a young literary lion, he had been taken up by her socially ambitious mother) and he had proved a valuable addition to Eugenie's circle. By his wit, his worldliness and his scholarship, he had lent an aura of distinction to the somewhat harum-scarum imperial Court; the presence of this eminent man of letters had tended to make it less philistine. For all his renowned scepticism, however, Mérimée had a compassionate heart, and it was never more valuable to the Empress than it was now. Day after day, in spite of having suffered a stroke earlier that month, he came limping into her apartments. There he would sit, part-confessor, part sounding-board, while Eugenie held forth unabated. Not that her impassioned flow of talk was considered to be anything but superb by her listener.

'I know of nothing more admirable,' wrote the enraptured Mérimée of the Empress. *'Elle me fait l'effet d'une sainte.'*

This was all very well, but not every Parisian shared Mérimée's estimate of the Empress. She might be a saint to her entourage but her heroics were making very little impression on the population as a whole. In fact, they hardly knew about them. Beyond the threshold of the Tuileries, no one seemed to be paying much attention to her. She was like some great trage-dienne playing to an empty house. Her frequently repeated vows that she would never desert her post, her appeals to all Frenchmen to work together, her doggedly conducted negotia-tions with the foreign ambassadors, her nights without sleep and her days without food did not really alter the situation. She was magnificent but she was expendable. With the great mass of the people she had no contact whatsoever. Nor, with the best will in the world, could she hope to have any. Dissatisfied, inflammable and uncompromisingly republican, the great majority of the Parisian working-class people were not prepared to rally to her side. She might protest that she had cast aside all thought of the dynasty and was fighting only for France, but they never really believed it. The Parisians had been opposed to the régime far too long to associate themselves with it now. No matter how admirable, how patriotic, how genuinely un-selfish Eugenie's present stand might be, it could not alter the fact that she represented the hated Empire. In her heart of hearts she knew it. While her luck—or rather Napoleon's luck— had held, they had tolerated her; now that the Empire had fallen on bad times, they could hardly wait to jettison it. *'En ce pays,'* complained Eugenie bitterly, *'on n'a pas le droit d'être malheureux.'* 'All things in this world may cause envy—except a crown,' she wrote to her mother. 'One gives up everything— repose, happiness, affection, to find oneself surrounded by nothing but weakness or worse.'

The army which she feared most, she one day admitted, was not the Prussian army, but 'the army which M. de Bismarck has in Paris'.

Indeed, this particular army was ready to go into action at the first sign of collapse of the imperial authority. Until such time, however, its leaders were busily undermining that authority as best they could. Radical journalists and street-corner orators railed ceaselessly against the mismanagement of the war and the inefficiency of the régime. In the *corps législatif* the Republican deputies—such men as Jules Favre, Ernest Picard and Jules Ferry—were planning to gain power by constitutional means. The fact that the governing party, composed of right-wing Bonapartists, moderate Bonapartists and some of the independents, was beginning to lose its cohesion, gave them reason for optimism. First the Republicans tried to get nine extra deputies added to Palikao's cabinet ('we distrust the men of the Empire,' explained Picard, 'and if you expect the Left to support the cabinet, you must put some of our members in a position to see what the ministers are doing'), but the assembly voted against this proposal. Then they appealed to the independent deputies, who formed a considerable section, to ditch Palikao's ministry and to assume power themselves by making the *corps législatif* the sovereign body—something in the nature of a convention. The Left, always more dynamic than the deputies of the Centre, could then gradually gain control of this body. Against this proposal, too, Palikao just managed to scrape together a majority vote. 'However,' as the Emperor was afterwards to remark, 'the wind had been set in that direction.'

What Favre and his fellow Republicans were hoping for was to gain power without a revolution. Although the threat of a revolution was very useful for frightening more moderate deputies into giving them what they wanted, they themselves stood to lose as much from a revolution as did the government. A popular insurrection could so easily get out of control. Leadership of the movement would almost certainly pass from them to the men of the extreme Left—those violent 'Red' revolutionaries such as Blanqui, Delescluze and Pyat. These men were to be feared more than the Imperialists.

The great hope of the Republican deputies was General

Trochu. The new governor of Paris was at one and the same time a nominee of the Emperor and the idol of the masses. Although he was not a Republican, neither was he an Imperialist; he would thus be worth cultivating. On the morning of 21 August, a deputation of the leading members of the Left called on the General. The meeting was inconclusive but the visitors sensed that they were dealing with a man who longed for position and whose vanity had been wounded by the off-hand manner in which he was being treated by the Empress and her ministry. 'I really believe he is our man,' remarked one of the deputies after the meeting.

He was a strange man, Trochu. The Empress and her circle certainly did not know what to make of him. 'I still seem to see him,' wrote Filon years afterwards, 'an upright figure, tightly buttoned into his uniform, but fidgety and agitated in his demeanour, his proud, refined expression, his large bald head, his compressed lips, his eyes, ever shifting, full of fire, the eyes of a visionary. One felt him to be a mixture of incompatibles. . . .' He seemed far too bombastic to be taken seriously; his verbosity bored them and his hyperbole embarrassed them. He one day repeated to a gathering of ministers a speech which he had just delivered to the National Guard. In it, so he told his bored audience, he had exhorted the men to 'die well' and to maintain 'in the supreme agony that proud and tragic attitude which alike becomes men, citizens and soldiers'.

'Good God, General,' interrupted the exasperated Empress, 'one dies as one can.'

His protestations of loyalty were no less highly coloured. 'Madam, I am a Breton, a Catholic and a soldier,' he once cried out, flinging himself to his knees before the Empress, 'and I will serve you to the death.' When the embarrassed Eugenie put out her hand to gesture him to his feet, he clasped it in his own and kissed it passionately.

'An honest man has no need of such a flood of words to express his readiness to do his duty,' the Empress afterwards remarked.

Her opinion was shared by the ministry. Trochu might behave like a buffoon, but they suspected that he was up to some mischief. In a letter to *Le Temps* soon after his appointment as

154

governor, he had declared that he would use 'moral force' only to keep order in the capital. The ministers, living in daily expectation of revolution, asked him to clarify the statement. With his wordy explanation doing little to enlighten them, Clément Duvernois asked him point-blank, 'Then, General, if the Regent were attacked, what would you do?'

'I should lay down my life on the steps of the throne,' replied Trochu fervently.

But they did not believe him. As a result, both Eugenie and her ministers thought it wisest to have as little to do with him as possible. They tolerated him, but that was all. Whenever he subjected them to one of his extravagant speeches, they scarcely bothered to hide their amusement. They never referred to him and they never took him into their confidence. His task, assigned to him by the Emperor, was the defence of Paris, but the government gave him no information to help him in the preparation of this defence. 'I have received from the Government, neither verbally nor in writing, neither directly nor indirectly, neither in confidence nor otherwise, any communication whatsoever relative to the movement of the Prussian Army,' wrote Trochu in a justifiably aggrieved tone to Palikao. He had to judge, he complained, by what he read in the newspapers. His complaint was ignored.

Yet the government should, perhaps, have fought down its distaste and worked in close conjunction with him. They should, like the men of the Left, have flattered him and made him feel important. After all, he was their one sure link with the opposition. Although the Republican deputies had remained deaf to the Empress's appeals for a political truce, she might have been able to reach them through Trochu. Even if men like Favre had not been prepared to meet her half-way, someone like Gambetta, who was afterwards to conduct the country's defence with something of Eugenie's own vigour and purposefulness, might well have responded to an approach by the governor. But then neither Eugenie nor her ministry wanted any truck with Gambetta; to them he was nothing better than a revolutionary firebrand. And as for Trochu's contacts with the Left, they could see them in a treasonable light only. When he explained to the Empress that he was seeing the Republican deputies in order 'to keep in touch with public opinion', his frankness did nothing to disarm her.

In a way, she was right to be suspicious of him. Trochu seems to have been playing a waiting game. Favouring neither the Imperialists nor the Republicans, but being ambitious for power, he kept a foot in both camps. Lest a victory at the front strengthen Palikao's government, he dare not openly oppose the Regency, but with the opposition going from strength to strength he must needs keep friendly with them as well. Whichever way the cat jumped, he would be safe. 'Up to the very last moment,' said the Emperor afterwards, 'he let circumstances decide whether he would be the saviour of the dynasty or the man of the revolution.'

It was not until 28 August that Eugenie realized that the Prussian Third Army had turned away from Paris and that almost the whole of the enemy force could now be concentrated against MacMahon's army. With this news, all hope of Mac-Mahon and Bazaine ever joining hands faded and Eugenie's stubborn belief in an ultimate victory began to falter. 'In a few days from now there will probably be a great battle,' she wrote to her nieces. 'How terrible war is!' And although, even now, her courage did not fail her, her nerves began to give way. She alternated between periods of deep depression and spurts of almost frightening feverishness. She looked pitiful.

One evening she went out into the gardens of the Tuileries for a breath of air. With a white lace scarf thrown over her hair, she walked, pale and silent, under the tall chestnut trees. The setting sun had turned the sky a fiery red; against it the domes and gables and balustrading of the palace stood out in sharp relief. 'Look!' cried the Empress suddenly in a loud voice to her companion Madame Carette, 'one would think the Tuileries were on fire.' When she re-entered her apartments, her companions were appalled by her anguished expression. 'Only those who have lost all that life is worth living for,' wrote Madame Carette, 'can form any idea of the Empress's state of mind at this moment, seeing before her, as she did, the abyss into which France was about to fall, threatened both by revolution and defeat.'

'She is worn out with fatigue and emotion,' reported Metternich to his government. 'The day before yesterday she said to me that all night long she had been telling herself that she was mad, that all this was not true, was only the working of a disordered brain. The conviction was so strong that on waking she shed tears of despair to find that she was not mad.'

4

Late on the afternoon of 26 August, the Prussian scouts discovered MacMahon's army among the dripping trees of the Argonne.

At the sight of the Prussian patrols, the stark madness of the whole operation became suddenly and frighteningly clear to MacMahon. The Crown Prince was much closer than he had imagined; Bazaine was obviously not planning a break-out from Metz; and in a great arc to the south of the French lay three German armies. By now the enemy was in front of him, to the south of him and behind him. MacMahon's only hope lay in calling off the advance and retreating to the north. Orders to this effect were sent out and MacMahon wired his decision to Paris.

Palikao's answer was both prompt and predictable. 'If you abandon Bazaine, revolution will break out in Paris, and you yourself will be attacked by the entire enemy forces. . . . You have at least thirty-six hours' march over [the Crown Prince] perhaps forty-eight; you have nothing in front of you but a feeble part of the forces which are blockading Metz. . . .'

To back up this message, Palikao sent a further, more forceful one. 'In the name of the Council of Ministers and the Privy Council, I order you to aid Bazaine. . . .'

MacMahon countermanded his latest orders to retreat northwards and, ignoring a feeble protest from the Emperor, continued on towards the Meuse. With this particular manifestation of lunacy on the part of Palikao, the Empress is said not to have associated herself. Filon claims that 'this time the Regent, whatever may have been her personal opinion, made no comment'.

On 30 August MacMahon's army began to cross the Meuse.

For the northernmost corps, the crossing was not too hazardous. But in the south the 5th Corps, under General de Failly, was dangerously close to the advancing enemy. Failly had already, the night before, had a brush with the Prussians and now, in a state of utter exhaustion, his men were encamped on the slopes outside the village of Beaumont. No sentries had been posted, the horses were unsaddled and the men, enjoying the unaccustomed sunshine, were in no hurry to break camp and move on.

It was upon this peaceful, if haphazard, scene that the Germans stumbled on that morning of 30 August. They could scarcely believe their luck. Within minutes their artillery opened fire. The result was pandemonium. Here and there the German onslaught was met by desperate resistance, but for the most part the French simply turned tail and fled. Officers were said to have gone on their knees to the men in an effort to get them to stop this headlong flight, but it was no use. By sunset the valleys between Beaumont and the Meuse were a chaos of overturned vehicles, abandoned guns, riderless horses and thousands upon thousands of wildly fleeing men. A last-minute cavalry charge, ordered by the desperate Failly, did almost nothing to check the advancing enemy. In the fast-fading light his demoralized troops swarmed over the Meuse bridges. Those who despaired of ever getting across simply plunged into the river and were drowned. The French lost over 7,000 men at Beaumont that day.

There could now be no question of continuing the march towards Bazaine. At a loss to know what to do, MacMahon ordered his army to fall back on the nearest refuge. This was a small fortified town lying astride the Meuse, a few miles to the north-west of their present position. The town was called Sedan.

5

All the while, the Prince Imperial, with his three aides-de-camp, Duperré, Clary and Lamey, and his escort of *Cent Gardes* under Lieutenant Watrin, was being hurried from one town to the next. No sooner had they arrived at Mézières on the day that they left the Army of Châlons, than a message from the Emperor urged them to quit Mézières and make for Sedan. At Sedan, to which, in three days' time, the Emperor himself would be forced to retreat, they put up at the *sous-préfecture*. As the guests of M. and Mme Petiet, Louis was kindly received and sympathetically treated, but that evening their game of piquet was disturbed by a violent uproar in the town. The clanging of the alarm bell and a shout of *'Les Prussiens!'* sent a stampede of local inhabitants through the streets. Lieutenant Watrin and his *Cent Gardes* were sent galloping off on reconnaissance but they reported that there was nothing to be seen and the panic soon died down. Duperré, however, remained uneasy. Sedan was obviously too close to the fighting line and that night he decided that his charge must be taken back to Mézières. They left early the following morning. At Mézières things were no better than at Sedan. The town was seething with rumours of the approach of the enemy and that evening, after Louis had gone to bed, his aides agreed that he must once more be moved—this time to Avesnes, a town lying some miles to the north-west of Mézières. They decided to set out at once.

Duperré went off to wake Louis. He found that the boy was not yet asleep. When Duperré told him that he must get up and dress so that they could leave at once for Avesnes, Louis refused to do any such thing. Usually so obedient to commands, he simply would not listen. Nothing could persuade him to make a move. He had had enough of running away; he would flee no farther. Duperré was appalled. There was a strong possibility, he told him, that the Prussians were about to attack Mézières.

'Well, then,' answered Louis shrilly, 'we will defend ourselves!'

With the boy obviously on the verge of hysteria, Duperré changed his tactics. He spoke about discipline. The Emperor, he said, had put Louis in his charge; if Louis disobeyed him, he would be disobeying the Emperor. His reasoning finally wore the boy down and Louis, in black despair, agreed to go.

At Avesnes things were slightly better. The atmosphere was less panicky and the townspeople were sympathetic. Louis was accommodated in the Maison Hannoye (it was the very house in which Napoleon I had lodged on his way to Waterloo), and the three days which they spent there were days of comparative calm. *Pompiers* guarded his door, *mobiles* paced the ramparts and the *Cent Gardes* patrolled the outskirts. For the moment, Louis's frantic wanderings seemed to have ceased. 'In a word,' says Filon, 'among all the stations of that calvary, Avesnes was the least dolorous.'

But Duperré was still not happy. He could not for the life of him see why Louis should be kept so close to the fighting line. Now that he had left the army, why could he not be sent well away from the danger area? Could they not go to Amiens? Nor did the conflicting orders with which both the Emperor and the Empress kept bombarding Duperré make his task any easier. When he ventured to complain to the Empress of this divided duty, she lost no time in letting him know which advice he was to follow.

'For the Prince's safety,' she wired, 'ignore orders from the Emperor, as he cannot judge.'

As a matter of fact, Eugenie was not at all sure that the Emperor had done the right thing by allowing Louis to leave the army. When her mother suggested that Eugenie should send the boy to the safety of Spain for the duration of the war, the Empress vetoed the suggestion in typical fashion. 'My cruellest affliction is to see Louis exposed to all kinds of dangers,' she wrote to her mother, 'but I can't change his destiny. He must remain in this country as long as it wants us. One can't think of oneself in moments of danger and then turn up again when it is all over. Our fate is in the hands of God. We will do our duty, each of us. . . .'

To Duperré she was more specific. 'I do not approve of these wanderings from town to town. You must make a stand where you are. If the town were captured, it would be time enough to hide your charge and get him away secretly. If Avesnes is impossible, go to Laon: that is a fortified place and in the theatre of war.

'You have a duty more urgent than security. It is that of honour, and I consider this retreat on Amiens unworthy of it and us. Each of us must sustain, within the limits of his power, the harsh duties which fall upon us.

'My heart is rent but resolved. I have had no news of my husband nor you since yesterday. I am suffering the most terrible anguish, but my will is, first and foremost, that each of you should do his duty. Remember this: I could weep for my son dead or wounded, but a fugitive! I should never forgive you. It is, therefore, to your honour as soldiers that I appeal. Act for the best, but act like soldiers. I cover you and take full responsibility.'

It was stirring stuff but it could not really have done much to enlighten poor Duperré. Nor could the Emperor be looked to for more practical commands. Since midnight on 30 August, no word had reached Avesnes from the Army of Châlons. To Duperré it was 'as if the Emperor and his army had vanished behind an impenetrable fog which was concealing them from every eye and cutting them off from the rest of the world'. No one knew what had happened to them. Except for Louis, they all expected the worst. He, of course, was living in feverish expectation of a great victory.

On the afternoon of 1 September, Duperré decided to take Louis out for a drive. For three days now he had been cooped up in the Maison Hannoye and his aides imagined that an outing might take him out of himself a little. It might also give them some respite from his anguished and continual questioning. It was a day of brilliant sunshine. The hood of the carriage was lowered and, escorted by the giant *Cent Gardes* with their glittering breastplates and jogging lances, Louis went driving out of the Porte de France into the open countryside. Passing through the village of Sainte-Hilaire, he was enthusiastically greeted by the inhabitants. As their shouts of '*Vive l'Empereur! Vive le Prince Impérial!*' died away on the summer air and the cortège was out on the open road once more, there came another sound. It was a slow rumbling noise, as though of distant thunder. The aides-de-camp recognized it immediately but, not wanting to upset the boy, said nothing. But he had heard it. Hearing it again, he leapt to his feet in the carriage.

'*Mon Dieu, on se bat!*' he cried out in excitement. '*C'est le canon!*'

He clasped his hands together and stood there in the lurching carriage, praying to God, silently and fervently, for a victory.

He had heard the guns at Sedan.

CHAPTER NINE

Sedan

1

As the Germans moved relentlessly forward from one victory to the next, so did they begin to lose the sympathy of the other European powers. The unbroken chain of German successes, the realization that the contestants were not evenly matched and, above all, the increasingly aggressive spirit of the conquerors, was swinging neutral opinion towards the French. The German Press, echoing the growing belligerence of all Germans, conservatives and liberals alike, was being especially arrogant; the truculence of its tone was alienating many erstwhile friends. Even the London *Times*, which had consistently championed the Germans against the French, was beginning to wonder whether the victors would show proper magnanimity towards the enemy. Germany was new to 'such enormous victories . . .' noted *The Times*; could she 'feel that mercy becometh most the strong'?

Few Germans were more conscious of this loss of sympathy than the Crown Prince Frederick of Prussia. Possessed of a much more sensitive nature than men such as Bismarck, Moltke or King Wilhelm himself, the Crown Prince was incapable of simply ignoring adverse criticism. He was particularly upset by British disapproval. 'The discord between us and England grieves me deeply,' he wrote in his diary a few days before the battle of Sedan, 'all the more as the tone of our Press encourages it daily. . . .' Within a few months he would be admitting that the Germans were by then considered 'capable of every evil'. 'That is not the result of this war alone—' he was to write, 'it is the theory of blood and iron, invented and acted upon by Bismarck, which has brought us to this pitch. He has made us great and powerful, but he has robbed us of our friends, of the sympathies of the world, and of our conscience. . . .'

After the war, in conversation with his mother-in-law, Queen Victoria, the Crown Prince would own that Bismarck's part in promoting the conflict had been considerable. In his opinion, Bismarck was 'energetic and clever, but bad, unprincipled and all-powerful'. He had been as much to blame for the war as had Napoleon III.

'This corroborates and justifies what many people have said,' noted Victoria.

Her daughter, the Crown Princess, was suffering no such pangs of conscience about the responsibility for the war. Her adopted country's every move was above reproach. In these days before and after Sedan she was in full patriotic spate. Her husband might be regretting the loss of international goodwill but she could see no justification for it.

'The exasperation against the French grows every day,' she wrote to Queen Victoria, 'which is but natural, seeing that it is they who brought on this war, and not we who would have it, that we are obliged to sacrifice almost all the most valuable lives in the country to resist their overbearing and unjust interference. . . . They will never own themselves in the wrong, and go on making the most outrageous inventions.'

Even as the Crown Princess was dashing off her justifications, the German army was closing in to strike the death-blow to Imperial France. On the last day of August, General von Moltke ordered his men to begin surrounding the fortress of Sedan, and by that evening the encirclement was well under way. 'Now,' he cried out later that night, 'we have them in a mousetrap.'

On the morning of 1 September, King Wilhelm of Prussia, escorted by a detachment of brightly uniformed Life Guards and trailing a retinue of princes, generals and courtiers, rode up to the summit of a hill above the village of Frénois, outside Sedan. Here, in a stubble-field, the glittering assembly—which included Bismarck, Moltke, Roon, as well as General Sheridan of the United States—took up their positions to watch the day's battle. It was an excellent vantage point. Below them, just over a mile away, astride the blue waters of the River Meuse, lay the little walled town of Sedan. Its steepled churches and tall houses could be seen quite distinctly; with field-glasses one could watch the people in the narrow streets. Wooded hills and

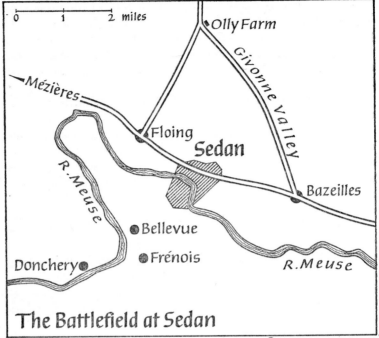

0   1   2 miles

Olly Farm

Givonne Valley

Mézières

Floing

Sedan

Bazeilles

R. Meuse

Bellevue

Frénois

Donchery

R. Meuse

The Battlefield at Sedan

© CASSELL & CO LTD 1969.

valleys, dotted with hamlets and farm buildings, lay all around,
and to the north, as a backdrop, rose the pine-covered slopes of
the Ardennes. The Belgian frontier was a mere seven miles
away.

That day's battlefield, stretched out like a map below the
uniformed group on the hilltop, was in the shape of a triangle.
The base of this triangle faced the spectators. In the centre of
this base line lay Sedan; at its western end lay the village of
Floing and at its eastern end the village of Bazeilles. From
Floing a road running north-east formed the left-hand side of
the triangle; from Bazeilles, a road running north-west (along
the Givonne valley) formed the right-hand side. These two
roads converged, making the apex of the triangle, at Olly
Farm. The terrain contained within this triangle was hilly and
wooded and sloped down towards the base, where Sedan lay in
the valley of the Meuse.

By dawn on that first day of September, the Germans were in command of the hills which lay to the south of Sedan and were fast moving up the left-hand side of the triangle—from the village of Floing to Olly Farm. At the same time they were closing up the right-hand side of the triangle—the Givonne valley—but it would not be until about noon that the two forces would meet at Olly Farm, thus completing the encirclement. Had the French wanted to escape the swiftly closing trap, they might have been able to do so during the early hours of the day when the way towards Mézières, via Olly Farm, was still open. By the early afternoon all hope of retreat would be gone. To General von Blumenthal, watching, from that hilltop above Frénois, the great masses of grey-uniformed German soldiery closing in, the unfolding battle could have only one outcome. 'This evening will end with the hoisting of the white flag,' he predicted.

The prophecy of the French general, Ducrot, was more trenchant. '*Nous sommes dans un pot de chambre, et nous y serons emmerdés,*' he said.

2

It was at Sedan that the Emperor Napoleon III came once more into his own. Realizing, perhaps, that it was in this old walled town on the River Meuse that the final scene of his tragedy was to be played out, he forsook his purely passive role and prepared to take part in the forthcoming battle. He had very little doubt that Sedan would see the destruction of the Army of Châlons; because of this, he was anxious to acquit himself in a manner worthy of so great a débâcle. If this was to be the end, then let it be an honourable one.

He had arrived at Sedan towards midnight on 30 August. With the troops just beginning to take up their positions in that great triangle on the plateau beyond the walls of the town, Sedan itself was still dark and quiet. The Emperor went limping through the deserted streets to the *sous-préfecture* and here, where three days before the Prince Imperial had played piquet with Mme Petiet, he established himself and his suite. He had

not been there long, however, before MacMahon—all too conscious of that ominous semicircle of enemy camp fires on the
hills outside—advised the Emperor to escape to Mézières while
there was still time. But Napoleon was retreating no farther. 'I
have decided not to separate my lot from that of the army,' he
announced quietly.

The battle of Sedan began before dawn on 1 September. The
Germans moved up through the mist to attack the French position around the village of Bazeilles, at the eastern point of their
defensive triangle. By the time it was light, almost every house
in the village was blazing, but the French were holding their
own.

It was now that Napoleon made his appearance. Mounting his
horse Phoebus and attended by his staff, he rode out from the
sous-préfecture. He was wearing the uniform of a general, ablaze
with decorations, and on his head was his gold-braided *képi*.
He looked slightly better that morning but the appearance was
deceptive. A touch of rouge had put a little colour on to his pale
cheeks and his freshly waxed moustache had given him back
something of his old martial air, but he was in great pain.
Every minute spent on horseback was torture for him and he
was to spend almost five hours in the saddle that day. 'What!'
a surgeon examining the Emperor was afterwards to say. 'Did
that man actually endure five hours on horseback on the battlefield at Sedan? He must have suffered agonies!' But Napoleon
was sustained, perhaps, by the certainty that this was to be his
last day on earth. There is no doubt that he intended to get
himself killed that morning. Only by his death on the field of
battle could he hope to atone for his failures and win back some
measure of glory for his discredited dynasty. Only by his death
could he put an end to his terrible sufferings. It was thus in
search of a monumental climax to his career that the painted
Emperor rode out towards the sound of gunfire at Bazeilles that
morning.

It seemed, for a moment, as though Marshal MacMahon (no
less in need of a boost to his reputation) had beaten him to it.
As the Emperor went cantering along the road towards Bazeilles
he met MacMahon being carried back to Sedan. The Marshal
had been wounded in the leg by a shell fragment and was unable

to remain on the battlefield. He had delegated the command to General Ducrot. The first thing that General Ducrot did was to order an immediate retreat from Sedan. Better than MacMahon, he realized that they would soon be entirely surrounded. Only the road to Mézières was still open and he was determined to take it. When his fellow officers objected, claiming that the French were successfully resisting the enemy attack at Bazeilles, he refused to listen. Soon after 8 a.m. the retreat was under way.

But at this moment there appeared on the scene a relatively unknown general by the name of Wimpffen. To the astonishment of his fellow generals, he announced that *he* was now in command of the Army of Châlons. He thereupon drew from his pocket an order from Count de Palikao in Paris. 'In the event of any mishap befalling Marshal MacMahon,' read the dispatch, 'you will take command of the troops now under his orders.' Until recently Governor of Oran, General de Wimpffen had arrived at Sedan, direct from a luncheon appointment with Palikao in Paris, just a short time before. Confident, blustery and energetic, Wimpffen was very much a man after Palikao's own heart; the Minister of War had no doubt that Wimpffen would be able to inject a little much-needed stamina into MacMahon's demoralized forces. Wimpffen lost no time in attempting to do this. The order to retreat on Mézières was countermanded and General Ducrot was told to use all his 'energy and skill to ensure a victory'. When Ducrot tried to explain the desperateness of the situation to the new commander, Wimpffen remained unconvinced. 'We need a victory,' he said stoutly.

'You will be lucky, *mon Général*,' replied Ducrot, 'if this evening you even have a retreat.'

When General de Wimpffen came galloping up to the Emperor to announce his appointment, Napoleon advised him to follow Ducrot's plan and retreat on Mézières while there was still time. To emphasize his point, the Emperor drew Wimpffen's attention to the enemy troops even then massing above the Givonne valley which formed the eastern side of the French triangle. 'I beg Your Majesty not to be alarmed by what you see,' answered Wimpffen airily. 'In a couple of hours I will have pitched them all into the Meuse.'

'Pray God,' said General Castlenau in an aside, 'we shall not be thrown into the river ourselves.'

'It was most unfortunate,' Napoleon was afterwards to say in his restrained fashion, 'that . . . the chief command changed three times within a few hours, which naturally gave rise to a great lack of continuity in the direction of manœuvres.' For even as the little party sat their horses above the Givonne valley, the enemy were moving up along the western side of the French triangle, from the village of Floing to the farm of Olly, cutting off the very last avenue of escape. By noon the encirclement was complete. There could be no talk of retreat now.

All morning the Emperor courted death. Accompanied by his staff, which included his aide-de-camp General Pajol, his orderly officer Captain d'Hendecourt and his principal *écuyer* Count Davilliers, he made for wherever the fighting was heaviest. He went first to Bazeilles. Not wishing to subject his staff to unnecessary danger, he insisted that they shelter behind a wall while he, escorted by his three principal officers, rode up to an exposed crest above the village. The little group of horsemen presented an easy target for the enemy, and to render the target easier still, the Emperor urged his own horse forward. Shells crashed down until the clouds of dust and smoke became blinding. 'The Emperor,' says Pajol, 'remained immovable as if waiting for one of the shells to hit him.' But at Bazeilles it was his orderly officer, Captain d'Hendecourt, who was hit and killed.

Slowly, 'under a ceaseless rain of shells', the Emperor made his way northwards along the ridge above the Givonne valley. When the agony of riding became unbearable, he would dismount and lean his head against a tree. Then he would walk a little way. He never complained. 'His clenched hand,' says Pajol, 'was the sole indication that what he was enduring was almost beyond his strength to bear.' Sometimes, with his hand clutching the hilt of his sword, he would walk behind a line of gunners. At one stage he tried his hand at firing a *mitrailleuse*. Sitting his horse on the heights near the wood which crowned the plateau, he was exposed to a particularly concentrated attack. Shells, exploding on either side of him, caused the horses of two of his officers to rear and fall; both men were hurt but the Emperor emerged from a cloud of acrid dust unscathed. 'Death passed very near me,' he murmured.

By now the French resistance was beginning to crumble. Bazeilles had fallen and Napoleon doubted if the ridge above the Givonne could be held much longer. He decided to cross to the far side of the plateau to talk to General Douay but, finding his way blocked by a disorderly crowd of fleeing men, he made for Sedan instead. He would confer with MacMahon. There is no doubt that by now Napoleon was deeply distressed, not only by the utter hopelessness of the situation, but by all that he had seen during the morning's fighting. He was said to have been particularly upset by the screams of the dying men. 'The wounded, the fleeing, the overturned cannon, burning wagons— all these things caught the eye of the Emperor, who was always more alive to what was to come than to what was actually happening in a battle,' said Pajol. 'His proverbial impassiveness was giving way to a deep feeling of pity for the wounded. During the [Italian campaign] it was noticed that he, the conqueror, was profoundly moved by the painful sights he witnessed after the struggle. How then could he remain calm in the presence of such a struggle as this then in progress at Sedan? It was a terrible conflict, he said later, "each stage of which was more fearful than its predecessor".' By visiting MacMahon, Napoleon hoped that the two of them might be able to decide on some way out of the impasse.

Sedan was crowded. Over thirty thousand soldiers and civilians were crammed into the narrow streets and already the enemy shells were crashing into the buildings. Fires were breaking out everywhere. As the Emperor was riding across a bridge over the Meuse which divided the town into two, a shell exploded directly in front of him. The impact flung one of his aides and his horse to the ground and a thick cloud of dust enveloped the Emperor. Assuming that he had been hit, his officers rushed forward to his aid, but as the air cleared, Napoleon was revealed sitting calmly astride his horse. His remarkable *sang froid* was greeted with loud cheers from the onlookers. 'But that strange mask gave no sign of emotion,' noted one witness. 'Napoleon simply, with a wave of his hand, strove to check the cheers.' He then rode on to MacMahon's quarters.

In spite of five hours in the firing line, he had not been granted the death which he so eagerly sought. 'I had no luck that day,' he afterwards remarked to General Pajol.

Having talked things over with MacMahon (who could, indeed, have had very little constructive advice to offer), the Emperor decided to continue on his way to see General Douay at his position above the village of Floing at the far western point of the triangle. Standing in the courtyard of the *sous-préfecture* he steeled himself for the ride. 'He was suffering terribly after those long hours passed in the saddle,' writes one of his staff. 'His aides-de-camp knew what resolution was necessary to prevent himself from falling from his horse through sheer pain; and to his physical suffering was added an equally cruel moral suffering.' He was to be spared the torture of any further riding, however, as by now it was impossible for him to get out of Sedan. The streets were jammed full of wagons, horses and panic-stricken people. There was simply no way of forcing a passage through the crowd. So they brought him a chair and, for want of anything better to do, he sat in the sunshine of the courtyard, while all about him, in the streets of Sedan, the noise and confusion increased a hundredfold.

By now even the buoyant General de Wimpffen was coming to some appreciation of the desperateness of the situation. If they remained at Sedan, they would be annihilated; the only hope, therefore, would be to force a break-out, saving as many of the troops as possible. Still obsessed with Palikao's idea that it must be towards Bazaine and Metz that any move must be made, Wimpffen decided that the break-out must be forced through the south-eastern corner of the battlefield, near Bazeilles. At about 1 p.m., after an altercation on the matter with General Ducrot, Wimpffen gave firm orders for the break-out and sent Captain de Saint Haouen to Sedan to fetch the Emperor. Napoleon was having none of it. He knew that it would be a hopeless venture; at best he and a couple of thousand men might be able to get through. This was hardly the way in which to refurbish his tarnished image. 'Tell General de Wimpffen,' he said, 'that I will not be party to the sacrifice of the lives of several thousand men in order that I may escape.'

But by now it was too late anyway. Almost the entire French

line was collapsing under the pounding of the German guns. The troops were streaming back through the woods towards Sedan in terrified disorder. Above Floing, General Ducrot played his last, desperate card. He ordered a cavalry charge. The great host of horsemen assembled on the crest of a hill and then, with a thunder of hooves and a flash of drawn sabres, went crashing down the slope in the last great flourish of the French Seeond Empire. They were shot to pieces by the unyielding German lines. As the survivors came galloping back, Ducrot asked their commander, General de Gallifet, whether they could possibly try again. 'As often as you like, *mon Général*,' answered the insouciant Gallifet, 'so long as there's one of us left.' It was no idle promise. The horsemen rallied and thundered down the slope again and again, leaving a pile of dead and dying in front of the German lines. King Wilhelm of Prussia, watching the suicidal charges, was moved to scarcely comprehending admiration. '*Ah! Les braves gens!*' he exclaimed. His words were afterwards to be carved on the memorial to the imperial cavalry that stands above Floing.

But the situation was beyond any such remedies, no matter how spectacular. By three o'clock a mob of panic-stricken soldiers was pouring into the little town. In desperation the gates were locked against them, but they flung themselves into the moat and swarmed over the walls. The Germans brought their guns up to the southern hills and started a massive bombardment of the town. 'I never dreamt of a catastrophe so appalling,' Napoleon afterwards told Eugenie. 'Just imagine an army surrounding a fortified city and itself surrounded on every side by forces far superior. After several hours' fighting our troops broke into a rout and tried to re-enter the town. The gates were closed; they clambered over them. The town was then full of a dense crowd, mixed up with vehicles of all descriptions, and on the cluster of human heads the shells rained down from all sides, killing the people in the streets, tearing off the roofs and setting the houses on fire.'

Worse still than the blazing buildings and the wildly shrieking townspeople were the signs of mutiny among the troops. Officers were threatened and the generals openly accused of inefficiency. All discipline in the army and self-control among the civilians was likely to snap at any moment. The town might soon become the scene of the most unspeakable savagery.

By now all the generals, with the exception of Wimpffen, had collected about Napoleon in the courtyard of the *sous-préfecture*. All were agreed that further resistance was useless; the carnage must be stopped. But General Ducrot was still anxious to get the Emperor away to safety. It would be impossible, he said, to save the army, but under cover of darkness they might be able to cut a way through the enemy lines for the Emperor, his suite and a small band of cavalry. Again Napoleon refused the offer. 'I desire to share the lot of my army,' he repeated, 'and I am absolutely opposed to any plan for effecting my escape which leaves the army behind.'

Indeed, far from wishing to save his own skin, the Emperor was about to make the greatest sacrifice of his life. Unable to die at the head of his troops, he decided on another, less glorious form of death. To have allowed the bombardment to continue and to have gone down in a gigantic holocaust might have been a more triumphant finale for a Napoleon, but the Emperor was incapable of any such selfishness. The slaughter must be stopped. No longer Commander-in-Chief of the army, it was not up to him to stop it; he could quite easily have left the agonizing decision to Wimpffen. But to save his generals from the stigma of capitulating, he decided to take upon himself the humiliation of the first step towards a surrender. Assuming the reins of authority once more, he ordered that the white flag be hoisted above Sedan.

'Nothing in his whole life became him more,' wrote Edmund d'Auvergne of the Emperor, 'than that humbling of himself to spare the lives of Frenchmen.'

For this act of valiant self-sacrifice, Napoleon III was henceforth to be labelled 'the coward of Sedan'.

Once the white flag had been raised, Napoleon arranged for a message requesting an armistice to be sent to the enemy. It was drawn up and General Lebrun was sent off to get General de Wimpffen, as Commander-in-Chief, to sign it. Wimpffen, whom Lebrun met on the road to Bazeilles, was having none of it. Angrily, he ordered the white flag to be hauled down. 'No capitulation! Drop that rag!' he shouted. 'I mean to fight on.'

With that he ordered a last desperate sortie in the direction of Metz. An hour later, the battle was still raging.

'Why does this useless struggle go on?' demanded the Emperor of Lebrun when he realized that the white flag had been cut down. 'It is absolutely necessary to stop the firing!'

By then, however, Moltke had seen the white flag and had sent two of his officers into Sedan under a flag of truce. Much to their surprise, for they had not known that Napoleon was at Sedan ('the old fox is too cunning to be caught in such a trap. He has doubtless slipped off to Paris,' Bismarck had said to General Sheridan), the two Prussian officers were led into the Emperor's presence. He told them that he would be sending General de Wimpffen to negotiate terms and that he would be writing a personal letter to King Wilhelm. The officers went galloping back to the King's headquarters on that hill above Frénois; one of them, spurring his horse forward, pointed in the direction of Sedan and shouted excitedly, *Der Kaiser ist da!*

A little while later General Reille came riding up the hill with the Emperor's letter for the Prussian King.

Monsieur mon frère,' it read, 'having failed to meet death in the midst of my troops, nothing more remains for me but to surrender my sword into Your Majesty's hands.'

This was to be a further sacrifice on the part of the Emperor. He imagined that in handing himself over as a prisoner to the King of Prussia, he might save his army from the humiliation of a surrender and win for them an 'honourable capitulation'. He hoped that he alone would be made a prisoner of war and that his men would be able to march out of Sedan with full military honours on the understanding that they did not take up arms against the enemy for the duration of the war. But to this the Germans would not agree. King Wilhelm told Reille that he would negotiate only if the whole French army laid down its arms. In a courteous letter to the Emperor, the King made this clear. He added that he would be designating General von Moltke to conduct the negotiations for Prussia. Reille went galloping down the hill to Sedan with the King's answer and the group of victorious Germans on the hilltop above Frénois dispersed.

With their going, says one of the British war correspondents, 'a strange, uncanny silence and stillness succeeded the thunderous noise and turmoil of the day'. It was a beautiful evening, warm and golden, with only here and there a drift of smoke to smudge the pellucid air. The still waters of the Meuse reflected the last flickers of burning villages. As it became darker and the circle of German camp fires began to flicker on the hills above the town, the words of an old Lutheran hymn, *Nun danket alle Gott*, rose into the stillness of the night. The sound 'so gripped my heart', admitted the Crown Prince Frederick, 'I could not keep back tears of pure joy.' The Germans were thanking God for a victory which, although still unsuspected by the majority of them, was to decide the history of Europe for the next seventy-five years.

3

No such sense of gratitude reigned in the French camp. There were heated scenes in the *sous-préfecture* that evening. Wimpffen was particularly upset. Having promised everyone a victory, he was faced with one of the most monumental defeats in the history of the French army. At first he tried to hand in his resignation and, when the Emperor refused to accept it, he began to blame his colleagues for the débâcle. 'Sire,' he said to Napoleon, 'if I lost the battle, if I am beaten, it is because my orders were not executed; it is because your generals refused to obey me.' At this General Ducrot lost his temper. 'To whom are you referring?' he shouted. 'Are you speaking to me? Alas, your orders were executed only too well! If you hadn't countermanded my orders to retreat, in spite of my urgent opposition, we would now be safe and sound at Mézières, or, at any rate, beyond the reach of the enemy.'

And not only was Wimpffen not prepared to accept any responsibility for the defeat, but he refused to conduct the negotiations with the enemy. Once again the angry Ducrot lashed out at him. 'You assumed the command when you thought there was some honour and profit in exercising it....' he thundered. 'Now you cannot refuse.'

It was left to the Emperor to bring the situation under control. Asking to be left alone with Wimpffen, he managed to convince the irate Commander-in-Chief that he had no choice but to go and discuss terms with the enemy. Wimpffen finally acquiesced and, together with Generals Castlenau and Faure, set out through the night for the near-by village of Donchéry. There, in a house just outside the village, he was met by Bismarck and Moltke.

General de Wimpffen, still hoping for an 'honourable capitulation'—for the army to be allowed to go free on the promise that they would not continue the fight—was not left to nurse his illusions long. The Prussians insisted that the entire French force, officers and men, lay down their arms and become prisoners of war. When Wimpffen haughtily protested that he would continue fighting rather than accept such humiliating terms, Moltke pointed out, only too accurately, the emptiness of any such threat. The French would simply be pounded, or starved, to death.

At this, Wimpffen was forced to try another line of argument. Whereas a harsh peace would lead to a period of 'unending strife between France and Prussia', he said, a generous one would win the gratitude of France. It was sensible reasoning but Bismarck could counter it. The gratitude of a people, he said, was nothing more than 'a myth'. 'It is possible to meet with the gratitude of a sovereign, sometimes even from a ruling family,' he claimed, 'and it occasionally happens that you may implicitly rely on such gratitude. But you must never count on a nation's gratitude. Were the French like other peoples; if they had firmly established institutions, such as ours: if they honoured and respected their institutions; if their sovereigns followed one another regularly on the throne—if all these things were so, why then we might have faith in the gratitude of the Emperor and his son, and estimate its worth. But during the last eighty years governments in France have been so unstable and so numerous; they have changed so rapidly, so curiously, so contrary to all expectation, that one can rely on nothing in your country. Consequently it would be madness, it would be building on sand, for any government to base any hopes on the friendship of a French sovereign.' How could he be sure, asked Bismarck, that a revolution might not tomorrow topple the Empire and that a new French government—as vainglorious, as aggressive and as anti-Prussian as all French governments—might not release the troops of their promise not to fight again and compel them to take up arms once more? It would be madness to let the men go free.

Then Bismarck touched upon another, rather more significant, point. It concerned the future relations between France and Germany. During the past two hundred years France had attacked 'peaceful, inoffensive' Germany no fewer than thirty times. This had to stop. The French must be taught a lesson. Germany must make certain that in future she would be safe from French aggression. 'We must have land, fortresses and frontiers which will protect us for good from enemy attack,' he declared. By this demand, Bismarck was sowing the seeds of a discord which was to bedevil European politics for the following three-quarters of a century. He was already contemplating that harsh peace which, as Wimpffen had predicted, would lead to 'unending strife' between the two countries.

At this point, General Castlenau, as the Emperor's personal representative, joined in the talk. 'I wish to remind you that the Emperor has just sent his word to the King and given himself up as a prisoner; and he has done this in the hope of saving the army from too severe terms of surrender. His Majesty, in a word, has sacrificed himself for the sake of his soldiers. It would seem, therefore, that the King should take this fact into consideration in fixing the terms of the surrender.'

Such a plea might have touched the heart of King Wilhelm but it did nothing to shake the resolve of either Bismarck or Moltke. In it, however, the Prussian Chancellor recognized a deeper issue. Now that the French had been so soundly beaten, Bismarck was quite ready to conclude peace. Not only did he want a harsh peace but he wanted a quick one. He was not in favour of a prolonged war. As far as he was concerned, the campaign had achieved what he had planned it should: the bringing together of all the German states in a fight against a common enemy. Once peace was concluded, the formal unification of Germany would not be long in following. Thus, when Castlenau spoke of the Emperor's sword, Bismarck wanted to know whether Napoleon was surrendering merely his own sword, or that of France. If it were the sword of France—if, in other words, the French state was about to surrender—then, said Bismarck, the negotiations could take on an altogether different complexion. His terms for this particular surrender 'could be modified'. Anxious for peace, Bismarck was ready to make concessions. But the French generals were in no position to speak on behalf of the government and they replied, quite honestly, that the sword was the symbol of the Emperor's personal surrender only. Moltke, who shared none of Bismarck's anxiety to finish the war, greeted the answer with scarcely veiled gratification. 'That being the case,' he said brusquely, 'the Emperor's act can in no way modify the conditions of the surrender.'

At this the headstrong Wimpffen declared that he had no choice but to continue fighting. Moltke's answer was that he would simply reopen the bombardment of the town on the expiry of the truce at 4 a.m. His bluff called, Wimpffen asked for additional time in which to consult his fellow generals. Moltke agreed to a prolongation of the truce until 9 a.m. It was the only concession he made. The Frenchmen called for their horses and rode back to Sedan.

The Emperor, who had never quite outgrown the lone habits of a conspirator, was a great believer in a personal approach. In the somewhat forlorn hope that the King of Prussia might respond to a private appeal to soften the terms of the surrender, Napoleon decided to by-pass the negotiators and address himself directly to his fellow-sovereign. Napoleon III himself, after his victory at Solferino in the Italian campaign, had treated the defeated Emperor of Austria in the most generous fashion; might King Wilhelm not show a similar generosity?

To this end, the Emperor set out from Sedan at five o'clock on the morning of 2 September. He was wearing his general's uniform under a blue cloak with a scarlet lining. Expecting to return in an hour or two's time, he made use of an open, two-horse carriage and as he went trundling out of the Porte de Torcy down the road towards Donchéry, a group of Zouaves cried 'Vive l'Empereur!' Gravely, he returned their salute. This little scene was to furnish the material for one of the many calumnies heaped upon the head of Napoleon III after his fall. He was said to have driven out from Sedan in a luxurious landau drawn by six horses, smoking a cigarette with callous non-chalance, while the wheels of his carriage ground over the bodies of his wounded soldiers.

Half-way to the village of Donchéry he was met by Bismarck. The Prussian Chancellor had been warned of Napoleon's approach and was making quite sure that the Emperor did not see King Wilhelm before he himself had questioned him. As the Emperor and the Chancellor met, there occurred a strange incident. 'When I approached the Emperor's carriage,' Bismarck afterwards recalled, 'His Majesty took off his cap to salute me. It is not the custom with us when in uniform to do more than touch the cap; however I took mine off and the Emperor's eyes followed it until it came on a level with my belt, in which was a revolver, when he turned quite pale—I cannot account for it.' Napoleon might simply have had a spasm of pain or perhaps—for he was a superstitious man—he had remembered a gipsy's warning that he would one day die by a bullet through the forehead.

Bismarck then suggested that they enter a wayside cottage in order to negotiate. They sat in two chairs by the door of the small, two-storeyed cottage and Napoleon at once brought up the question of better terms for the surrender. 'Moltke alone is competent to deal with these military matters,' said Bismarck, and promptly began to steer the talk into political channels. But the Emperor made it clear that he considered himself a political prisoner and that only the Regent and her government were in a position to negotiate peace terms. At this Bismarck lost interest. He returned to Donchéry to report to the King, leaving Napoleon to wait for Moltke. The Emperor wandered upstairs and sat down, quite alone, in one of the rooms. When Madame Fournaise, the owner of the cottage, came in to ask him if there was anything he needed, Napoleon asked her to pull down the blinds. After sitting in the half-light for a little while, he returned downstairs and began pacing up and down a potato patch, taking care to keep to the path. 'His whole appearance was a little unsoldierlike,' noted one witness. 'The man looked too soft, too shabby, I may say, for the uniform he wore.' He maintained an 'almost unbroken silence', in marked contrast to his officers, who 'spoke and gesticulated with great animation'.

When Moltke arrived, the Emperor asked him whether he would allow the French army to withdraw to Belgium for the duration of the war or at least to leave the terms of the capitulation open until the Emperor had seen King Wilhelm. Moltke promised to discuss these matters with the King and the Emperor was asked to continue on to the near-by Château de Bellevue where he was to await the arrival of King Wilhelm. By now Napoleon realized that he would not be allowed to see the King until the capitulation had been signed. He realized, too, that his own imprisonment had already begun. His mission had failed.

When the Emperor left that little yellow cottage on the road between Sedan and Donchéry, he made a point of thanking Madame Fournaise for her kindness. 'This is probably the last hospitality which I shall receive in France,' he said. With characteristic generosity, he gave her four gold *louis*. Three of them she kept to pay for her funeral and the fourth she had buried with her. However, this was not to be all that the astute Madame Fournaise was to make out of the historic meeting. She sold the table at which the Emperor had sat to Bismarck, the cane-bottomed chairs on which Napoleon and Bismarck had rested to General Sheridan and Sir Beauchamp Walker, and thereafter copies of the chairs, in the pretence that they were the one in which the Emperor had sat, to anyone who visited her. Her little cottage stands there to this day.

While the Emperor had been talking to Bismarck, his generals had been discussing the terms of the capitulation. By nine o'clock, the time at which the truce was due to end, they were still undecided, but a German threat to reopen the bombardment soon made up their minds. General de Wimpffen rode out to the Château de Bellevue and at 11 a.m. he signed the surrender. The terms were those upon which Moltke had all along insisted: the Army of Châlons, with all its arms and material, was to surrender as prisoners of war.

For years afterwards, visitors to the panelled dining-room at Bellevue would be shown an inkstain on the table at which the capitulation had been signed and would be told that General de Wimpffen, in his 'shame and grief', had overturned an inkpot while signing his name. In fact, the 'historic inkstain' was made the following day by the British war correspondent Archibald Forbes.

Only now, with the capitulation signed, would Bismarck allow the Emperor to meet the King of Prussia. While Napoleon waited at Bellevue for Wilhelm's arrival, his suite urged him to eat something. The Emperor demurred, saying that he did not want to be found at table 'like an ordinary mortal on an ordinary day'. But they insisted and one of his generals fetched him a flask of wine and a small loaf of bread.

When King Wilhelm came riding over to Bellevue, Napoleon was waiting to greet him on the glassed-in veranda of the château. 'The contrast between the two sovereigns was strange and painful,' noted one eyewitness, 'the German tall, upright, square-shouldered, with the flash of success from the keen blue eyes from under the helmet, and the glow of triumph on the fresh cheek; the Frenchman, with weary stoop of the shoulders, his eyes drooping, his lips quivering, bare-headed and dishevelled.'

It was a short embarrassed meeting with the Emperor betraying his nervousness by repeated twirlings of his waxed moustache. His eyes shifted continuously. King Wilhelm was his usual polite self. They spoke of the battle (Napoleon envied Wilhelm his artillery) and the Prussian King asked after the Empress and the Prince Imperial. It was arranged that the Emperor would spend the night at the château and that he would leave the next day for his place of detention. His prison was to be the palace of Wilhelmshöhe, near Cassel, where Napoleon I's youngest brother Jerome, the father of Plon-Plon, had once reigned as King of Westphalia. Napoleon asked only one favour of King Wilhelm, and that was that he be allowed to go into captivity by way of Belgium and not have to pass through the ranks of his defeated army. He wanted to avoid being seen, and possibly insulted, by his own men. This the King granted.

After Wilhelm had left, the Emperor sent a telegram to Eugenie informing her that the army had been defeated and that he was a prisoner. He then wrote to her, heading the letter *Quartier impérial, 2 Septembre 1870*.

My dear Eugenie, I cannot tell you what I have suffered and am suffering. We made a march contrary to all the rules and to common sense; it was bound to lead to a catastrophe, and that is complete. I would rather have died than have witnessed such a disastrous capitulation; and yet, things being what they are, it was the only way of avoiding the slaughter of 60,000 men.

Then again, if only all my torments were concentrated here! I think of you, of our son, of our unfortunate country. May God protect you! What is going to happen in Paris?

I have just seen the King. There were tears in his eyes when he spoke of the sorrow I must be feeling. He has put at my disposal one of his *châteaux* near Hesse-Cassel. But what does it matter where I go? I am in despair. Adieu: I embrace you tenderly.

Napoléon

By the evening his habitual calm seems to have reasserted itself and he went to bed with a copy of Bulwer Lytton's *The Last of the Barons*, which he had found in a bookcase in the bedroom. His unmade bed, says someone who saw it the following morning, showed no signs of nocturnal restlessness. The Emperor had obviously slept quietly.

He left for Wilhelmshöhe on 3 September. By now his carriages and his *fourgons*—all marked *Maison militaire de l'Empereur*—had been brought from Sedan and the courtyard of the château was alive with the jingle of harness, the clash of hooves, and the scurryings of liveried *piqueurs* and bewigged postilions. Over a hundred horses were included in the Emperor's train. Napoleon, wrapped in his blue cloak, was seen to be shivering as he took his seat. In a grey blur of rain the cortège moved off down the hill. As it passed a column of French prisoners trudging along the road, one of the men, catching sight of the pale, impassive face of the Emperor, cried out, 'You sold us to save your carriages!'

Having watched the imperial procession disappear down the narrow, rain-lashed road, Bismarck turned to his companions.

'There is a dynasty on its way out,' he said.

4

Eugenie heard the news at five o'clock on the afternoon of

3 September. The Emperor's telegram was handed to her by Henri Chevreau, the Minister of the Interior.

At that moment Augustin Filon was sitting with Eugène Conti, one of Napoleon's secretaries, in the Empress's study, waiting for her to return from the council meeting then in progress. Both men had already heard the news. Their sad and desultory conversation was suddenly interrupted by the appearance of the Empress at the head of the little spiral staircase which connected her apartments with those of the Emperor below. They rose and hurried towards her. One glance at her face was enough to tell them that she knew all. 'She was pale and terrible,' says Filon, 'her eyes were hard and brilliant with anger, her face distorted by emotion.'

'Do you know what they are saying?' she shouted. 'That the Emperor has surrendered, that he has capitulated! You don't, surely, believe this infamy?'

Appalled by her anger, they dared not answer. At this, her tone became even more vehement, almost threatening. 'You don't believe it?' she repeated.

'Madame,' stammered poor Conti, 'there are circumstances where even the bravest . . .'

'But without waiting to hear more,' says Filon, 'the Empress cut short his words, and her soul, stirred to its innermost depths, poured forth its anger in a torrent of incoherent and mad words. What she said then Conti never repeated to anyone, and I shall die, like him, without repeating it.'

The outburst, of course, was a violent attack on the Emperor. She did not at that time realize, says the devoted Filon, 'all that the Emperor had suffered'. But he confesses that he could remember nothing of the terrifying scene but the sound of the words. 'I was so overcome at the time that my memory was as if paralysed. I know, however, that it lasted five long, terrible minutes.'

The paroxysm of rage over, the Empress turned and swept down the staircase.

'We remained speechless and stunned,' says Filon, 'like men who have come through an earthquake.'

CHAPTER TEN

The Fourth of September

1

Sunday, 4 September, dawned clear and luminous. It was obviously going to be a day of radiant sunshine. After the tumult of the night before, when an exhilarated crowd had roamed the boulevards, shouting *'Vive la République!'* and *'A bas l'Empire!'*, the morning seemed curiously quiet, almost languorous. To young Filon, looking out from the windows of the Tuileries at the dawn sky above the roofs and chimneys of the Rue de Rivoli, it seemed as though the previous night's revolutionary clamour had been nothing more than a feverish dream. The new day would surely find everything as before. But his reverie did not last long. He knew that by now the news of Sedan was placarded all over the city and that last night's riotous crowds would soon be preparing to flood the streets once more. 'A soft and glorious summer morning is as suitable for a revolution as a tempestuous night,' he mused and wondered whether the Empress would still be alive by sunset.

Eugenie, too, rose early. She put on a simple black silk dress and over her shoulders—for she was always cold these days—she threw a violet shawl, braided with gold. At half past seven she heard Mass in her private chapel. Only half a dozen of her little Court were present, the men kneeling in troubled meditation, the women weeping softly. After Mass, Filon approached her and begged her to leave Paris. She could transfer the government to some provincial city and he would go north to fetch the Prince Imperial. She would not hear of it.

'That would mean civil war,' she said. 'The strength of our resistance against the Prussians would be broken in half—and to what purpose? If one does not have Paris, one has nothing. No, I shall not move from here.'

'Your Majesty, then, will defend herself?'

'I shall not stir, but I will not allow a shot to be fired.'

What, Filon wondered, was she planning to do? Perhaps she meant to combat the revolution single-handed. Was she going to dare the Parisians to commit, on her person, a crime that would go down in history; or else, by that personal magnetism which had made fanatics of her entourage during the past month, win them to her side? Whatever her intention, there was one thing that she would not do: she would never leave Paris. There were too many precedents of monarchs who had fled the Tuileries in the face of the storm; she did not intend to follow their shameful example. 'I will never run away in a cab like Charles X and Louis Philippe,' she declared stoutly. 'I will never fly from the Revolution.' Nor, like the Empress Marie Louise at the fall of the First Empire, would she allow herself to be shuffled aimlessly from town to town. She was in Paris and in Paris she would remain.

When her cousin, Ferdinand de Lesseps, hurried across to the Tuileries that morning to urge her to save herself by handing over all her powers to the *corps législatif*, she refused to discuss the idea. 'One can only give up that which is one's own, but never that which has been received in trust—the Sovereignty is not mine to give,' she said. 'I shall never abdicate.'

At eight o'clock she presided over the council of ministers. There had been a rowdy sitting of the *corps législatif* the night before at which Jules Favre had introduced a resolution proposing dethronement. That today's meeting of the assembly would bring things to a head, there was no doubt whatsoever; of this the ministers now gathered around the council table were only too conscious. Indeed, matters were already being taken out of their hands. In the face of the arguments of the highly articulate Opposition and, still more important, of the menacing attitude of the Paris mob, the deputies had last night begun to waver; even if the government could still command a majority in the Chamber, it was unlikely that the revolutionary crowds would leave them in peace long enough to do any such thing. The Palais Bourbon, in which the *corps législatif* was to meet at one o'clock, was bound to be invaded.

To forestall any such invasion, Clément Duvernois proposed

a *coup d'état*. The leaders of the Left should be arrested and the revolutionaries 'terrorized'. His proposal was hardly worth listening to. To employ force, it was first necessary to have it in one's own hands. This the government did not have. There was a mere handful of troops at the government's disposal and most of these were of doubtful loyalty. Their commander, General Mellinet, was not at all sure that they would obey a command to open fire on the populace. Then someone came up with another idea. This was to form a Council of Regency chosen by the *corps législatif* and armed with absolute powers. It would be presided over by the Empress and headed by Palikao under the impressive title of Lieutenant-General. Why the ministers imagined that this idea would find favour with the deputies is obscure. It was hardly more practical than the proposed *coup d'état*. It was expressly to get rid of the Empress, Palikao and the imperial côterie that the crowds were even now beginning to surge once more through the streets. In the face of this popular feeling the *corps législatif* was hardly likely to agree to the set-ting-up of any such council. None the less, the ministers adopted the plan with the intention of proposing it to the assembly when it met at one o'clock. Their course of action decided on, the ministers took their leave of the Empress.

There were two men in Paris that September day who could quite possibly have averted revolution. One was Thiers and the other Trochu. Thiers, the doyen, and the most moderate, of the Opposition deputies, commanded considerable respect both in and out of the Chamber. He was popular with the Parisian middle class and often found himself in accord with the Bona-partist deputies who made up the Centre of the *corps législatif*. And, as an opponent of the Empire, he was extremely valuable to the men of the Left. If, during these confused days after Sedan, Thiers had appealed to the Chambers to support Palikao's government until the hour of danger had passed, he might well have rallied the wavering Bonapartist deputies and won over the more moderate Republicans. But Thiers was not prepared to take any such step. He had always been opposed to the Empire and, having remained deaf to Eugenie's earlier appeals, he was hardly likely to come to her aid now that the Empire was tottering. With both his popularity and his influence on the increase, he was not going to risk all by helping to prop up a collapsing régime. When Metternich, representative of monarchial, anti-revolutionary Europe, asked Thiers how France could avoid the coming insurrection, the veteran politician answered that he had no advice to give. 'I am waiting to see what turn events take,' he said frankly.

But he was not averse to giving events a guiding hand. By the morning of 4 September he had worked out his own solution to the problem. It was not nearly as drastic as Jules Favre's call for dethronement. As the deputies began to assemble in the Palais Bourbon for the one o'clock sitting, they were handed the text of Thiers's resolution. With the Emperor's imprisonment having rendered the throne vacant, Thiers proposed that the Chamber nominate a Council of National Defence. That way power would be taken out of the hands of the Empress and her ministers without actually enforcing dethronement. His plan would ensure the substance, if not the form, of abdication. 'I neither suppress nor maintain the Empire,' he said. 'I leave the future to God and circumstances.' However, on reading the proposal, the Bonapartist deputies became uneasy. They had, after all, sworn an oath of allegiance to the Emperor; might it not be perjury thus to deprive him of his powers? It was up to the Regent, as the Emperor's representative, to abdicate her powers to the *corps législatif* and not for them to take those powers from her. They did not want to be accused of usurpation.

Such speculations were already becoming idle. The deputies would soon have their minds made up for them by the mob. That this contingency was becoming more and more likely was due, almost entirely, to the behaviour of General Trochu.

As soon as the news of Sedan had become known in Paris the day before, Palikao had set about preparing for an insurrection. He had been determined, however, that Trochu should have no hand in these preparations. General Trochu might be the governor of Paris but Palikao did not put any faith in his ability to check a Parisian uprising. He simply did not trust him. Palikao therefore wrote a note to General Soumain, one of Trochu's subordinates, making this distrust quite clear. 'I know for a fact that trouble is brewing,' he wrote. 'This matter being entirely outside the defence of Paris, which is your special concern, any steps you may take for public order are to be reported direct to me. You will, furthermore, receive your orders direct from me if the public peace is disturbed.' General Trochu, in other words, was not to interfere.

General Soumain, faced with Palikao's order to ignore his superior—General Trochu—lost no time in covering himself by sending the letter on to Trochu. Thus the governor, on returning from a tiring tour of inspection of the city's fortifications, found the letter waiting for him. His reactions can be appreciated. To the most forbearing of men the contents of the letter would have been insulting; to one as self-opinionated and touchy as Trochu, they acted as a calculated slap in the face. He was furious. His staff officers were no less indignant. One of them suggested that the governor send in his resignation immediately. But Trochu decided against this. Instead, he washed his hands of the whole business. If Palikao did not need him, then well and good. Let *him* handle the coming disturbances as best he could. True to Palikao's instructions, Trochu would concern himself with the external defence of Paris only.

It was with Trochu in this state of injured pride that Henri Chevreau, the Minister of the Interior, arrived at the governor's office with a message from the Empress. Would the governor please come to the Tuileries, so that he could consult the Empress on the best way to control the rising agitation in the capital? 'I told him,' said Chevreau, 'of the Empress's anxiety, that his place was at her side, that all faithful friends and followers should group themselves around her. . . .'

To this eleventh-hour plea from one who had consistently ignored him during the past fortnight, Trochu gave an evasive reply. He was tired after his long tour of the forts and he had not yet dined. He would call on the Empress later that evening.

He never did. And whether or not he called the following day is uncertain. Filon, who was with the Empress for most of the day, claims that he did not. Filon's version of the controversy is that the Empress, in the early hours of 4 September, sent for Trochu once more. Her messenger came back alone. General Trochu was too busy to come in person but he would be sending his chief-of-staff to call upon her. The chief-of-staff, like Trochu, never turned up. Other sources, however, claim that Trochu did call early that morning but that he merely treated the Empress to one of his non-committal orations and then left. Whatever the truth, the one thing which is certain is that Trochu made no determined effort to come to the Empress's assistance that day. He was still playing a waiting game. Smarting from his treatment at the hands of the Imperialists, he had decided to make no move towards defending them. A show of strength, or even an appeal to the largely good-natured crowds, by someone of Trochu's popularity would probably have saved the day but he saw no reason why he should align himself with the government. Indeed, he stood to gain a great deal more by siding with the insurgents. For this duplicity, the Empress was never to forgive him.

'Had Thiers and Trochu come forward at this moment to the support of the regency,' claimed Metternich, 'they would probably have saved the Empire and minimized the national disaster. But they both refused their aid, and the Empress was left alone with her ministers to struggle against the revolution.'

That the revolution was getting under way was becoming increasingly clear to the anguished company at the Tuileries. Watching from the windows of the palace, their worst fears seemed about to be confirmed. All morning the cries of '*Déchéance!*'—the call for dethronement—came floating through the summer air. They had no way of judging the temper of the crowds that were streaming past the Tuileries in the direction of the Palais Bourbon for the sitting of the *corps législatif*. Nor did they know what reliance to place on the National Guard now massed in the Place de la Concorde. This National Guard, assembled by order of Trochu, was a Parisian militia, at one time made up of dependable bourgeois, but now containing numberless republicans. If, urged on by the mob, the National Guard were to attack the palace, there were only a few troops at the Empress's disposal and the loyalty of these was questionable. For the last few days these regular troops had been sharing the duties of guarding the Tuileries with the National Guardsmen, with the result that their own fidelity towards the régime had been severely undermined. Some of them regarded the members of the Court, says Filon, 'with a mocking air, as much as to say

"Your minutes are numbered!"' But even if their loyalty had been above reproach, it would not have brought much comfort to the imperial circle, for the Empress had given orders, not only once but twice, that no shot was to be fired into the crowd. With a regard for human life that was to be notably lacking in those who were to hold power after her, she insisted that no French blood be spent in her defence.

If there was some doubt about the loyalty of the imperial troops, there was none whatsoever about that of the imperial Court. The shameful way in which the first Napoleon and his family had been deserted on the fall of the First Empire was not to be repeated on the fall of the Second. A Court which has so often been dubbed shallow, frivolous and insincere, proved itself to be remarkably worthy on this, its last, assembly. Throughout the morning of 4 September, in spite of the clamour in the streets, the faithful arrived at the Tuileries to give their support to the Empress. Almost all the names that for eighteen years had been associated with that most glittering of courts were now represented; by noon the drawing-rooms—dust-sheeted and bare of ornaments and flowers—were packed with an anxious, ever-shifting crowd of sympathizers. There was nothing that they could do, other than to wait and hear what was happening at the Palais Bourbon.

At half past twelve a deputation arrived from the *corps législatif* to see the Empress. With the historic sitting almost due to begin, the deputation had come in a last-minute attempt to stave off the dissolution of the Empire. Terrified of the mob that had already begun to force its way past the uncertain troops into the Palais Bourbon, the deputies felt that they must make all possible concessions short of dethronement. It was by now quite obvious that the *corps législatif* would never agree to Palikao's scheme for a Council of Regency. Nor, on the other hand, were the deputies prepared to adopt Thiers's motion whereby power would simply be wrenched from the Empress's hands. They doubted if so illegal a move would command the support of the bulk of the nation. To counter Jules Favre's drastic demand for a dethronement, these deputies of the Centre were planning to propose an alternative—if only slightly less drastic—one. The Empress must voluntarily hand over her executive powers to the *corps législatif*. The assembly would then nominate a provisional government which would work solely for the salvation of the country, without concerning itself with the dynasty. The dynastic question could be settled at a later date. What the deputation wanted from Eugenie was —to all intents and purposes—an act of abdication, tempered by the possibility that her powers might be handed back some time in the future. That way the deputies would not be breaking their oath of allegiance to the Empire, and the new government, nominated by them, would be a legal one.

The deputation of seven men was headed by Louis-Joseph Buffet. Buffet, an Independent, had once been a member of Ollivier's ministry. Eugenie, attended by Admiral Jurien de la Gravière and the Countess de la Poëze, received them in the Blue Drawing Room. Taking a chair, she invited the deputies to sit down. In silence, and with a dignified calm that characterized her attitude throughout the interview, she listened to their proposal.

This was to be Eugenie's last great scene as Empress of the French. In many ways, it was her finest. She sat there in her black dress and her violet shawl, her copper-coloured hair drawn back from her sad and lovely face, never revealing (as she afterwards admitted) that 'each sentence uncovered a new danger and each word struck as a knife into my anguished heart'. Free of melodrama, free of histrionics, the scene revealed her at her most admirable. Her unselfishness, her strict regard for legality, her sincere desire to do what was best for France, shone through everything that she said. It was almost as though the terrible trials of the past month had tempered and refined her; no less spirited, she was considerably more rational.

Buffet put the proposal to her: with consummate tact, he asked her to abdicate. 'If,' he said in summing up, 'a government is nominated by the *corps législatif* at the invitation of the Regent, we deputies will not be violating our oath and our government will be perfectly legal; one can then expect all lovers of order and all patriotic citizens, irrespective of party, to come to the support of the government in its efforts to steer the nation safely through the present terrible crisis.'

Count Daru backed up Buffet's arguments by appealing to

190

the Empress to avoid the revolution which her refusal to abdicate her powers to the *corps législatif* would certainly bring.

When Daru had finished, Eugenie gave her answer.

They had assured her, she said quietly, that their proposal
would leave open the question of the future of the Empire. To
achieve this safeguard for the dynasty, she was now being asked
to abandon, in the hour of greatest peril, the post with which she
had been entrusted. 'I cannot, I dare not consent to this.' The
future—not of France, but of the dynasty—was, at the moment,
the very least of her worries. 'Believe me, gentlemen, the ordeals
to which I have been subjected have been so painful and so terrible that at present the thought of preserving the Crown for the
Emperor and my son weighs very little with me.

'My only desire, my one ambition, is to carry out faithfully
the duties which have been imposed upon me. If you think—if
the *corps législatif* thinks—that I am an obstacle and that the
name of the Emperor is an obstacle rather than a rallying point
and a symbol of resistance, then let them pronounce our deposition; I shall not complain. I can then quit my post with honour.
I shall not have deserted it. But I am convinced that the only
sensible and practical course is for the country's representatives
to rally round me and my government, to put aside for the
moment all internal questions and to unite our efforts to repel
the invader. . . . As for myself, I am ready to face all dangers and
to follow the *corps législatif* to wherever it decides to form a
nucleus of resistance. If this resistance becomes impossible, I
believe that I could still be useful in obtaining better peace
terms. Yesterday the ambassador of a Great Power offered to
propose a mediation of the neutral states on the following two
bases: first, that no territory be taken from France and second,
that the imperial dynasty be maintained. I replied that I was
ready to accept the first condition, but that I was absolutely
opposed to the second. The maintenance of the dynasty is a
question which concerns this country only and I will never
permit a foreign power to intervene in our internal affairs.'

Buffet, obviously impressed by these arguments, agreed that
the maintenance of the regency would be the most sensible plan
but that the state of public opinion, both inside and outside the
corps législatif, made it utterly impractical. Count Daru, showing

more subtlety, appealed to the Empress's patriotism. 'You fear, Madam,' he said, 'that you may be accused of deserting your post, but you will have given greater proof of your courage by sacrificing yourself for the public good and in sparing France the horrors of a revolution—and a revolution, moreover, in the face of the enemy.'

By now the discussion was being constantly interrupted by notes from the *Préfecture de Police*. The crowds were obviously getting out of hand and each new message revealed that they were moving nearer and nearer the Tuileries. The atmosphere in the room was becoming increasingly tense. The deputies, obviously nervous, began pressing their arguments on the still unyielding Empress. When one of them again stressed that the handing over of her powers would be the only way to safeguard the future of the dynasty, Eugenie showed a flash of her usual temper. 'Do you think that I am so anxious to retain power?' she exclaimed. 'My crown is no longer what it was in the days of glory and festivity. Nothing will ever efface the heart-rending memories of the present. I shall bear the woes of France eternally in my heart.'

At this point a messenger burst into the room to say that the imperial eagles had been ripped off the Palais Bourbon and that the mob had invaded the Chamber. The *corps législatif* would soon be powerless to adopt any sort of motion. If Eugenie wanted to avoid a full-scale revolution, she had no choice but to yield. 'Personally, I think this is a mistake,' she said, 'but you wish it, gentlemen, and I am ready to give up my opinion for yours. But I must act legally. I desire that my cabinet be consulted in the matter. If my ministers agree with you as to the wisdom of the proposed course, no further opposition will come from me.'

She rose, and the deputies, deeply impressed by the attitude of a woman whom most of them had hitherto thought of as high-handed virago, took their leave. At the door each bowed to kiss her hand. Buffet's eyes were seen to be wet with emotion. 'I could not help shedding tears,' he afterwards admitted, 'in the presence of so much disinterestedness and greatness of soul.'

It had been magnificent but, like so many of Eugenie's *grandes gestes*, quite valueless. In common with almost all her best scenes, it had been played *in camera*. She had impressed seven men but no one else. Her nobility had had no bearing on the situation whatsoever; it made not a scrap of difference to the course of events. What she consented, or did not consent, to do was by now quite immaterial. The drama of the fourth of September was not played out in the Blue Drawing Room of the Tuileries, it was to be enacted—such as it was—in that symbol of republican Paris, the Hôtel de Ville.

2

The scene at the Palais Bourbon was chaotic. Early that morning, on Palikao's instructions, a cordon of regular troops had been thrown around the building and the great iron gates leading to the forecourt shut. The forecourt itself was filled with police. In the ordinary way, such precautions should have been sufficient, but General Caussade, who commanded the troops, had very little taste for the role which he was expected to play. Ageing, ill and bemused by the turn of events, he was the very worst choice of man to control an unruly mob. Whether or not he could trust his troops, he simply did not know. He was hamstrung, moreover, by the Empress's firm injunction that no shots were to be fired. The police were every bit as unreliable as the soldiers. They seemed to be allowing the most extraordinary people to slip through the gates and enter the building; by mid-morning the trickle had become a flood and the corridors and public galleries were swirling with an assortment of rowdy strangers. Tickets for admission were being applied for, and granted, by the hundred. 'My wife and daughter desire to be present at the invasion of the Assembly,' scribbled one earnest citizen on his application form.

At noon a detachment of the National Guard came marching up the building to relieve—so they explained to the harassed General Caussade—the police within. Assuming the Guard to have been sent by some higher authority, Caussade let them through. In their wake trailed an army of riff-raff. They forced their way through the doors, they scrambled through the windows, they swarmed up the stairways. By the time the session

opened the noise within the hall was deafening and it was wondered how much longer the iron gates would hold against the
press of people beyond.

To try and hold a debate on the various motions—on Palikao's
for a Council of Regency, on Thiers's for a Council of National
Defence, even on Favre's for deposition—was quite impossible
against the clamour of the crowd. Gambetta, raising his powerful
voice above the uproar, begged for order. Never the revolutionary firebrand of the imperialists' imaginings, Gambetta tried
to introduce some legality into the proceedings, but his efforts
were simply howled down. M. Schneider, the President, having
repeatedly cried out for silence, left his seat in disgust. Soon
after he had done so, a great roar announced that the mob had
forced the gates and was pouring into the building. At this
Jules Favre, anxious to direct rather than to be at the mercy of
the crowd, made himself heard above the shouts of '*Vive la
République!*'

'This is not the place for proclaiming the Republic,' he cried.
'It should be done at the Hôtel de Ville. Follow me there! I will
lead the way!'

His suggestion was greeted by a roar of approval and, followed
by the Republican deputies and the cheering mob, he made his
way out of the Palais Bourbon. In the courtyard he was joined
by the National Guard. With flowers stuck into the barrels of
their rifles, the Guardsmen took up position on either side of
the procession and they all went marching along to the Hôtel
de Ville.

At the Pont Solferino they met General Trochu. With the
possible exception of an early morning visit to the Empress, this
was his first appearance that day. Throughout the morning's
excitements he had remained firmly shut up in his office. Nothing could induce him to go out. When, towards two o'clock that
afternoon, an alarmed deputy begged the governor to save the
corps législatif from the mob, Trochu answered that it was
quite out of the question. 'During the past few days,' he said,
'I have not been called upon to take command anywhere but
on the contrary, have been pushed to one side. General de
Palikao has tried to crush me completely, and has succeeded in
doing so. It is now too late to call upon me; I can be of no help.'

It was thus not until Jules Favre and his flower-garlanded escort came tramping across the Pont Solferino that General Trochu was seen in the streets. Favre shook the governor firmly by the hand. 'There is no government yet,' said Favre, 'but we are going, my friends and I, to set up one at the Hôtel de Ville; and we would be glad if you would return to your quarters and there await news of us.'

Trochu needed no second bidding. Without asking what had happened at the Palais Bourbon, he turned his horse and rode back to his office in the Louvre. On the way he passed the Tuileries. Within, the woman whom he had voted to 'serve until death', was still waiting for him to keep his word.

Things at the Hôtel de Ville were hardly less chaotic than they had been at the Palais Bourbon. Favre and his friends were not the only ones intent on setting up a new government. They arrived to find that the men of the extreme Left—the 'Reds' or 'Ultras'—had reached it before them. The names of such revolutionaries as Blanqui, Delescluze, Flourens, Millière and Pyat were already being circulated among the crowds as possible leaders of a new government, and Favre and his more moderate republicans had to act swiftly in the matter of getting themselves elected. Lists of names of proposed ministers were drawn up by whoever happened to have forced their way into the Hôtel de Ville and were then flung out of the windows on to the heads of the waiting crowd below. Whoever grabbed the fluttering pages would shout out the list; the louder the acclamation of the mob, the more likely was a particular candidate to be elected. To bring some sort of order out of this impossible situation, Favre (who was not a lawyer for nothing) proposed a simpler method: the new government should be composed exclusively of the existing Republican deputies for Paris. To this the Paris mob gave its vociferous approval.

The business settled, Léon Gambetta climbed on to a window-sill and, in his great voice, proclaimed the Third French Republic.

There followed a wild scramble for ministries. By running as fast as they could to the various ministry buildings, the members of the new government were able to stake their claims. Gambetta, arriving at the Ministry of the Interior at the same time as Picard, only just managed to beat him to it by sending off a batch of telegrams signed 'The Minister of the Interior, Léon Gambetta'. Jules Favre helped himself to Foreign Affairs.

To find a head for this hastily assembled government, the new ministers did not have far to look. Before long a delegation arrived at the Louvre to offer the post of President to General Trochu. Putting on civilian clothes (it would not do for him to head the new Republic in his old imperial uniform), Trochu made his way to the Hôtel de Ville. Having first treated his new colleagues to one of his long-winded speeches (they, like Eugenie, were assured that he was 'a Breton, a Catholic and a soldier') he accepted the post of President. His first, and no doubt highly gratifying, duty was to tell Palikao that he, Trochu, was now the head of the new French Republic.

So fell the Second Empire. Less than four months before, some seven and a half million Frenchmen had voted for its continuance; now not one voice could be found to speak out firmly in its favour. The Empire had been brought down by a few thousand noisy Parisians. The crowd was not even the terrifying, blood-thirsty rabble of previous revolutions; its behaviour, throughout the day, remained unruly rather than violent. It might have been very different, of course, had the mob not gained its way. It could quite easily have turned dangerous. A single incident, a shot fired into the crowd, could have provoked the most savage reaction. The blood which was spared on 4 September was to be spent, in horrifying abundance, six months later. When set beside the excesses of the Commune of the spring of 1871, the revolution of 4 September was about as dramatic as a Sunday school picnic.

But all was not quite over. The imperial standard still floated above the great dome of the Tuileries. The Empress had not left Paris. Nor had she the slightest intention of doing so.

3

For the better part of that Sunday, the crowds had concentrated on the Palais Bourbon. Only towards mid-afternoon did they turn their attention to the Tuileries. Two lines of ornamental railings protected the palace from the surging mob: the first divided the Tuileries Gardens from the Place de la Concorde; the second separated the private from the public part of the Gardens. By half past three the Place de la Concorde was a close-packed mass of heads, with here and there the bayonets of the National Guardsmen flashing in the afternoon sun. A sound like distant thunder filled the ears of those who stood waiting in the Tuileries. Every now and then a rhythmic chanting of '*Dé-ché-ance!*' would be heard above the ominous and continuous roar. The gilded eagles crowning the gateposts had already been ripped off. How much longer the railings would hold, no one could tell.

Within the Tuileries, the Empress refused to budge. They all begged her to leave. To the entreaties of her ministers, her Court and her Household, were added those of Prince Metternich and Count Nigra, the Ambassadors for Austria and Italy, who had just arrived. But still she refused. Even when the railings of the Place de la Concorde finally gave way and with a great cheer the mob came flooding into the Tuileries Gardens, she would not stir. The Prefect of Police warned her that the last line of railings would not long hold back the crowd and that all their lives were in real danger. General Mellinet assured her that unless he was allowed to fire into the mob, they would be in the palace within fifteen minutes. But she would allow no shooting. She would not lift a finger in self-defence. What was she planning to do? To face the mob as they came surging up the stairs? To reduce them to silence by her calm and dignified manner? To stand, proud and unprotesting, as they raised their weapons to kill her? Such dauntlessness is easier in theory than in practice. 'I had no fear of death,' she afterwards said. 'All I dreaded was falling into the hands of viragoes, who would defile my last scene with something shameful or grotesque, who would try to dishonour me as they murdered me. I fancied them lifting my skirts, I heard ferocious laughter. . . .'

The prospect undoubtedly weakened her resolve. So did the reasoning of one of her suite. 'You will not abdicate?' he argued. 'Well, in an hour you will be in the hands of those who will make you abdicate by force, and you will thus have sacrificed the rights which you hold in trust. If you get away, no matter where you go, you carry these rights with you.'

Such logic was bound to appeal to Eugenie. This, coupled with Nigra's pleadings not to endanger the lives of her friends, decided her. She suddenly announced that she would go. Unhurriedly, she moved into the adjoining salon to take leave of her ladies. At the sight of her, so calm and sad, they burst into tears, begging her to let them go with her. But she refused. 'No,' she said softly, 'I cannot take you with me. You have your husbands and your children. I do not wish to involve anyone in my own misfortune. Happier times will come again to France. *Adieu*, or rather, *au revoir*.'

She put on a small black hat with a heavy veil and over her shoulders she threw a black travelling cloak. As she had not eaten since early morning, one of her ladies begged her to take something from her untouched luncheon tray. She ate a little bread and then, hurried along by Metternich and Nigra, who had made themselves responsible for her safety, she left her apartments.

Accompanied by the two Ambassadors, her reader Madame Lebreton, Admiral Jurien de la Gravière, Eugène Conti and young Lieutenant Conneau, Eugenie descended to the ground floor and made for the door leading into the courtyard of the Tuileries. This vast courtyard, formed by the meeting of the wings of the Tuileries and the Louvre, was divided in two by a line of railings. If the Empress took the Court carriage which stood waiting on this side of the railings, she would be able to make her escape through a side entrance which gave on to the quay beside the Seine. But the carriage was emblazoned with the imperial arms and Metternich considered its use too risky. He sent Conneau for his own carriage which was standing farther along the quay. As they stood in the doorway waiting for Conneau to return, the courtyard was suddenly filled with noise. The crowd, having broken into the courtyard by way of the archway through the Louvre, was even now dashing towards the line of railings which divided the courtyard into two. Conneau came running back to say that it would be impossible to get out that way. If the Empress as much as moved out of the doorway, she would be seen. While the Admiral went out to try and calm the mob crowding the railings, the rest of the party hurried back up the staircase. The only thing to do would be to traverse the length of the palace and try to get out by way of the adjoining Louvre.

Moving more swiftly now, they passed through the Salle des États—so recently the scene of the triumphant proclamation of the plebiscite results—and reached the door leading to the picture galleries of the Louvre. It was locked. Their frantic knocking brought no answer from the museum attendants beyond. As the little party stood in agonized confusion, they could hear the sea-like roar of the crowd behind them. Had the palace been invaded? Then someone came rushing up with a master key and they hurried on. With the best paintings having been stored for safety, the galleries were almost empty. Reaching Géricault's dramatic picture of the wreck of the *Méduse*, Eugenie paused to look at it for a second. 'How strange!' she said quietly. Then, remembering that there might be some members of the palace staff who had not yet realized that she had left, she asked Lieutenant Conneau to go back and see that they left as quickly as they could. She reminded him to change his conspicuous uniform before he himself left the palace. He kissed her hand and left.

On the landing above the great staircase leading to the ground-floor galleries, she took leave of Conti. She did not want him to run any further risks for her sake. Now, with only Madame Lebreton and the two Ambassadors as escort, she descended the stairs and walked through the hall of Egyptian antiquities. From here they emerged through the main door of the Louvre into the Place Saint German l'Auxerrois.

A noisy crowd was milling about the square. Cries of '*Vive la République!*' and '*A bas l'Espagnole!*' filled the air. The fugitives stood rooted in the doorway. But the crowd surged past and for a moment the pavement was almost deserted.

'Now let us go,' urged the Empress.

But Nigra was apprehensive. 'I think we had better wait a little while longer,' he said.

'No, no,' cried Eugenie, 'one must be bold!' Saying this, she opened the door fully and stepped out into the sunshine.

Metternich went off to find a carriage but at that moment

an urchin, recognizing the Empress, rushed back to tell the crowd of his discovery. His excited shrieks were lost in the general din. Just then a *fiacre* came jogging by and Nigra quickly bundled the two women into it. As it drove off, the urchin came dashing back but Nigra caught him by the arm and pulled him back. He stood arguing with him until the *fiacre* had disappeared in the direction of the Rue de Rivoli.

In the meantime, the palace was quickly emptying of the last members of the imperial Court. The Countess de la Poëze was hurrying about, reminding various officials and ushers to change their uniforms before going out into the streets. At the top of the staircase leading to the Empress's private rooms, the Countess discovered one of the *Cent Gardes*, still standing sentinel at the door. She told him that the Empress had gone.

'Is there no one left in the rooms?' he asked.

'No one,' answered the Countess.

He brought down his rifle with a crash that echoed and re-echoed through the now empty corridors and, having positioned it in a corner by the window, he followed the rest of the company out of the palace.

Madame Lebreton had given the cab driver the address of M. Besson, a *conseiller d'état*, who lived on the Boulevard Haussmann. As they drove through the crowd, with the cab bobbing like a cork on the river of excited people, Eugenie, through her heavy veil, was taking in every detail of the scene. At the Louvre barracks, the young members of the Imperial Guard were joining lustily in the shouts of '*A bas l'Empire!*' and '*Vive la Nation!*' At a corner of the Boulevard des Capucines, the Empress noticed an imperial crest being ripped off a shop front. 'Already,' she said with a shrug to Madame Lebreton.

They reached M. Besson's apartment to find that he was not at home. As they had already dismissed the cab, the two women walked through the deserted streets of the *quartier* until they could find another. This time they drove to the home of the Marquis de Piennes. He, too, was out. The Empress then suggested that they throw themselves on the mercy of the Minister for the United States, Mr Elihu Washburn. But they did not know his address. This reminded Eugenie of her dentist, an

American by the name of Dr Evans, who lived in the Avenue de l'Impératrice. They would try him.

Dr Evans, too, was out but as he was expected back at any moment, his servant asked the two callers to wait in the study. It was an hour before Evans returned. When he did, he could scarcely believe his eyes. Speaking rapidly, Eugenie told him of her escape from the Tuileries. 'And I have come to you,' she said, 'for protection and assistance, because I have full confidence in your devotion to my family. The service which I am asking on my behalf and on that of Madame Lebreton will be a severe test of your friendship.'

Evans assured her that he would be only too happy to help her in every way he could. He would give her all the protection and assistance that she needed. Clearly touched by his fervency, Eugenie thanked him and said that she would like to make her escape to England as soon as possible. Then, sitting in an armchair with 'the pale light from the window by her side falling upon her still paler face, careworn and sad, but singularly beautiful', the Empress spoke of the train of events which had brought her so swiftly from the pinnacle of power to her present predicament.

'You see,' she said haltingly, 'I am no longer fortunate. The evil days have come, and I am left alone. . . .'

At this, she broke down. The extraordinary courage which had sustained her during the last few days suddenly gave way and she burst into tears.

CHAPTER ELEVEN

Into Exile

1

It was on that very day—Sunday, 4 September—that the Prince Imperial heard of the surrender at Sedan. His equerries had known about it since the previous evening but, apprehensive of his reaction, had put off telling him. By that Sunday their wanderings had brought them to the town of Maubeuge, close to the Belgian frontier and, on driving through the streets, Commander Duperré had noticed a placard announcing the surrender. That decided him. Louis would have to be told at once. As soon as they had settled themselves in the home of Madame Marchand, the widow of an Imperial senator, Duperré set about his painful task.

Louis heard him out in silence. Duperré, who had been expecting hysterics, was amazed—and not a little alarmed—at the boy's control. When the officer had finished his piece, the Prince asked to be left alone.

Duperré withdrew but he did not dare leave the boy unobserved. He was afraid that Louis might try to commit suicide. So he left the door slightly ajar and, calling his fellow officers to his side, remained just outside the room. What they saw was not the Prince Imperial fumbling with a weapon but his slight figure hunched in an attitude of heart-rending grief. The tears were streaming down his cheeks. He sat with his face buried in his hands, trying his best to stifle the sobs that were racking his whole body. Even in this extremity of grief he did not want the others to know that he had given way to tears. It would not do for a soldier and a Napoleon to be seen crying.

When it was over, and he was obliged to join his hostess at the luncheon table, his officers were astounded at the poise with which Louis conducted the conversation. But he would eat nothing.

Outside, in the streets of Maubeuge, the situation was turning dangerous. The revolutionary fervour which was even then bringing down the Empire in the capital was setting remote Maubeuge aflame as well. As it was a Sunday, the town was packed with the peasantry from the surrounding countryside. They massed about the cafés, listening open-mouthed to local Republican orators raging against the Emperor, or else collected under Louis's window in the Rue Royale in the hope of catching a glimpse of the illustrious visitor. But the Prince's party remained firmly indoors; it would be far too risky to show themselves. Already the *Cent Gardes* had been jeered at as they passed through the streets. Their commander, the massive young Lieutenant Watrin, had had to haul one particularly voluble officer of the *mobiles* off to the police station. As long as the crowd confined itself to insults it would not be too bad, but if they were to resort to physical violence, the soldiers would not have a chance. With each hour the situation was becoming more hazardous.

Within the Marchand house, Duperré was in an agony of impatience. The only sensible course would be to make for the Belgian frontier, but without orders he dared not move. Napoleon, telegraphing by permission of his captors, had urged Duperré to make for Belgium and England immediately, but Eugenie, who at that stage had still not fled the Tuileries, had told Duperré to ignore Napoleon's instructions ('The Emperor cannot appreciate the situation') and to await further orders from her. He would receive them, she promised, before nightfall. All that Duperré could do was to make sure that when the Empress's instructions did finally come, he would be ready to act on them immediately. It was decided that the Prince and his three officers would slip away from the town unobserved, leaving the escort of *Cent Gardes* to conceal their departure. To this end Duperré arranged for a small horse-drawn omnibus to be waiting at a side entrance of the house and for four suits of civilian clothes to be delivered to them. One can imagine with what heartbreak Louis must have put aside his uniform in order to dress himself in ordinary clothes. More than anything, perhaps, this would have brought home to him the humiliating truth that it was all over; that he was being forced to fly, not from the enemy, but from his own beloved Frenchmen. Only with the utmost effort could he restrain himself from giving way to a second storm of tears.

Not until five o'clock that afternoon did the orders arrive from the Empress. They had been telegraphed by Filon from the Tuileries at half past three, just before Eugenie had made her escape. 'Leave at once for Belgium,' they read.

Duperré lost no time in carrying them out. Louis bade a hurried farewell to his hostess and then, followed by his three sober-suited equerries, he climbed into the waiting omnibus. As it was about to pull away, he suddenly caught sight of Lieutenant Watrin. He leapt out of the vehicle, flung his arms about the young man's neck and cried out, '*Allons! du courage*; good-bye, Watrin! Good-bye!...'

Watrin watched them go. Then, having put on full dress uniform, he showed himself to the crowd outside the house before returning to Louis's brightly lit rooms. The townsfolk assumed that he was dining with the Prince Imperial whereas Louis, by then, was safely in Belgium.

He would never again set foot in France.

They reached Namur, by train, at midnight. Here Louis spent the night as the guest of Count de Baillet, the Governor of this particular Belgian province. Unbeknown to the Prince, the Emperor was not far off. He was at Verviers, *en route* to his captivity at Wilhelmshöhe, and he had sent a message to Duperré, asking him to bring his son to Verviers. Duperré decided against it. With Louis in so wretched a state, the sight of his father—a captive of the Prussians—would be too much of a shock. So Count Clary went across to Verviers and explained to the Emperor, whom he found sitting on a bench at the railway station in a state of utter dejection, that Louis had not been well enough to come. Napoleon was deeply disappointed, particularly as he had been toying with the idea of taking Louis with him to Wilhelmshöhe. But when Clary protested that the boy's health would not stand the strain, the Emperor gave way. He agreed that they must take Louis to England. Clary took his leave and returned to Namur.

On the morning of 5 September, while Louis was waiting for the afternoon train that would take him from Namur to Ostend, Duperré told him that the Empire had fallen and that France was now a Republic.

They left for the railway station in a closed cab at three that afternoon. A great crowd had collected at the station to see Louis off. Looking pale and nervous, he hurried from the cab to the station-master's office and, once the door had been closed, asked to be left alone. He then burst, once more, into floods of tears. By the time the train drew in, however, he had gained control of himself. Emerging from the station-master's office, he passed slowly through the curious crowd, bowing royally from left to right and even managing a ghostly version of his old radiant smile. The train drew out in almost complete silence.

That night he slept at the Hôtel d'Allemagne at Ostend and the next day he boarded the *Comte de Flandres*, bound for Dover. The quay was crowded with interested spectators but he remained below until the steamer was under way. Only when the vessel was well out to sea did he emerge from his cabin. He then sat on deck, his face 'pale and impassive like the Emperor's', until he could see the land no more.

2

It was on that same platform at Verviers, where he had waited for the Prince Imperial, that Napoleon III heard that his Empire had fallen. A newsboy, dashing along the platform, was heard yelling, *'Chute de l'Empire! Fuite de l'Impératrice!'* The sight of the headlines, although not entirely unexpected, came as a profound shock to the Emperor. Could it be possible that the Empire which he had created, cherished and made powerful had simply collapsed overnight? 'Could I imagine,' he afterwards said, 'that this nation, formerly so chivalrous and generous, would take advantage of the moment of my misfortunes to avenge itself for imaginary injuries? No, it is not the nation which has done this . . . it is certain men—but, *mon Dieu*, what men!'

Too physically and emotionally exhausted to travel any farther that day, the Emperor asked to be allowed to spend the night in a hotel at Verviers. Permission was granted. In point of fact, Leopold II, the King of the Belgians, had been in two minds about letting the Emperor pass through Belgian territory at all. Unnerved by the battles that had been fought within sight of Belgian territory, King Leopold was anxious to avoid any action which might jeopardize his country's neutrality. Then, with Verviers lying in the French-speaking part of Belgium, but close to the German frontier, there was an additional risk of some sort of demonstration—and counter-demonstration—by the townsfolk. General Chazal, Commander of the Belgian forces, felt it necessary to appeal to the crowd that had collected outside the Emperor's hotel, to behave with restraint. He asked them 'in the name of Belgian hospitality and in the name of the city of Verviers', to treat the Emperor with 'the respect due to his great misfortunes'. It was therefore in almost complete silence that Napoleon, the following morning, came down the steps of his hotel on the arm of General Chazal and took his seat in the waiting carriage. The crowds at the station were equally mute but, as the train drew away, with the Emperor framed in one of the windows of his saloon, a great shout of '*Vive l'Empereur!*' suddenly burst forth from the people on the platform. 'It was a moving sight which I shall not soon forget,' wrote one of his suite.

It was raining when the Emperor reached Cassel that evening. General Monts, the Governor of Cassel, into whose charge the Emperor had been assigned, was waiting at the station platform to meet him. Napoleon was introduced to the Governor's suite and then drove, through the streaming rain, to Wilhelmshöhe.

On the first day of his captivity, the Emperor told his aides that he had once visited Wilhelmshöhe fifty-seven years before, when it had been the pleasure pavilion of his uncle Jerome, whom the First Napoleon had made King of Westphalia. He wondered whether it contained 'some souvenirs of the past'. While they were walking slowly through the rooms, the Emperor seeming almost indifferent to his surroundings, he suddenly stopped short. On the wall hung a portrait of a young woman in all the seductive grace of her First Empire clothes. It was a painting of his mother, the Empress Josephine's daughter, Queen Hortense. Deeply moved, Napoleon gestured his companions away, and remained for almost an hour, standing alone in front of the picture. When he reappeared, he seemed, says one eyewitness, 'comforted, encouraged, resigned, calm and strong'. Napoleon III had loved his mother very dearly; perhaps, with his strong streak of mysticism, he really had drawn comfort from this unexpected sight of her portrait.

Indeed, it was to be her qualities—the Beauharnais qualities of charm and adaptability—rather than any Napoleonic traits, that were to characterize the Emperor's behaviour during the six months of his captivity. Wilhelmshöhe would know none of the temperamental eruptions of the first Napoleon's captivity on Saint Helena. To General Monts, Napoleon III's jailer, the Emperor's personality came as a complete surprise. He had expected someone altogether more forceful; more like one of the *'vieux grognards'* of the First Empire. 'His features express kindliness and goodwill, and his voice does not belie that impression,' wrote Monts. 'His whole attitude is characterized by a certain lassitude, which only disappears when he is talking about things which particularly interest him, such as the Empress's and the Prince Imperial's wellbeing. He then looks almost captivating.'

But that was to be much later. On the first day of his captivity the Emperor knew nothing of the Empress's wellbeing. He did not even know if she was alive.

3

Eugenie had left Paris at dawn on the morning of 5 September. Dr Evans, in consultation with the Empress and a fellow American, Dr Crane, had decided that they would make for Deauville, on the Normandy coast, where Mrs Evans was on holiday. From here the Empress might be able to hire a yacht to take her across the Channel. Considering any means of public transport too risky, they agreed to travel by relays of carriages, starting off in Evans's own landau. The four of them—the

Empress, Madame Lebreton, Dr Evans and Dr Crane—hoped to reach Deauville within two days.

That the journey was to be fraught with danger, they had not the slightest doubt. Eugenie knew something of the feeling against her in France—that she was looked upon as the chief instigator of the war, that she was accused of having 'recklessly sacrificed the French nation in an attempt to consolidate the Imperial dynasty'. As Regent (and Eugenie never for a moment doubted that she was still Regent) she would be extremely valuable to the revolutionary leaders; they would, she imagined, do anything to stop her from becoming a rallying point for the Imperialists. Were she to be recognized, she would probably be attacked and almost certainly arrested. The little party of fugitives were only too conscious of the fact that their journey had a precedent in the flight of Eugenie's heroine—Queen Marie Antoinette—to Varennes. What the revolutionaries had done to *l'Autrichienne*, they were quite capable of doing to *l'Espagnole*. 'Had not the Empress reason to be alarmed?' asked Evans.

Wearing her black dress, her travelling cloak, a black Derby with a veil and carrying no luggage other than two handkerchiefs in a small handbag, Eugenie took her seat in the carriage. She had refused to listen to Madame Lebreton's entreaties that she disguise herself in some way. To be arrested in disguise would be too humiliating. She had even drawn those bold and characteristic black lines—'the Empress's signature'—around her eyes. This was a matter of pride rather than of vanity. 'Her beauty was her sole weapon, her only defence,' says Filon, 'and by its aid she knew she would be enabled to play the Empress to the last.'

Once safely through the gates of Paris (the *mobiles* on guard had shown only the most perfunctory interest) Eugenie's spirits rose. In fact, Evans was to be amazed at her resilience, her vitality and the ease with which she adapted herself to the dangerous and uncomfortable circumstances of the journey. She was certainly much more animated than poor Madame Lebreton. In spite of all the discomforts—the frequent changes of carriage, the inadequacy of the carriages themselves, the squalor of the accommodation, the coarseness of the meals, the nearness of the crowds singing the *Marseillaise* and shouting '*Vive la Répub-*

lique!'—she never once complained. She washed her handkerchiefs and dried them against the window panes, she cut her
bread and Bologna sausage with a pocket knife, she walked
through the pouring rain and scuttled to safety up dark stairways. 'When we are not driven by hard necessity,' she once
explained, 'we never suspect our capacity for doing certain
things.' Indeed, she seemed, at times, to be positively enjoying
herself. With her love of action, this escapade had become almost
pleasurable. More than once she burst out laughing at the
extraordinariness of the whole situation. 'Ah, *mon Dieu,*
Madame,' whispered the terrified Madame Lebreton as they took
refuge in some sordid hotel room, 'how can you laugh at this
wretched situation we are in?'

Evans was hardly less amazed. He had seen her the year
before, during her state visit to Constantinople *en route* to the
inauguration of the Suez Canal, being rowed across the Bosporus
in the Sultan's superb barge, 'sitting alone in evening dress, a
light mantilla over her head, wearing a diadem and many rich
jewels, radiant and beautiful, and supremely happy and proud to
accept this magnificent tribute paid to the glory of France. . . .'
Now, as he saw her huddled in a doorway of a factory at
Lisieux, drenched to the skin as she waited for him to bring up
yet another carriage, he imagined that he must be dreaming.
'It is impossible,' he later claimed to have thought to himself,
'that she, who was the recipient in a foreign land of all those
honours . . . was the same person who today is a fugitive, without
a shelter even from the inclemency of the weather, forgotten,
unnoticed by her own people as they pass by her in the street,
and so completely lost, in this very France where she was once
so honoured, that her existence is known to but two men—and
those two Americans!'

But Eugenie herself wasted no time on regretting past glories
or bewailing present discomforts. For the most part her thoughts
were on the events of the past few days in Paris. She never tired
of explaining, and justifying, her behaviour to the two men.

'They asked me to abdicate,' she said, 'but how could I? How
could I, who have acted only as a delegate, abdicate a sovereignty that is not my own?' She had been quite willing, she
claimed, to hand over her powers to the *corps législatif,* but

THE FALL OF THE THIRD NAPOLEON

surely it would have been much more sensible for the Regency to have continued and for everyone to have concentrated their energies on winning the war. One of the troubles, of course, lay in the character of the French people. They 'have great and brilliant qualities, but they have few convictions and they lack constancy. Their minds are supple but their characters are fickle. They love glory and everything that is brilliant and showy, but they do not know how to endure the strokes of misfortune. For them right is confused with success. In France you are honoured today and banished tomorrow. . . . There is no country in the world where there is so little distance between the sublime and the ridiculous. And how history repeats itself! For a hundred years every government in France has ended in revolution and flight. Only the other day when some persons expressed the fear that a fresh defeat might bring about the fall of the Imperial government, I declared to them that I would never leave the Tuileries in a cab like Louis Philippe. And that's exactly what I have done!'

Yet she had meant so well. There was no risk that she would not have run, no sacrifice that she would not have made, no suffering that she would not have endured. 'I could have been useful in so many ways. I could have been an example of devotion to my country. I could have visited the hospitals. I could have gone to the outposts. I could have encouraged and stimulated the defence at every point. Oh, why could they not let me die before the walls of Paris!'

When they stopped at Mantes, Evans bought her the *Journal Officiel* and she learnt, for the first time, that Trochu was now the President of the Government of National Defence. She refused to believe it.

'No, no, that is impossible!' she cried out. 'How could he go over to the revolutionaries after the solemn declarations of loyalty and personal devotion which he made to me? I cannot believe it!'

She went on to read the names of the other members of the government, but it was Trochu's name alone that seemed to interest her. Again and again she subjected her travelling companions to an impassioned tirade against Trochu's treachery. She seemed far more concerned about that than about the setting up of the Republican régime. 'Whom could I have trusted if not him—a soldier selected by the Emperor himself as especially trustworthy, who had accepted the duty of defending me, who to the very last moment swore to be faithful to me?' So incensed was she by Trochu's behaviour that she burst into tears. But they did not last long. Her natural optimism soon reasserted itself and, smiling through her tears, said, 'I shall soon be in England, and then I shall know what is to be done.'

They reached Deauville at three o'clock the second afternoon. While the Empress, who had slipped in at a side entrance of the hotel, remained with Mrs Evans, the dentist went off to find a vessel to carry her across to England. There was a yacht belonging to an Englishman, Sir John Burgoyne, in the harbour and, after some initial hesitation (a violent storm was brewing) Sir John agreed to take the Empress. Towards midnight Eugenie and her little party made their way on foot through the dark, rain-lashed streets to the quayside.

'On that gloomy night of 6 and 7 September,' wrote Evans, 'there were no flags waving, no cries of "Vive l'Impératrice!" or "Vive Eugénie!" nor any admiring crowd to witness the departure, perhaps for ever, of this great lady from the home she had so long made radiant by her presence; only the clouds in black masses, spread over the heavens like mourning drapery; there were no offerings of fresh flowers, only the scattered leaves of autumn driven before the wind; there were no attending courtiers at her side, only one follower and friend accompanying the deserted Empress to the place where she was to embark; and the only voices to be heard were those of men singing the Marseillaise in the wineshops, and of the howling storm, and of the rolling waves breaking against the shore. The world, which had hitherto been so accurately informed as to every movement of Her Majesty, did not know that she was about to leave her country; and her subjects were so busy in smashing to pieces the whole fabric of the Imperial government, or in seeking their own personal safety, that nobody in the capital from which she had fled seemed to have even thought of her.'

There, indeed, was the rub. France, by now, had lost interest in her. The excessive caution of the last two days had been quite unnecessary. No one had been watching out for her. Her flight, in the words of one of her less sympathetic biographers, had 'every element of the dramatic, except pursuit'.

One bit of real drama remained, however, and that was the crossing of the Channel. It was terrifying. The yacht left Deauville at dawn on 7 September and that afternoon it ran into the most violent storm. The storm lasted for over twelve hours and it seemed as though the mountainous waves must dash the little ship to pieces. Farther down the Channel, H.M.S. *Captain* went down with over five hundred men. Eugenie, who was never afraid of the sea, bore up bravely, but poor Madame Lebreton spent most of that horrifying night on her knees in prayer. At one stage the two women heard a desperate cry of 'We are aground!'

'What are they saying?' asked Madame Lebreton, whose English was not perfect.

'They are saying,' replied the Empress deftly, 'that we are near the land.'

Even in this extremity of danger, Eugenie remained alive to the dramatic potential of her position. 'The little vessel,' she afterwards said, 'was jumping on the waves like a cork. I thought we were lost. Death in that great tumult seemed to me enviable and sweet. I reflected that I was about to disappear, and that, as my crossing to England had been a secret, no one would ever know what had become of me. Thus an impenetrable mystery would have enwrapped the end of my fate.'

What a finale to her tumultuous career! She would have provided history with one of its most fascinating enigmas. But she was to be denied so magnificent an epilogue. At dawn on 8 September, in a calm sea, Sir John Burgoyne dropped anchor off Ryde in the Isle of Wight.

Part Four

CHAPTER TWELVE

The Peacemaking

1

The fall of the Second Empire did not mean the end of the war. Not by any means. Within five days of the Emperor's surrender at Sedan, the German army was marching towards Paris. Leaving Prince Frederick-Charles and his army to see that Bazaine did not get out of Metz, the bulk of the German forces marched south. With the taste of victory sweet in their mouths, the Prussians were determined to teach the French a lesson. 'We ought to crush them,' noted one fervent Prussian general, 'so that they will not be able to breathe for a hundred years.' The German advance was incredibly swift. By 20 September, the capital was surrounded and, to the astonishment of the civilized world, Paris—that charming, insouciant *ville lumière*, so recently the gayest city in Europe—was in a state of siege.

How long the siege was likely to last, no one could predict, but of its ultimate outcome there was very little doubt. Sooner or later, Paris would have to capitulate. The new Government of National Defence, viewing the situation in the sober light of day which followed the intoxicating establishment of a republic, began to think in terms of a negotiated peace. It was, after all, against Napoleon III's régime that Prussia had gone to war; now that the Empire had fallen, might Bismarck not be prepared to call a halt?

With this in mind, Jules Favre, the new Minister of Foreign Affairs, sought an interview with the Prussian Chancellor, now installed in the Rothschilds' great château at Ferrières. However, before setting out to meet Bismarck, Favre informed the various European chancelleries that in any proposed settlement, France was not prepared to yield 'an inch of her soil or a stone of her fortresses'. It was a short-sighted boast. Favre should

215

have known Bismarck better than that. Soil and fortresses were precisely what Bismarck was interested in. What the Prussian Chancellor demanded of Favre was the whole of the province of Alsace and part of Lorraine and, with them, the fortresses of Strasbourg and Metz. Only thus could Germany be rendered secure from any future French aggression. These harsh terms appalled Favre. 'You want to destroy France!' he cried out, and left Ferrières in tears.

The failure of Favre's mission had the effect of strengthening the new French government's resolve to fight on. As professional armies had proved unsuccessful, the Government of National Defence decided on a *levée en masse*. France must become a Nation in Arms and, fired with the revolutionary spirit of 1792, rise up as one man to drive the invader from French soil. From now on it was to be *guerre à outrance*.

To instil the somewhat apathetic provinces with the same sense of purpose which characterized besieged Paris, it was agreed that the new Minister of the Interior, Léon Gambetta, must go to Tours. From this provincial city he would organize a new centre of resistance. Unable to slip through the German lines, Gambetta was obliged to make his escape from Paris in a balloon. It was a suitably theatrical introduction to a performance that was to inspire all France. By his eloquence, his energy and his example, Léon Gambetta came to epitomize the spirit of the French resistance to the enemy. There must be no more talk of a negotiated peace.

In the meantime, Bismarck was not at all sure that it was with the Government of National Defence that he should be negotiating at all. The batch of Left-wing lawyers who now ruled France was certainly not his idea of a properly constituted government. They had not even been elected to power; they had simply snatched it. At this stage, Bismarck still felt that he should be dealing with the imperial régime. There had been no formal act of abdication and although the Emperor himself was a prisoner, there remained two representatives of Imperial power. The one was Bazaine with his still unbeaten army besieged in Metz—an imperial island in a republican sea—and the other, of course, was the Regent, the Empress Eugenie. In an announcement made a few days before the investment of

Paris, Bismarck let it be known that he was quite prepared to talk peace with either of these imperial deputies.

The announcement would have come as no surprise to the Empress. She still considered herself very much the Regent. Already, from the modest hotel at Hastings where she had been reunited, on British soil, with the Prince Imperial, she had written letters to the Tsar Alexander II and the Emperor Franz Josef of Austria, asking them to do what they could to secure an honourable peace for France. Their replies had been polite but non-committal. For all her conviction that she was still a political force ('She remained conscious—I could see it at once —of the position she had occupied and which she still occupied,' noted Filon, who had joined her at Hastings), Eugenie was careful to do nothing to embarrass or hamper the new French government. She knew that she must move with caution; she had been blamed for far too much as it was. In this she was supported by the Emperor. Even better than she, he realized that they could not afford to sign any peace treaty dishonourable to France, and in his letters to her he was always counselling patience and circumspection.

Eugenie, by now, was quite prepared to listen to him. The sudden fall from power had opened her eyes afresh to her husband's many admirable qualities and she may well have been feeling some prick of remorse for her often high-handed treatment of him. It had taken a 'day of storm', she admitted in one of her letters to Wilhelmshöhe, to prove to her that the ties between them had not been broken. '*Pauvre cher ami*,' she wrote, 'if only my devotion can bring you an instant's forgetfulness of the trials through which your great soul has passed. Your adorable long-suffering makes me think of Our Lord. . . .' It was all a far cry from her recent outpourings, on the staircase in the Tuileries, against the *lâche de Sedan*.

Her behaviour during the Regnier affair, which took place during those confused September days, was every bit as prudent as Napoleon would have wished it to be. When Monsieur Regnier, an unknown, middle-aged Frenchman, suddenly arrived at the Marine Hotel, Hastings, with a plan whereby the Empress would board a warship, land at a French port, convoke the Chambers and negotiate peace, she refused to receive him.

Young Filon, however, proved much less impervious to the stranger's tempting scheme and allowed Regnier to talk him into arranging for the Prince Imperial to write a few words on a postcard which Regnier could use as a means of gaining access to the Emperor at Wilhelmshöhe. Armed with the signed card Regnier presented himself to Bismarck at Ferrières and asked to be allowed to proceed to Wilhelmshöhe. Bismarck, who was indeed anxious to negotiate with the imperial régime (or, at least, to play the old French government off against the new) received this self-appointed peacemaker warmly and arranged for him to go, not to Wilhelmshöhe, but to Metz, where he was to persuade Bazaine to sue for peace in the name of the Emperor. The Empress could then return to France and, supported by the Army of Metz, overthrow the Government of National Defence and negotiate peace.

Bazaine welcomed Regnier no less warmly. As yet, there had been no agreement between the Army of Metz and the Republican government in Paris, and Regnier's plan offered more hope of avoiding utter disgrace than did the prospect of a prolonged siege followed by an inevitable capitulation. Bazaine, moreover, was always pleased to have his mind made up for him. It was therefore arranged that General Bourbaki should be allowed to leave Metz and go to England to discuss the proposed scheme with the Empress. When Bourbaki, who was the brother of Eugenie's companion-in-flight, Madame Lebreton, duly presented himself to the Empress, she was appalled. She assured the bewildered Bourbaki that Regnier's mission had not had her sanction and lost no time in letting the Prussian government know the same thing. She would do nothing to weaken the hand of the Government of National Defence. To the persistent Regnier, to whom she granted an audience once the affair was closed, she made her position clear. The French, she said, 'will never pardon one who gives up a portion of France; they will always say, and their sons will say after them, that if only they had struggled to the end they would have triumphed; and furthermore, the peace would not be recognized, and after the foreign war we should have civil war'.

Bismarck, in spite of the failure of Regnier's mission, was still anxious to treat with the imperial rather than the revolutionary régime, and when Bazaine, who was by now getting desperate, sent an aide-de-camp, General Boyer, to try and reach an honourable settlement with the Prussians, Bismarck arranged for Boyer to go to England to consult with the Empress. By now Eugenie had moved from Hastings and had taken a house in the village of Chislehurst in Kent and it was here that she received General Boyer. From him she learnt that Bismarck wished Bazaine to issue a *pronunciamiento* in favour of the imperial régime and for the Empress to return to France in order to sign a treaty of peace. The terms of the peace would be decided once she had agreed to the plan. When Eugenie realized that she was being asked to sign what she called a blank cheque, she burst out, says Filon, 'into splendid and flaming anger' and refused to do any such thing. A personal appeal from the Empress to the King of Prussia brought no modification of these conditions and the talks fell through.

By now Bazaine had reached the end of the road. Metz, demoralized and without food, could not hold out much longer. A Council of War, called by Bazaine on 24 October, agreed to ask the investing Prussian army for terms. These turned out to be severe: the fortress must be surrendered, the army must become prisoner and all war material must be handed over. There was nothing for it but for the French to agree to these humiliations, and five days later the fortress capitulated. The Army of the Rhine went off into captivity and with it went the last hope of the imperial dynasty being asked to play any part in the negotiations for peace. From now on Bismarck would be obliged to deal with the Republicans.

But still Eugenie did not give up hope. In December, with besieged and starving Paris in the grip of winter and the new, hastily scraped-together French army fighting valiantly but ineffectively on the River Loire, she thought of a way by which she might be able to put an end to the terrible struggle and at the same time re-establish the imperial authority. She would return to France, establish herself in some provincial city, convoke the pre-war *corps législatif* and sue for peace. Prussia would surely grant her, as Regent of the Empire, more generous terms than it would to the Republic. This more favourable peace treaty she would then submit to the French nation in a plebiscite. The Emperor had always consulted the nation on major issues; why not on this?

Napoleon, on hearing of her scheme, immediately condemned it. It was utterly impractical. In the first place she would simply be arrested and sent back to England; in the second, the old imperial senators and deputies would neither care nor dare to answer her summons; in the third, no peace treaty, no matter how generous, could ever be anything but disastrous. And as for a plebiscite, it would not be honest. The country would be being asked to vote, not on the actual peace treaty, but on whether they would prefer peace or war. No, wrote the Emperor firmly, the two of them must keep clear of any such schemes and allow events to take their course.

It was sound advice but the Emperor could hardly be said to be following it himself. Throughout his captivity he seems to have been involved in various secret negotiations with the enemy. It is claimed that he knew more about the Regnier affair than Eugenie ever realized and to the very end of his time at Wilhelmshöhe, his agents were flitting about Europe peddling imperial peace proposals. But then his moves were always clandestine. What he was warning Eugenie against was some impulsive, public gesture which might cover them in ridicule. All their actions, he told her, 'must bear the stamp of dignity and grandeur in accordance with the position we have held. . . .'

2

On 18 January, 1871, in the Palace of Versailles, where the German army now had its headquarters, King Wilhelm of Prussia was proclaimed Emperor of Germany. In the glittering *galerie des glaces*, whose walls had so often mirrored the great *fêtes* of the Second Empire, the Second German *Reich* was inaugurated. Bismarck's dream had come true.

Ten days later the French asked for an armistice. This was granted on the understanding that the country would elect a new government which would then either accept or reject the German peace terms. The result of the elections, held on 8 February, came as a discouraging surprise to the Republicans:

it was a massive victory for the Royalists—both Legitimate and Orleans. It proved once again—if proof were needed—that revolutionary Paris was by no means representative of France and that the provinces, who less than a year ago had given the now discredited Napoleon III an overwhelming vote of confidence, had remained conservative.

The natural choice as head of this new ultra-conservative government was the veteran Thiers (he had been elected by twenty-six constituencies) and it was therefore he who had to accept the German peace terms. These were extremely harsh. France was to cede Alsace and most of Lorraine, including the fortresses of Strasbourg and Metz, and to pay an indemnity of five thousand million francs. Until this was paid, France was to be partially occupied. Thiers had very little choice but to accept the terms and on 1 March, the National Assembly ratified the treaty. 'Such a peace,' declared the Emperor Napoleon on hearing the news, 'can only be a truce. . . .' Within twenty or thirty years' time, Prussia would be forced to become aggressive and then, he added prophetically, 'Europe will crush her.'

The conclusion of the war meant his own release from captivity. Towards the middle of that month he left Wilhelmshöhe and on 20 March 1871 he landed at Dover where he was met by the Empress and their son. As, with the welcoming cries of the townsfolk ringing in his ears, he and his family made their way along a narrow passage-way leading to the railway station, there occurred an incident of considerable significance and poignancy. The defeated Emperor, about to begin his exile, came suddenly face to face with some members of the Orleans family, about to end theirs. It was Napoleon III's reign that had prolonged their exile; now that he had fallen and the Royalists had gained so massive a victory in the elections, they were able to return to France. For a few seconds the two opposing groups of royalties stood rooted to the ground in embarrassed silence. Then Eugenie, who had always had a weakness for legitimate monarchies as well as a strong sense of occasion, moved slowly to one side and dropped a curtsy. She straightened and, followed by the Emperor and the Prince Imperial, passed on without a word.

CHAPTER THIRTEEN

Exile

1

'When I am free,' the Emperor had once written to Eugenie from Wilhelmshöhe, 'I should like to go to England, and live with you and Louis in a little cottage with bow-windows and creeper.'

It was a charming thought but hardly one that could be taken seriously. The house which Eugenie had chosen as their place of exile was a solid, three-storeyed, red-brick mansion set in a large park in the village of Chislehurst in Kent. It was known as Camden Place. Secluded, close to a Catholic church and a mere half-hour's train journey from London, Camden Place seemed ideal for what Eugenie at first imagined was to be a temporary place of refuge. Even the inscription—*Malo mori quam foedari* —cut into the stone above the main entrance, suited the Empress. 'It might be my own!' she exclaimed on first seeing the motto, and when Marie de Larminat translated it for the Prince Imperial as 'Death rather than desertion', he was no less enthusiastic.

'Ah, that's fine,' he answered, 'that is the kind of Latin I like.'

A band of faithfuls had already collected about the Empress and when the Emperor arrived from Wilhelmshöhe he brought a small suite of his own. It was thus a not inconsiderable company that was housed in the somewhat tastelessly furnished rooms at Camden (*'on dirait un café'* was Duperré's comment) and which found itself obliged to adapt, not only to the strangeness of exile, but to the slow-dawning realization that the exile might prove permanent.

Another aspect of exile to which they had to accustom themselves was a reduction in their standard of living. Until Eugenie was able to sell some of her magnificent personal jewellery (which she had prudently entrusted to Pauline Metternich before her flight from the Tuileries) and the Emperor some of his French and Italian properties, they had to live carefully, almost frugally. But the Empress, unlike her husband, had always been thrifty and by careful budgeting and shrewd investing, she was able to build up their fortune.

By a strange coincidence, Camden Place was not new to the Emperor. In the 1830s when, as a young man, Napoleon had been spending the first of his periods of exile in England, he had often visited Camden Place. The house had then been owned by people named Rowles and the daughter of the house, Emily Rowles, had been one of the dozens of women with whom Napoleon III had imagined himself to be in love. 'I used to be here frequently in former years,' he would now tell his visitors. Another coincidence was that the man from whom the Empress had leased the house, the owner, Mr Strode, had once been the trustee of one of Napoleon's mistresses. It is unlikely that Eugenie, who had taken the house on the recommendation of Dr Evans, was aware of these piquant links with her husband's past.

Another reminder of earlier days was in the form of a little circular building which the exiles discovered half buried in a hollow at the back of the house; it was an exact copy of a monument which had once crowned a hill-top at Saint Cloud. 'It struck,' sighed one of them, 'an incongruous note under the misty sky and unceasing rain in the melancholy sadness of that drab country.' To the homesick company, it merely served to underline the contrast between the golden past and their present mournful state.

For the Emperor it was not so difficult. He had spent more of his life in exile than out of it. Besides, he had always been the most long-suffering of men; he had never been one to fret. But even allowing for this, those who met him after the fall of the Empire were astounded at the ease with which he accommodated himself to the changed circumstances of his life. His philosophical acceptance of his misfortunes was little short of miraculous. His old friend Lord Malmesbury, visiting him at Camden Place on the day after his arrival from captivity, claimed that the Emperor's 'quiet and calm dignity and absence of all nervousness and irritability were the grandest examples of human moral courage that the severest Stoic could have imagined'. The two men had known each other for many years and through numberless changes of fortune and now, says Malmesbury, 'all those memories crowded upon me as the man stood before me whose race had been so successful and so romantic, now without a crown, without an army, without a country or an inch of ground which he could call his own, except the house he hired in an English village. I must have shown what I felt as, again shaking my hand, he said: *A la guerre, comme à la guerre. C'est bien bon de venir me voir.* . . . During half an hour he conversed with me as calmly as in the best days of his life, with a dignity and resignation which might be that of a fatalist, but could hardly be obtained from any other creed; and when I left him that was, not for the first time, my impression.'

Queen Victoria, who invited the Emperor to Windsor a week later, was likewise struck by his stoicism. It was an emotional meeting, for the two sovereigns had not seen each other since the halcyon days of the Anglo-French *entente*, over a decade before, when Victoria had been more than a little carried away by the dashing and seductively-mannered Emperor. Things had changed a great deal since then. The Queen had lost her husband and Napoleon his throne, and Victoria could not help comparing their earlier, enchanting meetings with this present doleful occasion. Much of the Emperor's magic had worn off since those days. 'He is grown very stout and grey and his moustaches are no longer curled or waxed as formerly,' noted the Queen, 'but otherwise there was the same pleasing, gentle and gracious manner.'

'He bore his terrible misfortunes,' she subsequently claimed, 'with meekness, dignity and patience.'

It was not only to occasional visitors that Napoleon III revealed this nobility of temperament. In the confused atmosphere of Camden Place he proved no less amiable. He lived a quiet life, spending most of his day in his little study on the first floor, reading, writing or working on some new invention. Sometimes, with his head tilted and a cigar between his lips, he would stroll slowly up and down the long gallery on the ground floor and occasionally, if the weather were good, he would take a turn on Chislehurst Common. Unlike the majority of his fellow-exiles, he never complained. Renowned, during the good years, for his generosity, his charm and his simplicity, these years of exile found him quite unchanged. On that bored, irritable and often despairing company at Camden Place, his presence had a soothing and inspiring effect. He was an example to them all. 'The Emperor,' wrote one of the Household after his death, 'was like an oak tree round which everybody gathered, listening to wise words.'

Most remarkable of all was the way in which he refused to defend himself against the outrageous calumnies that were being heaped upon him—'the coward of Sedan'—by his former subjects. In the face of these slanderous attacks, not only on himself but on the Empire and the imperial circle, he kept a dignified silence. He would never indulge in recriminations. 'You should have seen him during those last years at Chislehurst,' said the Empress in later life, 'never a word of complaint, or blame, or abuse. I often used to beg him to defend himself, to repulse some imprudent attack or the vile execrations hurled at him, to check once and for all the flood of insults that were endlessly pouring over us. But he would reply gently: "No, I shall not defend myself . . . sometimes a disaster falls upon a nation of such a kind that it is justified in blaming it all, even unfairly, upon its ruler. . . . A sovereign can offer no excuses, he can plead no extenuating circumstances. It is his highest prerogative to shoulder all the responsibilities incurred by those who have served him . . . or those who have betrayed him."'

One day the Empress was sorting through a box of papers recently arrived from Paris. It contained private letters belonging to the imperial family, which had somehow escaped the eyes of the Republican government. For the most part they were unimportant. Suddenly Eugenie, who had been on her knees beside the box, leaped to her feet and pressed a letter into her husband's hands. 'Look,' she exclaimed triumphantly, 'I have been searching for this for hours. Read it!'

It was a letter from the French statesman, François Guizot, who, since the fall of the Empire, had spared no effort to defame the late régime. While Napoleon III had still been in power, Guizot—although hostile to the Empire—had one day come to him with a tale of a son's debts which he was unable to pay. The Emperor, without question or comment, had given Guizot the money he needed and the grateful father had written an effusive letter of thanks, saying, 'Sire, you have saved more than my life, you have saved my honour.' It was this letter which Eugenie had discovered. The Emperor read it in silence and then murmured, 'I had forgotten all about it.'

He was about to crumple it when Eugenie snatched it from him, crying, 'Let me have it; it will be my revenge!'

'No, no, Eugenie,' said Napoleon softly, 'one does not take that kind of revenge.'

With that, he left the room.

However much Eugenie might try—and she did try—she could never match Napoleon's great qualities of resignation and forgiveness. Whereas he was naturally phlegmatic, she had always been restless, highly strung and impulsive. It needed a conscious effort on her part to keep her robust, avenging nature in check. She did not always succeed and there were times when the Household was subjected to a seemingly endless tirade against those who had betrayed the Empire. Sometimes Napoleon, exhausted by her railings, would say wearily, 'Eugenie, you do not possess an idea, the idea possesses you.'

The infamy of General Trochu was something which she could never forget. Night after night, for hour after hour, she would discuss every nuance of Trochu's behaviour, working herself up into a state of almost hysterical indignation. One evening, at about midnight, when she had, as usual, spent several hours re-examining Trochu's treachery, she noticed poor Marie de Larminat struggling to keep her eyes open.

'Good heavens, what time is it?' demanded the Empress.

'Madame,' answered the exhausted maid of honour, 'it is forty-five minutes past Trochu.'

'You are quite right, I think of nothing else,' admitted Eugenie frankly, 'but how could I forget it?' And the next night would bring the same diatribe.

But in spite of her irritating and, at times, almost maddening qualities, they loved her. They understood the essential honesty of her character. 'Her impetuous, passionate nature must have made her suffer more intensely than many . . .' said Marie, 'and I pitied her with all my heart.'

Almost worse were the evenings when Eugenie had nothing to say. Then they would sit in the large drawing-room, the women bent over their needlework and the men over their patience, with no sound other than the clash of balls in the billiard room to break the oppressive silence. The Emperor, 'wrapped in a cloud of cigarette smoke', would sit musing in a big armchair by the fire while the Empress read or worked at her embroidery. Time, on nights like this, would pass with agonizing slowness. Finally, at eleven o'clock, the Empress would rise and, on reaching the doorway, acknowledge the obeisances of the company by dropping a deep curtsy. With this famous curtsy ('an exquisite sweep down to the floor and up again, all in one gesture . . . like a flower bent and released by the wind' as one witness put it) the Empress had always taken her leave at the Tuileries. It remained, says Filon, 'the last and only vestige of Imperial etiquette which the Empress retained in her exile'.

These years at Camden saw a reconciliation between Napoleon and Eugenie. It is unlikely that the Empress was ever in love with the Emperor but during the Empire he had lost even her affection. His persistent unfaithfulness, both sexual and political, together with what Eugenie considered to be his lack of fibre, had often exasperated her. This exasperation had reached its climax in that scene on the staircase after Sedan. But at Camden, says Filon, she gave back the Emperor her old affection and forgot completely—much as a drunkard or a madman might forget—the terrible things that she had said about her husband in that moment of all-consuming rage. When tactfully reminded of them, in an account of those dramatic days written by one of the witnesses and presented to her for her approval, she was profoundly shocked. 'If among these observations there is one that above all others touches Her Majesty's heart,' she commented, 'it is that which concerns the Emperor and the feelings which she has never ceased to entertain for him. The thought that your account represents her as having imagined for one instant that the Emperor was unworthy of her fills the Empress with sorrow.'

And many years later, when she happened to be reading aloud a newspaper article which mentioned 'the profound affection that the Emperor had never ceased to feel for her', she was so overcome that her eyes filled with tears and she was unable to continue reading.

As for Napoleon, he had never ceased to be fond of her. A brief reference to their relationship, made in his Will, has a strangely touching quality. 'I trust that my memory will be dear to her, and that after my death she will forget the griefs I may have caused her.'

Thus, whatever other discord might have marked life at Camden Place, there existed, 'during those last hours of married life,' says Filon, 'perfect sympathy and understanding . . . between the Emperor and the Empress.'

2

For the Prince Imperial, exile was perhaps harder than for any of the others. Both Napoleon and Eugenie were unquestioningly cosmopolitan; Louis had known no country other than France. His whole life had been lived as the heir to the Imperial throne of France; he had never had cause to question his destiny. Now, quite suddenly, it was as though the bottom had dropped out of his world. He was utterly disorientated. Nothing that poor Filon could do (for the young man had by now resumed his tutorship of the Prince) seemed to arouse the boy's interest. He remained moody, listless and deeply perplexed. He refused to show any awareness of his new surroundings. He simply could not accept the fact of his exile. All his thoughts were concentrated on France. Louis was a Frenchman, claimed Filon, 'even before he was a Bonaparte'. When, on his fifteenth birthday, one of the Empress's ladies asked the Prince what happiness she should wish him, his reply was instantaneous. 'I'll tell you what,' he exclaimed. 'I would give my name, rank, prospects—everything I have in the world—only for a commission as Lieutenant in the French army!'

On another occasion, when his old history teacher, Ernest Lavisse, who had often given him lessons at the Tuileries, came to Camden Place to see him, Louis again revealed something of this anguish. The Prince appearing abstracted, Lavisse asked him what he was thinking about; Louis, suddenly remembering the sight of Paris spread out in the sunshine beneath the windows of the Tuileries, blurted out, 'I'm thinking what I would give to see the Grenelle–Porte St Martin omnibus coming out of the Rue du Bac.'

Perhaps the only consolation of this new life was that Louis was able to spend more time with his parents. He had always been *en rapport* with his mother and he adored his father. Whatever other disillusionments he may have suffered during and after the fall of the Empire, the boy had not lost faith in his father. To him the Emperor was as wise, as brave, as honourable as he had ever been. Nor, in his turn, did Napoleon have any doubt of Louis's capabilities. Filon might complain of the boy's lack of concentration and the Empress might fear his fits of reckless generosity, but to the Emperor his son was perfection. He would one day consolidate his father's work; of this Napoleon was certain. Already the Emperor was initiating the Prince into the world of politics and he would encourage him to remain in the room during the political discussions which were such a feature of life at Camden Place. 'Continue, M. Rouher,' said the Emperor one day to the visiting statesman as the Prince Imperial entered the room. 'You can speak before Louis. He is very interested in our affairs.'

In the meantime, the boy's more conventional education was being organized. In the autumn of 1871, at the end of his first year of exile, Louis went to King's College in London. This turned out to be a mistake. The Prince was too young, too backward, too much of an odd man out to reap any benefit from King's College. The only advantage gained from his months there was that he began to take an interest—not in his studies— but in his surroundings. Life in the streets of London fascinated him. To walk into a café and order an ice was an adventure; to be jostled by the crowds at Charing Cross station was a joke; to stare without being stared at was a positive delight. Slowly, he was beginning to come alive again. His curiosity was aroused and the natural buoyancy of his nature was reasserting itself.

Towards the end of the following summer the course of his life took a more interesting turn still. He entered the Royal Military College at Woolwich as a cadet. Now that he was sixteen years of age, it was important that he should begin his military training. If Louis was one day to be Emperor of the French he must, as a Napoleon, prove himself a soldier first. And it was equally imperative that he should train in the traditional service of the Bonapartes—the artillery. Enchanted at the prospect, Louis set out for Woolwich in the highest spirits. For the next few years he would be living at Woolwich and coming home at week-ends only.

His leaving plunged the household into a still deeper gloom. 'The days were sad indeed,' sighed Marie de Larminat of the period following Louis's departure, 'under the misty sky, in that great kingdom of fog and rain.' Indeed, to the bored company at Camden Place, it seemed always to be raining. Up and down, up and down the long gallery they would pace, pausing now and then to look out at the dripping trees or the heavy clouds. 'The pearly-grey English sky is like a dish that has been cooked without salt,' mused Eugenie. 'One must be very hungry to appreciate it.'

Some relief from this caged atmosphere was provided by visits from friends, relations and sympathizers. There would be calls from members of the Bonapartist party over from France and the arrival of an occasional opportunist ready to turn the misfortunes of the family to his own advantage. Queen Victoria returned the Emperor's visit (a hint was dropped that she found the rooms too stuffy) and once the royal call was over, county society and the Emperor's old English friends followed her example. Sometimes the routine was varied by holidays. One summer the Empress went to Spain to visit her mother, the ageing Countess de Montijo, while the Emperor and the Prince Imperial spent a month at Torquay. The following year Eugenie, the Prince, and a party of young Spaniards did a lightning tour of Scotland, during which time the Emperor was enjoying a more leisurely holiday at Brighton and Cowes. But such outings were exceptional; during most days of the year the exiles were obliged to fall back on each other's company. The result was inevitable. 'Here we are on the raft of the *Méduse*!'

exclaimed the Empress one day. 'There are moments we feel like eating each other.'

'By degrees,' says Marie de Larminat frankly, 'we began to rasp one another's nerves.'

The Emperor alone seemed unaffected by any domestic tensions. In truth, he was barely conscious of them. For most of the day he would sit in his little study, with the fire blazing and the windows shut tight, working on what was, in effect, his apologia for the débâcle of 1870. This was to be the answer to his vociferous critics. It took the form of two monographs: *The Military Forces of France 1870*, published in 1872, and *The Campaign of 1870*, published the following year. The Emperor had asked Filon to give him advice on style and grammar and never, claims the Prince's tutor, had any pupil accepted proposed corrections with more 'simplicity, good feeling and gratitude'. On one point, however, the Emperor would accept no advice. He refused to clarify a certain diffuseness of reasoning by simply laying blame where it was due. He would not point out the mistakes of some of his compatriots. When Filon spoke to him of the contrast between the lucidity of his verbal explanations and the obscurity of his writing, Napoleon replied with a sad smile, 'It is because I wish to justify myself without accusing others.'

That the finished products lacked force and conviction can be appreciated.

For many years after the Emperor's death, Filon kept a sheet of paper, written on in Napoleon's hand. It was one of the manuscript pages of *The Campaign of 1870*. The sight of it, with its dozens of untidy erasures and rewritten sentences, betraying the 'generous scruples which had agitated his soul' while writing it, always had the power to move Filon. It was the page on which Napoleon III had described the battle of Sedan.

3

The one thought that sustained the household at Camden through these lean years was that the Empire might be restored. Hardly had peace been concluded before they began looking, like gardeners for the first sign of spring, for indications of a reaction in their favour. That France might be content to remain a Republic seemed to them highly unlikely. She had tried Republics before; they had never lasted for more than a few years. Nor could monarchical Europe be expected to take a Republic seriously. Even if effervescent Paris favoured republicanism, solid France was monarchist. Had the recent elections not proved that? Nor was the behaviour of this same Republican Paris calculated to inspire confidence in the new régime: hardly had the conquering Germans marched out of the capital than the people of Paris—led by a band of dedicated revolutionaries —rose up in revolt against the government of Thiers, now established at Versailles. The reign of terror of the Paris Commune lasted for over two months and was crushed, with the utmost ruthlessness, by the Republican government. Over twenty thousand were killed during 'Bloody Week' alone, and when the victorious government troops reoccupied Paris, they found the city in ruins. Both the Hôtel de Ville and the Tuileries had been gutted by fire. When set against the horrors of the Paris Commune, the more notorious Reign of Terror of the 1790s was as nothing; the world had never experienced a bloodier revolution than this.

It was no wonder that the rest of France tended to look back with nostalgia to more placid days and more stable-seeming régimes: to the courtliness of the restored Bourbons, to the tranquillity of the July monarchy, to the prosperity of the Empire. That a monarchy of some sort would be restored seemed inevitable. It was merely a matter of which pretender would carry off the prize. They were all ready: the Count de Chambord with a Legitimate monarchy, the Count de Paris with an Orleanist, Napoleon III with an Empire. There were many (and not only Bonapartists) who thought that Napoleon had the best chance of all.

His chances were further enhanced by the attitude of the Legitimist Pretender, the Count de Chambord. Returning to France after his years of exile, the Count de Chambord promptly published a manifesto in which he refused—in the event of his assuming the crown—to accept the tricolour as the flag of France. 'The white flag of the Kings of France flew above my cradle at birth,' he declared, 'it is my will that it shall shade my tomb after my death.' On this issue he stood firm and his stand put an end to any hopes of a Bourbon restoration. As the Orleans family (who were a younger branch of the Bourbons) had agreed to recognize the childless Count de Chambord as having a prior claim to the throne, in the hopes that he would name the Count de Paris as his heir, Chambord's stiff-backed attitude put paid to their chances as well. This turn of events delighted Thiers. 'Henceforth no one will contest that the founder of the Republic in France is M. le Comte de Chambord,' he said.

But there remained the Imperialists. C. de B., the anonymous Paris correspondent of the London Rothschilds, reporting to his employers in October 1871, claimed that a group of eminent public servants had recently worked out a result of a hypothetical plebiscite on the choice of régime for France. Three million would vote for the Empire, two million for a Republic, two million for a Legitimist monarch and one million for an Orleanist monarch. Although an Orleanist himself, C. de B. rated Napoleon III's chances higher than that. He maintained that a plebiscite would give the Emperor between five million and six million votes; a mere one and a half million less than he had received in the last great plebiscite of his reign. Lord Lyons, the British Ambassador in Paris, shared this opinion.

So, it would appear, did the Republican government. They remained unquestioningly apprehensive of an attempted imperial restoration. The middle classes and the peasants were reported to be stubbornly sympathetic to the late Empire. A Republican deputy, driving one day through the countryside, was startled to hear a woman cry out to a couple of peasants in the fields, 'Ah! If only we could have our good Napoleon III back again, what splendid times we should have.' The country was being flooded with Bonapartist propaganda, including tracts to the army (Napoleon III, as ever, was working underground) and Bonapartist clubs were flourishing. In the Paris salons, reported C. de B., the question of a Napoleonic restoration was 'the one subject of conversation'. The exiled Emperor had only to leave Camden for a few weeks' holiday for the French government to get jittery. His visit to Torquay in the summer of

1871 gave rise to a rash of alarmist headlines in the French newspapers ('Plot for the restoration of Napoleon III'; 'The Emperor to make a descent from Torquay') and the authorities kept a close watch on the port of Rochefort at which he was expected to land. When the Empress Eugenie visited her mother in Spain, the French government kept an eye on all her movements. They even went so far as to employ a private detective to watch Camden Place; his agents, installed in a windmill on Chislehurst Common, compiled a list of all visitors to the house. When the Emperor's cousin Plon-Plon went to Corsica to canvass for a seat as deputy, the apprehensive Thiers dispatched a squadron of warships to the island to deal with any possible Bonapartist uprising.

All this, of course, was highly gratifying to the exiles at Chislehurst. The Emperor followed the French political scene closely; his agents were for ever crossing the Channel on secret missions. He is reported to have sent Count Fleury to St Petersburg to discover what the Russian attitude would be to an imperial restoration and when the Duke of Brunswick refused to lend him £330,000 for the purposes of a come-back, Napoleon is said to have applied to, and to have had more success with, Bismarck. The Iron Chancellor was obviously still unhappy with a black-coated government in Paris. The election of Rouher, *vice-empereur* of the late régime, as deputy for Ajaccio in the spring of 1872 was a straw in the wind indeed and by the end of the year the Emperor was ready to tell a visiting journalist that an imperial restoration was a 'historical necessity' and 'a progressive march which nothing can stop'. At a 'single word from me', claimed Napoleon, 'the flag of the Empire would be raised in fifty places at once from one end of France to the other. . . .' In fact, unbeknown to the Emperor's visitor, a plan had already been worked out.

It was to be another 'Return from Elba'; another triumphant and bloodless march to Paris. Napoleon III had spent too much of his life emulating the first Emperor to forsake him now. He would slip away from England in a yacht belonging to a Mr James Ashbury, join Plon-Plon in Switzerland and make for Lyons, where General Bourbaki was in command. From here he would set out for Paris and, while the hostile deputies in the

National Assembly were being packed into a train which was
to be left stranded in the Saint Cloud tunnel, he would ride into
the capital at the head of his acclaiming troops. The population,
presumably, would give him a rousing welcome. A list of ministers
was prepared, an imperial residence chosen (as Saint Cloud had
been destroyed during the war and the Tuileries burnt down
during the Commune, it would have to be the Louvre) and even
the tone of the restored Court decided upon: austerity was to be
the keynote of the new régime. A date was set for March 1873.
Spring was the time for restorations. A Napoleon always returned with the violets.

The plan had one important drawback; and that the most
important of all. The Emperor was very ill. The stone in his
bladder, from which he had had some relief since Sedan, was
beginning to torture him again. He could barely walk these days.
Any chance of his riding a horse at the head of a triumphal procession into Paris seemed remote indeed. When someone spoke
to him of the 'inevitable return of the Empire' he agreed but
added, 'It is a great pity that I am so ill.' Nevertheless, in order
to accustom himself to riding, he would each day mount a wooden
horse which the Empress had commissioned a French sculptor
to make for him. It was an agonizing exercise.

In the autumn of 1872 Plon-Plon visited Camden Place. A
professed Republican throughout the Empire, he was now knee-
deep in the conspiracy to overthrow the Republic and restore
the imperial régime. He had come to Camden to discuss final
arrangements. The sight of Napoleon appalled him. Was this
shambling, grey-faced creature the man who hoped to rally
France once more to the Empire? Would he even be able to
drive, let alone ride into his capital? The two men decided to
put things to the test. On the morning after Plon-Plon's arrival,
he and the Emperor set out in a carriage for Woolwich. Plon-
Plon observed his cousin carefully during the drive. His face
showed no signs of suffering, he never complained. But that was
never any guide to Napoleon's true feelings; that evening, when
he was alone with the Empress, he admitted that he had suffered
a little.

Something had to be done. Loath as was the Emperor to be
examined, he agreed to consult a doctor. 'My health will never

stand in the way,' he declared, 'I will do what it is my duty to do.' Later, with less heroism but with an eye to that triumphal ride, he exclaimed jauntily, 'In a month we shall be on horseback.'

The doctors examined him at Camden on 24 December, 1872. In the Emperor's bladder was discovered a stone the size of a large date. An immediate operation was decided on and Sir Henry Thompson, the renowned urologist, was installed in the house. The first operation took place on 2 January 1873. The stone was found, crushed and as many fragments as possible removed. Throughout the next two days the Emperor experienced considerable pain. A second operation was performed on 6 January. After careful manipulation, a further fragment was removed. For all the following day and the day after, the patient was sleepy and semi-delirious. The presence of yet another obstructing fragment was suspected and a third operation decided upon.

Once during that delirium-dazed day Napoleon asked Eugenie where Louis was.

'He is at Woolwich,' she answered. 'Do you want me to send for him?'

'No,' he murmured. 'His work mustn't be interrupted.'

When Sir Henry Thompson visited his patient the following morning—9 January—he found him so much better that he decided to perform the third operation at noon. Eugenie, reassured, prepared to drive to Woolwich to visit the Prince Imperial. As she was about to set out, she was suddenly called back. Sir Henry had noticed a marked change in the patient's appearance and realized that he did not have much longer to live. Eugenie sent someone to fetch the Prince Imperial and hurried to her husband's bedside.

'Louis is coming,' she whispered, knowing that this would give him the greatest comfort. He moved his lips, as though wishing to kiss her. At a quarter to eleven Napoleon III died. Eugenie lifted her arms and, uttering an ear-piercing cry, fell across the bed and kissed the dead face. Then, fainting, she was carried to her room.

Half an hour after the Emperor's death the carriage bringing Louis came clattering from Woolwich. It was met at the front door by several members of the Household. One look at their faces was enough for the Prince to realize that all was over. Pushing past them, he ran through the hall, across the gallery, up a broad flight of stairs, stumbling and falling as he ran. On the landing he met his mother. 'I have nothing left but you, Louis,' she sobbed. He went into his father's room. At the sight of the motionless figure on the bed, he fell to his knees and in a firm, fine voice, recited the Pater Noster.

'He knelt down a boy,' says Augustin Filon, 'and rose a man.'

It had been some time during that morning of 9 January, 1873, that Napoleon III had spoken his last coherent words. They had been to his old friend, Dr Conneau, who had been sitting beside his bed almost continuously during his illness. Waking for a few minutes from his drugged sleep, the Emperor had turned to his companion and whispered, 'Ah! It's you, Conneau. . . . It's true, isn't it, that we were not cowards at Sedan?'

4

The Empress Eugenie once declared that her idea of perfect happiness would be to see history avenge those whom she loved. It was to take almost half a century for history to avenge, if not actually the Emperor Napoleon III, then at least the battle of Sedan. And the Empress was to be there to see it. 'I died,' she used to say in her old age, 'in 1870.' In fact, she lived on for fifty years after the fall of the Second Empire. Her life had not run even half its course at the time of Sedan. When she died in July 1920, she was almost ninety-five years old.

After Napoleon III's death in 1873, all plans for an imperial restoration had to be put aside until the Prince Imperial had passed out from Woolwich and felt ready to attempt one. This re-establishment of the Empire became the ruling passion of his young life. It was a question, not of whether or not he would one day become the Emperor Napoleon IV, but of how and when he would do so. Although adventurous by nature, he did not wish to emulate his late father's youthful and unsuccessful attempts at restoring the Empire by leading an armed expedition against the existing French régime. Yet, to avoid becoming simply another half-forgotten pretender, he was always looking about for some way in which to draw French attention to himself; in which he could prove himself worthy of his destiny. And what better way, he reckoned, than on the field of battle? He was constantly on the lookout for a suitable war from which he could return covered in glory. 'He anxiously scanned the face of the earth, his sword burning in his hands,' writes Marie de Larminat, 'and if there was one thing evident about him, it was that, although he might be an aristocrat in the finest sense of the word, and even though he already gave promise of being a remarkable political leader . . . he was first and foremost a soldier.'

There was, of course, another reason why the Prince Imperial had to prove his military prowess: it was up to him to wipe out the stain of Sedan. He never forgot, nor was he ever allowed to forget, the accusations of cowardice levelled at Napoleon III after 1870. One day, when Louis was still at Woolwich, a Frenchman called there on some business or other and the Prince, who was always delighted at the opportunity of speaking to a compatriot, asked to be allowed to meet him. The man was presented and Louis, in his good-natured way, opened the conversation by asking him what part of France he was from. With studied insolence, the visitor folded his arms, looked the eager young man straight in the face and answered emphatically, 'From Sedan.'

Louis turned pale but, controlling himself, answered politely, 'That's a very pretty district.' With that, he walked away.

'He never forgot the insults and base culumnies which had been flung at his father's name after Sedan,' claims Marie. 'He never spoke about it, but his intimate friends knew only too well that he would never have either respite or repose until he had, even at the cost of his own blood, attested to his courage, and shown the whole world that a Napoleon knew how to fight and, if needs be, knew how to die.'

His opportunity came in the year 1879, when he was twenty-three years of age. He joined the British forces fighting against the Zulus in South Africa and it was here, on 1 June, that he was killed in an unimportant skirmish. Deserted by his companions and unable to mount his bolting horse, he turned to face about a dozen assegai-wielding savages. He fought, they afterwards testified, 'like a lion', and when they left his corpse lying naked in a little hollow, there were seventeen assegai wounds in his body—all of them in the front.

When they recovered his uniform they found, rolled up in his wallet, that vicious French newspaper article in which the story of 'the bullet of Saarbrücken' and the charge of Bonaparte cowardice had been raked up once more. It was taunts such as these, declared his heartbroken French servant, that had killed him.

'I thought how deep shall be the repentance,' wrote a French journalist with the British forces in Zululand, 'of those whose insults drove the unhappy Prince to prove his manhood even at the cost of his life, when history shall relate how, in this faraway land, the last of the Napoleons brought by his death honour to the banner of France.'

In that sunlit hollow, lost in the vastness of the South African veld, the Prince Imperial made his personal atonement for Sedan.

His coffin was brought home to England and he was buried beside his father in the little Catholic church on Chislehurst Common. A few years later both bodies were transferred to the mausoleum which the Empress had had built for them near her new home, at Farnborough in Hampshire.

With Louis's death, all hopes of an imperial restoration died also. In the terms of the Prince's will the succession passed, not to Plon-Plon whom Louis had always hated, but to Plon-Plon's eldest son, Victor Napoleon. The outraged Plon-Plon refused to recognize his son's rights and the Bonapartist party split into two bickering factions. Not until Plon-Plon's death in 1891 did Prince Victor become undisputed pretender, but as he proved to be singularly unambitious, the imperial cause became progressively weaker. Prince Victor's son, Napoleon, born in 1914, is the present pretender.

The Prince Imperial's death was the crowning sorrow of the Empress Eugenie's tragic life. Once the first terrible agony of her grief had worn off, she very seldom spoke of her son. When she did, no one could forget the heartrending phrase by which she referred to him: *'mon petit garçon'*. A visitor tells of the occasion when, on returning from a stay in Paris, she mentioned to the Empress that France seemed ripe for a dictator.

'If he had been alive,' answered Eugenie slowly, 'he had every quality they needed . . . now might have been his chance . . . but I often say to myself that I would rather he is dead than think of him as Emperor. . . .' She went on to tell her listener something of the hardships she had endured while still Empress of the French. 'Not for one second have I regretted losing my throne,' she declared. 'To think of his perhaps going through it all—to endure what I had to endure . . . Ah!' Then, her face contracting 'with an indescribable pain and horror which pierced one to witness', she cried out, 'I thank God that he has, at least, been spared that!'

The Empress Eugenie lived on for forty years after her son's death. Far from being the withdrawn, sorrow-steeped figure of popular legend, she was an active, intelligent and vivacious old lady, different from her earlier self only in that she had by now developed a magnanimity hardly less remarkable than that of the late Emperor. As restless as ever, she built herself a villa in the South of France in which she spent part of each year, and bought herself a yacht in which she cruised the Mediterranean and the North Sea coasts. She often visited Paris and when she did, she always stayed at the Hotel Continental, overlooking the Tuileries Gardens. Although the palace itself was gone, the formal garden, with its statuary and its fountains and its chestnut trees, was exactly as it had been in Eugenie's hey-day. When her visitors asked her how she could bear to overlook this scene of her former greatness, she answered that nothing made the slightest difference to her any longer. 'What matters one spectacle or another,' she would say, 'compared with the memories I bear in my innermost heart?' When acquaintances came to the hotel to pay their respects, she would afterwards remark, 'They come to see me like a Fifth Act.'

She was still alive when, in August 1914, France and Germany went once more to war. She lived through that bitter struggle, claims one witness, 'in the closest communion with the soul of France'; the memory of 1870 was interwoven with the course of the present struggle 'like a *leit-motiv*'. The *Union Sacrée*, the working together of all Frenchmen regardless of political beliefs, is said to have awakened all her old regrets. 'Why was not the same truce made round the Emperor and myself, under the shock of our first disasters?' she cried. 'Why were public passions let loose against us after Froeschwiller and Forbach? . . . Why, in fact, was I not listened to on 4 September, when I implored them to call a truce to domestic quarrels and to think only of France?'

When, late in 1918, the Germans began to give way before the Allies, she cried out, 'If Foch could only catch them at Sedan!'

The final victory filled her with elation. With almost hysterical pride and gratitude she thanked God for allowing her to live long enough to see this day. 'It makes up for everything,' she exclaimed, 'it obliterates everything, it repays me all my grief, it allows me to die with my head held high, in peace with France, which will have nothing to reproach us for. . . .'

In a less effusive moment she wished her son had been there; the news, she said quietly, would have made him so happy.

There is a story that after the signing of the armistice by which France regained the lost provinces of Alsace-Lorraine, the ninety-three-year-old Empress went down into the crypt of St Michael's Abbey in which, in two massive granite sarcophagi, lay the bodies of her husband and her son. She there read out, in a firm voice, the clauses of the treaty by which France was finally avenged for 1870.

'When I die, for I shall die soon . . .' she said to Dom Cabrol, the Abbot of St Michael's, 'when I die, how *they* will welcome me above, bringing them this news! They had left me behind on earth. For long, long years I have not known why. It was to await this day. I tell you, the day of the armistice will have been my first day in Paradise.'

CHAPTER FOURTEEN

Post-Mortem

1

Who was to blame, not only for Sedan, but for the collapse of the French Second Empire?

It was, of course, the Franco–Prussian war which was the immediate cause of the downfall of Napoleon III. Had France not gone to war against Prussia in 1870, there was no reason why the régime—recently regenerated by the transition to a Liberal Empire—should not have lasted for at least another few years. Napoleon III is said to have contemplated retiring in 1874, by which time the Prince Imperial would have been eighteen, and the accession to the throne of this alert, likeable and politically unsullied young man might have given the Empire a new lease of life.

But once Bismarck had made use of the Hohenzollern candidature to inflame French public opinion, war became almost inevitable. Yet it need not have been so. A cooler head than that of Gramont, Napoleon's Foreign Minister, and a more experienced mind than that of Ollivier, the leader of the government, could have turned the Hohenzollern incident to France's advantage. France should have made the most of the withdrawal from the scene of Prince Leopold of Hohenzollern and should not have pressed the King of Prussia for guarantees that the candidature would never again be raised. Napoleon realized this, but lacked the conviction, and the resolution, to force his will. With his Empress, his Court, his ministers and his capital swept by war fever, there was not one sane voice close to him to back him up in his reservations. He allowed himself to be persuaded that the régime would never survive this insult from Prussia and that only by threatening war could he keep his throne. In this he was probably being unduly pessimistic. He undoubtedly underestimated the strength of the support for the Empire in France. Not three months before he had been given a massive vote of confidence by the country; his position was surely secure enough for him to weather this particular crisis. There was a much better chance of his retaining his throne by sitting tight than by going to war.

Bismarck's editing and publication of the Ems telegram put paid to any hopes of a diplomatic settlement. After that Napoleon had little choice but to go along with the war party.

Within a few days of mobilization it was obvious that France could not win the war. It was not that the Prussians were better soldiers; it was simply that they were better organized. And organization, by 1870, was half the battle. Nor was France's old-style, professional army any match for the Prussian 'nation-in-arms'. The Prussians were also better led. Napoleon's ill-health, defeatism, ineptitude and utter lack of any of the qualities necessary to inspire men to superhuman action made him the worst possible choice for Commander-in-Chief. Yet, as a Napoleon, he felt compelled to assume command of the army; the name he bore was synonymous with the glories of war. It was the Napoleonic legend that had made possible his re-establishment of the Empire in the first place and for all Napoleon III's protestations of 'L'Empire, c'est la paix', such was the force of this legend that he felt obliged to abide by it. The result was disastrous.

Nor, when he was replaced by Bazaine, was there any improvement. Bazaine's conduct throughout the campaign was so negative as to appear little short of traitorous. The half-hearted fashion in which he first evacuated Metz, his seeming indifference during the battles that followed, the alacrity with which he scurried back into the safety of the fortress and his lethargy during the siege could be explained only, it was thought, in terms of treachery. Indeed, after the war, he was tried and imprisoned for treason. But Bazaine was not a traitor. He was simply too small a man for the immensity of his task. Nevertheless, because of his incompetence, Bazaine must bear his share of responsibility for the débâcle of 1870.

Marshal MacMahon, too, who became the country's leading general once Bazaine was besieged in Metz, showed a singular lack of drive and initiative. He was much too anxious to have his mind made up for him; like Bazaine, MacMahon was a born second-in-command.

Both men were hamstrung by the presence of the Emperor at the front. For eighteen years Napoleon III had been the unquestioned master of France; his word had been law. Neither Bazaine nor MacMahon could condition himself to the fact that, quite suddenly, the Emperor counted for nothing; that they were meant to behave as if, although still surrounded by the trappings of his imperial state, he were not there. Unconsciously, they felt that he still had the final word, that they were still responsible to him. The result was that there was no one at the front to speak in a firm, decisive voice. There were far too many cooks spoiling an already inedible broth.

Palikao, the man who replaced the discredited Ollivier as head of the government after the first reverses at the front, was another culprit. His refusal to allow the Emperor and Mac-Mahon to fall back on Paris (a stand in which he had the Empress's full support) and his insistence that they march northeast to relieve Bazaine, certainly accelerated the final disaster. What course events might have taken had the Emperor and MacMahon returned to Paris is difficult to say. The result could hardly have been more disastrous than it was. Palikao's appointment of the blustering Wimpffen to command the Army of Châlons in the event of anything happening to MacMahon was equally unfortunate. Wimpffen's countermanding of the order to retreat from Sedan guaranteed the French defeat. On the other hand, if the Germans had not beaten the French at Sedan, they would have done so somewhere else. The result would have been much the same. Once MacMahon marched towards Bazaine, Napoleon III's fate was sealed.

Trochu, the darling of the Paris mob, might have been able to avert the revolution of 4 September. Had he, the Empress and Palikao been working in close harmony, the Empire might have been saved. But the Regent and her ministers, rightly or wrongly, did not trust him, and Trochu, like Bazaine, MacMahon and the Emperor himself, simply allowed events to take their course.

Thiers, just before the end, might have saved the situation, but having opposed the Empire during the good times, he saw no reason to support it during the bad.

The Empress Eugenie, by her refusal to allow any bloodshed, left the field wide open to the mob, and the actual overthrow of the Empire was accomplished by a few thousand noisy Parisians. These mercurial Parisians, encouraged by a band of hard-core revolutionaries and guided by a handful of Republican deputies such as Favre and Gambetta, brought down the régime in an almost lighthearted fashion. It was 'more like the bursting of a soap-bubble than the fall of a mighty Empire', declared one witness. But the Empress was right to insist on no shooting. Humanitarian motives apart, shooting into the crowd would not have saved the Empire and it might well have led, as it did six months later, to scenes of unspeakable savagery.

To blame the Empress, as she has so often been blamed, as the chief culprit for the débâcle of 1870, is to overestimate her influence. Her personal unpopularity certainly added to the unpopularity of the Empire in certain circles ('If Paris was able to love me,' she exclaimed one day to Mérimée, 'I would give ten years of my life for that!') and she made no secret of the fact that she considered war preferable to any further humiliation from Prussia. But then so did almost all the people surrounding the Emperor. If France had won the war, no one would have accused her of being a war-mongering virago. In advising, indeed ordering, the Emperor not to return to Paris, she may have been mistaken, but again she was reflecting the opinion of the majority. They all assumed that Bazaine would be breaking out of Metz to meet the advancing MacMahon. For Napoleon and MacMahon to desert Bazaine and return to the safety of Paris would mean revolution. Had Eugenie thought differently, she could, no doubt, have persuaded the cabinet that Napoleon should return, but she did not consider such a step wise and, in this, she found her ministers in full agreement.

Had the Empress Eugenie been as negative a personality as Napoleon I's second Empress, Marie Louise, it is doubtful that the course of events of 1870 would have been any different. The Empire would have fallen with or without any help from her. She was never as powerful a figure as a great many people, herself included, imagined.

The ultimate responsibility must lie with the Emperor Napoleon III. Had he been younger, healthier, and more resolute in that summer of 1870, things might have been very different. His talents were for politics and diplomacy rather than for soldiering; he should have made full use of them. Even if he had not been able to avert the war, he should never have taken personal command of the army. He should have remained in Paris, or at least returned there once he had handed over the command to Bazaine. Plon-Plon's plan—for the Emperor, MacMahon and Trochu to return together to Paris—was not a bad one. It might well have prevented the revolution. Bold leadership was needed to save the Empire in 1870 but by then the Emperor was incapable of giving it. His defeatism permeated not only the French army, but the imperial régime itself.

Such were the leading personalities and such the events which led to the collapse of the French Second Empire. But these made up the surface causes only; there were several underlying reasons for the fall of Napoleon III's régime. After all, defeat of a sovereign in the field need not automatically lead to his dethronement; the Emperors of Austria were constantly losing battles, yet their hold on their throne, and on the hearts of a great many of their subjects, remained secure. One of the reasons was what the Empress Eugenie had called the 'fickleness', the 'lack of constancy' of the French; a national restlessness which tended—and still tends—to manifest itself every dozen or so years. The French, and particularly the Parisians, are too volatile, too questioning, too idealistic almost, to rest content with one form of government for long. It is unlikely too, that the revolutionary spirit which had erupted in 1789, in 1830 and again in 1848, could have been stilled for ever. Revolution, and the setting up of a Republic, had become almost inevitable.

'France is bound . . . to complete the French Revolution,' Gambetta had once claimed. 'It is the task of the nineteenth century; it is particularly the task of our generation. The centenary of 1789 must not dawn upon us without the reconquest by the people for itself, and for the rest of the world, of the political heritage of which it was depossessed [by Napoleon I] on 18th Brumaire.'

But perhaps, more than anything, the reason lay in the very

nature of the Empire. It was the creation of one man and as such, depended almost entirely on the personality, the wisdom, the skill, the courage, the luck and the health of that man. The Second Empire could be only as strong, and as weak, as the Emperor Napoleon III. This was one of the great faults of the régime: it produced no statesman of real stature capable, not only of supporting the Emperor, but of directing imperial policy. Napoleon III was too conspiratorial, too distrustful, too diffident ever to take his subordinates fully into his confidence. He tended, rather, to play one off against the other, to make use of their weaknesses rather than their strengths. There was thus no one on whom he could rely, no strong body of lieutenants in whose hands he could safely leave the running of the Empire. Without him, the régime was rudderless. When Albert, the Prince Consort, once tactfully suggested to the Emperor that he delegate some of his responsibility, Napoleon had answered, '*mais où trouver l'homme?*' The Empress was neither popular nor influential enough to stand in for him; the Prince Imperial was too young; Plon-Plon too irresponsible.

The Liberal Empire, had it had longer to establish itself, might have produced more competent men and have made the régime less dependent on the Emperor's strength of mind and state of health. By 1874 the Liberal Empire, like other constitutional monarchies, might have been running itself regardless of the fortunes of its sovereign. But as it was, the Emperor was the Empire and when he capitulated at Sedan, his régime came tumbling down like a house of cards. His disastrous foreign policy, his underestimation of Bismarck's Prussia, his faltering attempts to gain compensation after Sadowa, his loss of Catholic sympathy because he had helped the Pope too little and of Liberal sympathy because he had helped him too much, had all led to an irreparable loss of prestige. In his final failure, his previous successes counted for nothing. The early glories of his reign, the breadth of his vision, the goodness of his intentions and the warmth of his heart were all forgotten. Napoleon III was to be remembered, not for the very real benefits that he bestowed on France, but for his surrender at Sedan.

In France, as the Empress Eugenie once said, a ruler cannot afford to be unlucky.

247

2

What were the results of the fall of the Second Empire? In Italy the withdrawal of the French garrison allowed King Victor Emmanuel to march in and take possession of Rome, thus forcing the Pope to become a prisoner in the Vatican. In France, bloody civil war broke out between the Commune in Paris and the government at Versailles. The loss, to France, of Alsace-Lorraine left a wound that refused to heal. In the Place de la Concorde, the statue representing Strasbourg, the capital of Alsace, was draped in black as a constant reminder of the national humiliation. The massive monument, 'Germania', raised by the victors on a wooded crest above the Rhine, seemed to commemorate, not so much the unification of the German people, as the mortification of France. The French were thus determined not only to win back Alsace-Lorraine, but to have their revenge on Germany. 'Henceforth there are in Europe two nations which will be formidable,' wrote Victor Hugo, 'the one because it is victorious, the other because it is vanquished.' Defeated France, watching the self-confident swagger with which the conquerors celebrated Sedan Day each year, was resolved that the stain of 1870 had to be wiped out. For proud and sensitive Frenchmen, *revanche* became an obsession and a second war between the two countries almost inevitable.

'There's no Europe left now!' cried Count von Beust, the Austrian Chancellor, foreseeing that from henceforth the various countries of Europe would develop increasingly aggressive nationalisms. The old Europe of little kingdoms and duchies and principalities, with their dynastic rather than nationalistic allegiances, had been replaced by half a dozen or so rigid power blocs. Men would think of themselves as Germans or Frenchmen or Austrians or Italians rather than as Europeans. Indeed, it had been Napoleon III, in his eagerness to dismantle the Treaty of Vienna of 1815 and with his belief in 'completed nationalities' who had helped set this particular ball rolling. As a good European, he had assumed that national self-determination would lead to lasting peace in Europe; that once all

248

nations had won their independence, they would come together to settle their grievances at a conference table. Like so many of the Emperor's well-meant schemes, this one had turned sour. From now on the peace of Europe was to be an armed truce, and not the harmonious peace of Napoleon III's fond imaginings.

But the most significant result of the fall of the Second Empire was the establishment of the Second German *Reich*. Germany now became the most powerful nation on the Continent, and the centre of European gravity swung from Paris to Berlin. Napoleon III's experiment of a Liberal Empire which, had it proved successful, might have served as an example for Europe's more reactionary monarchial régimes, was crushed, and Europe dominated by a country with a very different philosophy. Napoleon had been quite correct in predicting that Germany would be 'forced to become aggressive'. Born out of military victory, the Second German *Reich* was convinced that continued militarism was the only sure way of safeguarding her new position in Europe. The German military caste, considered to be the most important in its society, became increasingly arrogant, showy, despotic and powerful. German militarism, allied to German nationalism, became aureoled in glory with the result that Germany twice plunged Europe, and the world, into war. Not until 1945 did she lose the dominance which she had snatched up seventy-five years before, from out of the ruins of the French Second Empire. The débâcle of 1870 is thus one of the great turning-points in the world's history. What the French Revolution was to eighteenth-century Europe, the Franco–Prussian war was to the nineteenth century. With the death of Napoleon III's Empire, a much more brutal world came to life.

Sedan 1940

Sedan has remained one of France's most bitter memories. Much more than Waterloo, it is symbolic of a period of deep national humiliation. The French triumph of 1918, when in that same *galerie des glaces* at Versailles in which the German Empire had been proclaimed, France imposed its peace terms on a defeated Germany, did not long obliterate the shame of Sedan. Victory in the Great War had cost France dear; it left her crippled. 'We don't give the impression of a victorious people, nor do the Germans look like a defeated one,' noted a Frenchman during the negotiations at Versailles. Indeed, the French triumph was short-lived. In just over twenty years the Germans again brought France to her knees.

And again it happened at Sedan.

In May 1940 the Germans, having lured the Allied forces forward by an attack on Belgium, launched a second and more powerful attack in their rear. They broke through the enemy defences, particularly thin at that point, and poured across northern France towards the English Channel, thus driving a wedge between the Allied forces to the north in Belgium, and the rest of the French army to the south. Within a few weeks France capitulated. The point at which the Germans forced this break-through was Sedan and, for the second time in seventy years, the name of the town became synonymous with a French defeat.

Sedan had a further significance, for the town saw not only the birth, but also the death, of the Third French Republic. The battle of 1870 had led to the proclamation of the Third Republic; the battle of 1940 led to its collapse. When France fell in June, Marshal Pétain established the Vichy régime. Sedan thus marks the grave not only of the Second Empire but of the Republic which followed it.

The town was almost completely destroyed during the fighting of May 1940. Rebuilt after the war, it stands today within its circle of hills—new, anonymous, undistinguished and somewhat forlorn-looking. It seems hardly worthy of its turbulent and tragic past.

Bibliography

Acton, Baron J. E. E. D., *Historical Essays and Studies*. Macmillan, London, 1907: Books for Libraries, Inc., New York.

Aubry, Octave, *The Second Empire*. Translated by Arthur Livingston. J. B. Lippincott Co., New York and Philadelphia, 1940. Arthème Fayard, Paris, 1938.

Baldick, Robert, *The Siege of Paris*. Batsford, London, 1964: Macmillan Co., New York, 1964.

Bapst, Constant Germain, *Le Maréchal Canrobert* (6 vols.). E. Plon, Paris, 1893–1913.

Barkeley, Richard, *The Empress Frederick*. Macmillan, London, 1956: St Martin's Press, New York, 1958.

Barthez, A. C. E., *The Empress Eugenie and Her Circle*. T. Fisher Unwin, London, 1912.

Bellessort, André, *La Societé Française sous Napoléon III*. Perrin, Paris, 1932.

Bicknell, Anna, *Life in the Tuileries under the Second Empire*. The Century Co., New York, 1895.

Bismarck, Prince Otto, *Bismarck: His Reflections and Reminiscences* (2 vols.). Smith, Elder, London, 1898.

Blumenthal, Field-Marshal Count von, *Journals for 1866 and 1870–1*. Translated by Major A. D. Gillespie-Addison. E. Arnold, London, 1903.

Bonnin, Georges (Editor), *Bismarck and the Hohenzollern Candidature for the Spanish Throne*. Chatto & Windus, London, 1957: Clarke, Irwin, Toronto, 1958.

Boon, H. N., *Rêve et realité dans l'oeuvre économique et sociale de Napoleon III*. s'Gravenhage, 1936.

Brogan, D. W., *The French Nation from Napoleon to Pétain, 1814–1918*. Hamish Hamilton, London, 1957: Harper & Row, New York, 1958.

Burghclere, Lady, *A Great Lady's Friendship: Letters to Mary, Marchioness of Salisbury, 1862–1890*. Macmillan, London, 1933: Macmillan Co., New York, 1933.

Bury, J. P. T., *Gambetta and the National Defence*. Longmans, London, 1936: Longmans, New York, 1936.

Busch, Dr Moritz, *Bismarck and the Franco-Prussian War, 1870–1871* (2 vols.). Macmillan, London, 1898: Charles Scribner's Sons, New York, 1879.

    Bismarck: Some Secret Pages of His History (3 vols.). Macmillan, London, 1898: Macmillan Co., New York, 1898.

Cambridge Modern History (planned by Lord Acton). Cambridge University Press, 1909: Macmillan Co., New York, 1909–12.

Carette, Madame A., *Souvenirs Intimes de la Cour des Tuileries* (3 vols.). Paris, 1888–91.

    The Eve of an Empire's Fall. Dean & Son, London, 1890.

Carey, Agnes, *The Empress Eugenie in Exile*. Eveleigh Nash & Grayson, London, 1922: The Century Co., New York, 1920.

Chapman, Guy, *The Third Republic of France*. Macmillan, London, 1962: St Martin's Press, New York, 1962.

Cheetham, Frank H., *Louis Napoleon and the Genesis of the Second Empire*. J. Lane, London, 1909.

Cook, Sir Edward, *Delane of* The Times. Constable, London, 1916: Henry Holt, New York, 1915.

Cope, Vincent Zachary, *A Versatile Victorian*. Harvey & Blythe, New York, 1951.

Corley, Thomas A. B., *Democratic Despot: A Life of Napoleon III*. Barrie & Rockliff, London, 1961: Clarkson Potter, New York, 1962.

Corti, Count E. C., *The English Empress*. Cassell, London, 1957.

Corvin, Colonel Otto, *In France with the Germans*. R. Bentley & Son, London, 1872.

Cowley, Baron Henry Wellesley, *The Paris Embassy During the Second Empire*. Butterworth, London, 1928.

Curry, T. (Translator), *Secret Documents of the Second Empire*. W. Tweedie, London, 1871.

D'Ambes, Baron, *Mémoires Inédites* (2 vols.). Societé des Publications Litteraires Illustrées, Paris, 1909.

D'Auvergne, Edmund Basil, *Napoleon the Third*. Eveleigh Nash and Grayson, London, 1929: Dodd, Mead, New York, 1929.

Deléage, P., *Trois Mois chez les Zoulus et les derniers jours du Prince Impérial*. E. Dentu, Paris, 1879.

Delord, Taxile, *Histoire du Second Empire* (6 vols.). Baillière, Paris, 1869–75.

Des Garets, Marie Comtesse (de Larminant) de Garnier, *Souvenirs d'une Demoiselle d'Honneur: Auprès de L'Impératrice Eugénie*. Calmann-Levy, Paris, 1928.

    Souvenirs d'une Demoiselle d'Honneur: L'Impératrice Eugénie en exile. Calmann-Levy, Paris, 1929.

Du Camp, Maxime, *Souvenirs d'un Demi-Siècle*. Hachette, Paris, 1949.

Ducrot, A. A., *La Journée de Sédan*. E. Dentu, Paris, 1871.

Eugénie, Empress of the French, *Lettres Familières de l'Impératrice Eugénie* (2 vols.). Le Divan, Paris, 1935.

Evans, Thomas W., *Memoirs of Dr Thomas W. Evans*. T. Fisher Unwin, London, 1906: D. Appleton & Co., New York, 1905.

Favre, Jules, *Le Gouvernement de la Défense Nationale*. H. Plon, Paris, 1872.

Filon, Pierre Marie Augustine, *Memoirs of the Prince Imperial*. Heinemann, London, 1913: Funk & Wagnalls, New York, 1921.
   Souvenirs sur l'Impératrice Eugénie. Calmann-Lévy, Paris, 1920.

Fleischmann, Hector, *Les Secrets du Second Empire: Napoleon III et les Femmes*. Paris, 1913.

Fleury, Comte Maurice, *Memoirs of the Empress Eugénie*. D. Appleton & Co., London and New York, 1920.
   and Sonolet, Louis, *La Societé du Second Empire*. A. Michel, Paris. (N.D.)

Forbes, Archibald, *Memoirs and Studies of War and Peace*. Cassell, London, 1895.
   My Experiences of the War between France and Germany. Hurst & Blackett, London, 1871.
   Souvenirs of Some Continents. Macmillan, London, 1885; Harper & Bros., New York, 1885.

Fraser, Sir William, *Napoleon III; My Recollections*. Sampson Low, London, 1895.

Frederick III, Emperor of Germany, *The War Diaries of Emperor Frederick III*. Stanley Paul, London, 1895: Frederick A. Stokes & Co., New York, 1926.

Frederick, Empress of Germany, *Letters of the Empress Frederick* (edited by Sir Frederick Ponsonby). Macmillan, London, 1928.

Fuller, J. F. C., *The Decisive Battles of the Western World*. Eyre & Spottiswoode, London, 1956.

Goncourt, Edmond and Jules de, *Journal*. Paris, 1887–96.

Gooch, Brison D. (Editor), *Napoleon III—Man of Destiny*. Holt Rinehart, New York, 1963.

Gooch, George Peabody, *The Second Empire*. Longmans, London, 1960: Verry, Lawrence, Inc., Mystic, Conn., 1960.

Gorce, Pierre de la, *Histoire du Second Empire*. Paris, 1896.

Grant, A. J. and Temperley, Harold, *Europe in the Nineteenth and Twentieth Centuries*. Longmans, London, 1953: Longmans, New York, 1952.

Greville, Charles, *The Greville Diary*. Heinemann, London, 1927: Doubleday, New York, 1927.

Guedalla, Philip, *The Second Empire*. Hodder & Stoughton, London, 1932: Verry, Lawrence, Inc., Mystic, Conn., 1957.

　　The Two Marshals. Hodder & Stoughton, London, 1943: Reynal & Hitchcock, New York, 1943.

Guerard, Albert, *Napoleon III*. Alfred A. Knopf, New York, 1955.

Guest, Ivor, *Napoleon III in England*. British Technical and General Press, London, 1952.

Hatzfeld, Melchior Paul, *Hatzfelds Briefe*. Leipzig, 1907.

Hegerman-Lindencrone, Lillie Moulton, *In the Courts of Memory*. Harper & Bros., New York, 1912.

Henry, Robert (Editor), *Letters from Paris 1870–1875*. J. M. Dent, London, 1942.

Herisson, Comte Maurice d'Irisson, *Journal d'un Officer d'Ordonnance*. P. Ollendorff, Paris, 1885.

　　Le Prince Impérial. P. Ollendorff, Paris, 1890.

Hesekeﬂ, J. G. L., *The Life of Bismarck: Private and Political*. James Hogg, London, 1870: Harper & Bros., New York, 1870.

Hoche, Jules, *Bismarck at Home*. J. Macqueen, London, 1899.

Hoffman, Wickham, *Camp, Court and Siege*. Harper & Bros., New York, 1877.

Holden, W. H., *The Pearl from Plymouth*. British General and Technical Press, London, 1950.

　　(Editor), *Second Empire Medley*. British General and Technical Press, London, 1952.

Hooper, George, *The Campaign of Sedan*. George Bell, London, 1887: Harcourt, Brace, New York. (N.D.)

Horne, Alistair, *The Fall of Paris*. Macmillan, London, 1965: St Martin's Press, New York, 1965.

Howard, Michael, *The Franco-Prussian War*. Rupert Hart-Davis, London, 1961: Macmillan Co., New York, 1961.

Hozier, Captain H. M., *The Franco-Prussian War: Its Causes, Incidents and Consequences*. W. Mackenzie, London, 1899.

Hubner, Count, *Neuf ans de souvenirs d'un Ambassadeur d'Autriche* (2 vols.). Paris, 1904.

Jerrold, Blanchard, *The Life of Napoleon III* (4 vols.). Longmans, London, 1874–82.

John, Katherine, *The Prince Imperial*. Putnam, London, 1939: G. Putnam's Sons, New York, 1939.

Kurtz, Harold, *The Empress Eugénie*. Hamish Hamilton, London, 1964: Houghton, Mifflin, Boston, 1964.

Labracherie, Pierre, *Le Second Empire*. Julliard, Paris, 1962.

Lano, Pierre de, *The Empress Eugénie: The Secret of an Empire*. Osgood, McIlvaine, London, 1895: Dodd, Mead, New York, 1894.

Lebon, André, *Modern France, 1789–1865*. T. Fisher Unwin, London, 1897: G. Putnam's Sons, New York, 1939.

Lee, Sir Sidney, *King Edward VII* (2 vols.). Macmillan, London, 1925: Macmillan Co., New York, 1925–7.

Legge, Edward, *The Empress Eugénie, 1870–1910*. Harper & Bros, London, 1910: Charles Scribner's Sons., New York, 1910.
    The Comedy and Tragedy of the Second Empire. Harper & Bros., London, 1911: Charles Scribner's Sons, New York, 1911.
    The Empress Eugénie and Her Son. G. Richards, London, 1916.

Loliée, Frédéric Auguste, *Les Femmes du Second Empire*. J. Tallandier, Paris, 1906.
    The Life of an Empress. Dodd, Mead, New York, 1909.

Malmesbury, James Howard Harris, 3rd Earl of, *Memoirs of an Ex-Minister*. Longmans, London, 1884: Longmans, New York, 1885.

Martini, Magda, *Une Reine du Second Empire; Marie Laetitia Bonaparte-Wyse*. E. Droz, Geneva, 1957.

Maupus, C. E. de, *Mémoires sur le Second Empire*. Paris, 1884.

Maurice, Major-General J. F. (Editor), *The Franco-German War, 1870–1*. Swan Sonnenschein, London, 1900.

Mercy-Argenteau, Comtesse Louise de, *The Last Love of an Emperor*. Heinemann, London, 1926: Doubleday, New York, 1926.

Metternich, Princes Pauline, *Souvenirs 1859–71*. Plon, Paris, 1922.

Meyer, Arthur, *Forty Years of Parisian Society*, Eveleigh Nash & Grayson, London, 1912.

Minon, A., *Les Derniers Jours du Prince Impérial sur le Continent*. Paris. (N.D.)

Moltke, Field-Marshal Count Helmuth von, *The Franco-Prussian War of 1870–1*. Osgood, McIlvaine, London, 1891: Harper & Bros., New York, 1892.

Monts, General Comte de, *La Captivité de Napoleon III en Allemagne*. Pierre Lafitte et Cie, Paris, 1910.

Morley, John, *The Life of William Ewart Gladstone* (2 vols.). Macmillan, London, 1905: Macmillan Co., New York, 1905.

Murat, Princess Caroline Letitia, *My Memoirs*. G. Putnam's Sons., New York, 1910.

Namier, Sir Lewis, *Vanished Supremacies*. Hamish Hamilton, London, 1958: Hillary House, New York, 1958.

Napoleon III, Emperor of the French, *The Political and Historical Works of Louis Napoleon Bonaparte* (2 vols.). Illustrated London Library, London, 1852.
    Oeuvres posthumes et autographes inédits de Napoléon III en exil. Recueillis et coordonnés par le Comte de la Chapelle. Paris, 1873.

Nicolson, Harold, *Kings, Courts and Monarchy*. Weidenfeld & Nicolson, London, 1962: Simon & Schuster, New York, 1962.

North Peat, Anthony B., *Gossip from Paris during the Second Empire*. Kegan Paul, London, 1903: D. Appleton, New York, 1903.

Ollier, Edmund, *Cassell's History of the War between France and Germany 1870–1871*. Cassell, London, 1872.

Ollivier, Émile, *L'Empire Libéral* (16 vols.). Garnier Frères, Paris, 1895–1912.

    The Franco-Prussian War and Its Hidden Causes. Sir Isaac Pitman, London, 1913: Little, Brown, Boston, 1912.

Oman, Sir Charles, *Things I Have Seen*. Methuen, London, 1933.

Paléologue, Georges Maurice, *Les Entretiens de l'Impératrice Eugénie*. Plon, Paris, 1928.

Pinckney, David H., *Napoleon III and the Rebuilding of Paris*. Princeton University Press, Princeton, 1958.

Regnier, Edmond, *Quel est votre Nom? What is your Name? N or M. 'A Strange Story' revealed*. London, 1872.

Richardson, Joanna, *The Courtesans*. Weidenfeld & Nicolson, London, 1967: World Publishing Co., New York, 1967.

Robertson, C. Grant, *Bismarck*. Constable, London, 1918: Henry Holt, New York, 1919.

Ryan, Charles E., *With an Ambulance during the Franco-Prussian War*. John Murray, London, 1896.

Sencourt, Robert Esmonde, *The Life of Empress Eugénie*. Ernest Benn, London, 1931: Charles Scribner's Sons, New York, 1931.

    Napoleon III: The Modern Emperor. Ernest Benn, London, 1931: Appleton, Century, New York, 1933.

Simpson, Frederick Arthur, *The Rise of Louis Napoleon*. Longmans, New York, 1925.

Smythe, Dame Ethel Mary, *Impressions that Remain*. Longmans, London, 1923: Longmans, New York, 1919.

    Streaks of Life. Longmans, London, 1921: Alfred A. Knopf, New York, 1922.

    As Time Went On. Longmans, London, 1936.

Stannard, Harold, *Gambetta*. Methuen, London, 1921: Small, Maynard, Boston, 1921.

Tascher, S. de la Pagerie, *Mon séjour aux Tuileries* (3 vols.). Paris, 1894.

Taylor, A. J. P., *Rumours of War*. Hamish Hamilton, London, 1952: British Book Centre, New York, 1953.

    The Struggle for Mastery in Europe, 1848–1918. O.U.P., 1954: O.U.P., New York, 1954.

Bismarck. Hamish Hamilton, London, 1955: Alfred A. Knopf, New York, 1955.

Thierry, Augustine, *Le Prince Impérial*. Grasset, Paris, 1935.

Thiers, L. Adolphe, *Notes et Souvenirs 1870–1873*. Paris, 1904.

Thompson, James Mathew, *Louis Napoleon and the Second Empire*. Blackwell, Oxford, 1954: W. W. Norton & Co., New York, 1967.

Twain, Mark, *The Innocents Abroad*. Chatto & Windus, London, 1912.

Vandam, Albert D., *An Englishman in Paris*. Chapman & Hall, London, 1893: D. Appleton, New York, 1912.

Undercurrents of the Second Empire. G. Putnam's Sons, New York, 1896.

Van Laun, Henri, *The French Revolutionary Epoch* (2 vols.). Cassell, London, 1878.

Vare, Daniel, *Twilight of the Kings*. John Murray, London, 1948.

Victoria, Queen of Great Britain, *More Leaves from the Journal of a Life in the Highlands*. Smith, Elder and Co., London, 1884: New York, 1884.

The Letters of Queen Victoria. John Murray, London, 1926.

Viel-Castel, Horace, Comte de, *Mémoires du Comte de Horace de Viel-Castel* (6 vols.). Paris, 1883–4.

Vizetelly, E. A., *The Court of the Tuileries*. Chatto & Windus, London, 1912.

My Days of Adventure. Chatto & Windus, London, 1914.

War Correspondence of the *Daily News* 1870 (2 vols.). Macmillan, London, 1871.

Whitton, Lt.-Col. F. E., *Moltke*. Constable, London, 1921: Henry Holt, New York, 1921.

Williams, John, *The Ides of May*. Constable, London, 1968.

William I, Emperor of Germany, *The Correspondence of William I and Bismarck*. Heinemann, London, 1913.

Wolff, Sir Henry Drummond, *Rambling Recollections*. Macmillan, London, 1908.

Zeldin, Theodore, *The Political System of Napoleon III*. Macmillan, London, 1958: St Martin's Press, New York, 1958.

Emile Ollivier and the Liberal Empire of Napoleon III. Clarendon Press, Oxford, 1963: O.U.P., New York, 1963.

Zola, Emile, *La Débâcle*. Paris, 1892.

Newspapers and Periodicals
Paris: *Le Temps, Figaro, Revue des Deux Mondes*.
London: *The Times, Daily News, Graphic, Illustrated London News*.

Index

Adam, Juliette, 60
Adelon, M., 108–9
Affaire Baudin, The, 61
Agout, Mme d', 60
Alba, Duke of, 23
Alba, Duchess of, 23, 66
Albert, Prince Consort of Great Britain, 72, 99, 146, 247
Albrecht, Archduke of Austria, 57, 58, 68
Alexander II, Tsar of Russia, 56, 217
Alice, Grand Duchess of Hesse, 100
Almanach de Gotha, 77
Antigny, Blanche d', 8
Anton of Hohenzollern-Sigmaringen, Prince, 77, 78, 80, 82, 83
Appleton, Tom, 65
Apponyi, Count, 99
Arc, Joan of, 151
Ashbury, James, 234
Augusta, Queen of Prussia, 71–2
Auvergne, Edmund d', 172

Bachon, M., 33
Baillet, Count de, 204
Barthez, Dr, 19
Bassano, Duke de, 9
Baudelaire, 7
Baudin, M., 61–2
Bazaine, Marshal François

Achille, 52, 103, 111–13; assumes supreme command, 120; retreats towards Verdun, 121–6; at Gravelotte, 131–3; besieged in Metz, 137–42, 146, 150, 156–8, 170; and peace negotiations, 215–19; capitulates, 219; responsibility for the fall of the Empire, 243–6
Bazeilles, 164, 166–70, 172
Beaumont, 158
Bellevue, Château de, 179–80
Benedetti, Count Vincent, 78, 82–4, 98
Bernstorff, Count von, 98
Berthaut, General, 128, 130
Besson, M., 200
Beust, Count von, 248
Bismarck, Count Otto von, 19, 21, 51, 54, 101, 153, 162, 163, 234, 242–3, 247; and the growth of Prussia, 70–3; and the Hohenzollern candidature, 78–87; publishes secret treaty, 97–8; at Sedan, 173, 175–81; and peace negotiations, 215–20
Blanc, Louis, 60
Blumenthal, General von, 165
Bonaparte, House of (*see also* Jerome, Napoleon, Pierre etc), 6, 37, 63, 110, 230
Borgias, the, 63

Borny, 123
Bouet-Willaumez, Admiral, 108
Bourbaki, General, 52, 83, 218, 234
Bourbon, House of (*see* also Chambord, Count de), 233
Boyer, General, 219
Brancion, Mme de, 35
Brunswick, Duke of, 234
Buffet, Louis-Joseph, 190–2
Burgoyne, Sir John, 211, 212

Cabrol, Dom, 241
Camden Place, 222–31, 233–6
Camp, Maxime du, 40, 41
Campaign of 1870, The, 231
Canrobert, Marshal, 82, 103, 120, 124, 133
Capoul, 115
Captain, H.M.S., 212
Carette, Mme, 156
Carlyle, Thomas, 56
Cassagnac, Paul de, 108
Castlenau, General, 168, 175, 176
Catherine of Württemberg, 38
Caussade, General, 193
Cavaignac, General, 35
Cavaignac, Mme, 36
C. de B., 233
Chambord, Count de, 43, 232, 233
Charles X, King of France, 184
Charles of Hohenzollern-Sigmaringen, Prince, 82
Chazal, General, 206
Chevreau, Henri, 135, 182, 187
Clarendon, Lord, 28, 54, 79
Clary, Count, 158, 204
Clotilde, Princess, 7, 38, 56
Comte de Flandres, 205
Concours général, 35
Conneau, Dr, 66, 67, 237
Conneau, Lt., 198, 199
Conneau, Louis, 66, 95

Conti, Eugène, 182, 198, 199
Cossé-Brissac, M de, 116
Courbet, Gustave, 7
Cowley, Lord, 18, 19
Crane, Dr, 207, 208

Daily News, 132
Daru, Count, 190–2
Davilliers, Count, 168
Delane, John, 100
Delescluze, Charles, 60, 61, 153, 195
Demidoff, Prince Anatole, 38
Donchéry, 175, 177–9
Douay, General, 169, 170
Ducrot, General, 165, 167, 170–2, 174
Dumanoir, M., 96
Dumas, *fils*, 7, 8
Dunant, Henri, 52
Duperré, Charles, 158–61, 202–5, 222
Duvernois, Clément, 155, 184

Edward, Prince of Wales, 99, 146
Elizabeth, Empress of Austria, 57
Ems telegram, 84, 85, 243
Essling, Mme d', 116
Eugenie, Empress of the French, 4–6, 16, 19, 43, 57, 67–9, 105–6, 114, 125, 129, 131, 140, 145, 146, 148, 160, 171, 178, 180, 194, 203, 204, 234, 242, 244, 246, 247; parentage, girlhood, 22, 23; marriage, beauty, character, 24, 25, 26; political activities, 26–31; and the Prince Imperial, 31–7; and Plon-Plon, 37–40; and the Liberal Empire, 45–9; her attitude towards the declaration of war, 81–96; at the

Eugenie—*cont.*
beginning of her Regency, 107–11: forms new ministry, 115–18; forbids Emperor to return to Paris, 134–9; expects siege, 150–5; reaction to the news of Sedan, 181–2; receives delegation from *corps législatif,* 183–93; escapes from the Tuileries, 196–201; escapes to England, 207–12; and peace negotiations, 216–21; at Camden Place, 222–31; and death of the Emperor, 235–7; widowhood, 237–41; and responsibility for the fall of the Empire, 245

Evans, Dr T. W., 201, 207–12, 223

Evans, Mrs, 207, 211

Failly, General de, 56, 158
Faure, General, 175
Favre, Jules, 47, 51, 54, 60, 118, 119, 153, 155, 186, 189, 195, 196, 216, 245; proposes dethronement, 184; leads deputies to Hôtel de Ville, 194; negotiates with Bismarck, 215
Ferry, Jules, 60, 153
Feuillet, Octave, 107
Feuillet, Mme, 67
Filon, Augustin, 26, 48, 65, 66, 68, 69, 90, 107, 116, 118, 134–7, 154, 157, 160, 183–4, 187–8, 204, 208, 219, 227, 231, 237; meets Empress for first time, 25; and Prince Imperial, 32–7, 93–6; and surrender of Sedan, 182; and Regnier affair, 217–18; resumes tutorship of Prince 228

Flaubert, Gustave, 7, 10

Fleury, Count, 52, 56, 234
Floing, 164, 165, 168, 170, 171
Flourens, Gustave, 195
Foch, Marshal, 241
Fonvielle, Ulrich de, 62, 63
Forbes, Archibald, 132, 180
Fournaise, Mme, 178, 179
Franz-Josef, Emperor of Austria, 17, 30, 57, 58, 109, 177, 217
Frederick-Charles, Prince, 101, 112, 124, 132, 146, 215
Frederick, Crown Prince of Prussia, 30, 72, 101, 111, 112, 115, 140, 145–7, 150, 157, 162, 163, 174
Frénois, 163, 165, 173
Froeschwiller, 111–13, 116, 120–2, 241

Gallifet, General de, 171
Gambetta, Léon, 7, 47, 59, 60, 62, 118, 155, 194, 196, 245, 246; proclaims Third Republic, 195; escapes from Paris by balloon, 216
Garibaldi, Giuseppe, 57
Gautier, Théophile, 10
Géricault, Jean, 199
Germania, 248
Givonne Valley, 164, 165, 167–9
Gladstone, William, 82, 98–100, 145
Goncourt brothers (Edmond and Jules de), 6
Goncourt, Edmond de, 115
Gramont, Duke de, 81–5, 114, 242
Gramont-Caderousse, Duke de, 7
Grand Duchesse de Gerolstein, La, 8
Granville, Lord, 99, 100, 145
Gravelotte, 124–5, 129, 132–3, 142

Gravière, Admiral Jurien de la, 190, 198
Greville, Charles, 18
Guizot, François, 225, 226

Hamilton, Duke of, 7
Haussmann, Baron Georges, 3, 10
Hendecourt, Captain d', 168
Hohenzollern-Sigmaringen, House of (see Anton and Charles and Leopold of)
Hohenzollern candidature, 77–86, 242
Hortense de Beauharnais, Queen of Holland, 16, 18, 95, 207
Hübner, Baron, 19
Hugo, Victor, 17, 60, 248

Imperial, Louis, Prince, 4, 25, 29, 30, 38, 40, 41, 48, 66, 69, 88, 89, 110–12, 136, 165, 180, 183, 207, 217, 218, 221, 222, 241, 242, 247; birth, 16; character and early life, 31–7; attitude towards war, 92–6; at Saarbrücken, 106; and first reverses, 121–5; leaves army, 147–50; wanderings, 158–61; leaves France, 202–5; goes to Woolwich, 228–30; and death of Emperor, 236–7; death, 238–9
Isabella, I, Queen of Spain, 30
Isabel II, Queen of Spain, 77

Jerome, King of Westphalia, 37, 180, 206
Josephine, Empress of the French, 16, 95, 207
Journal Official, 210

Khedive of Egypt, 30
Kirkpatrick, William, 23

L'Aigle, 30
Lambert, Tristan, 106
Lamey, Captain, 158
Lanterne, La, 60, 61, 62
L'Armee française en 1867, 129
Larminat, Marie de, 47, 65, 66, 87, 90–3, 109, 116, 135, 222, 226, 227, 230, 231, 238
Last of the Barons, The, 181
Lavisse, Ernest, 91, 228, 229
Leboeuf, Marshal, 54, 82, 85, 87, 111, 119, 120
Lebreton, Mme, 198–201, 208, 209, 212, 218
Lebrun, General, 58, 172, 173
Leopold I, King of the Belgians, 15, 55, 99
Leopold II, King of the Belgians, 82, 206
Leopold of Hohenzollern-Sigmaringen, Prince, 77–84
Lesseps, Ferdinand de, 30, 184
Longeville, 123, 124
Louis XIV, King of France, 17
Louis XVII (Dauphin of France), 148
Louis, King of Holland, 16, 18
Louis-Philippe, King of the French, 184, 210
Lucien, Bonaparte, Prince, 62
Lyons, Lord, 145, 233
Lytton, Bulwer, 181

MacMahon, Marshal, 52, 53, 103, 115, 120–2, 125, 137–41, 146, 147, 150, 156, 243, 244, 245, 246; and battle of Froeschwiller, 111–13; at Châlons, 127–30; agrees to fall back on Paris, 131; marches to relieve Bazaine, 142; falls back on Sedan, 157–8; at Sedan, 166, 167, 169, 170

Madamoiselle, La Grande, 157

Magenta, 52, 122

Malakoff, Duchess de, 110

Malmesbury, Lord, 49, 90, 223, 224

Marchand, Mme, 202

Marie-Antoinette, Queen of France, 69, 134, 148, 208

Marie-Louise, Empress of the French, 134, 184, 245

Marx, Karl, 49

Mathilde, Princess, 6, 19, 31, 38, 40, 67, 89, 91

Maugny, Count de, II

Mauguin, M., 8

Maximilian, Emperor of Mexico, 17, 21

Meduse, 199, 230

Mellinet, General, 185, 197

Mercy-Argenteau, Countess de, 19, 89, 90

Mérimée, Prosper, 66, 151, 152, 245

Metternich, Princess Pauline, 7, 9, 109, 110, 223

Metternich, Prince Richard, 22, 29, 57, 81, 109, 110, 157, 186, 188; helps Empress to escape, 197–200

Micheler, General, 104

Military Forces of France, 1870, The, 231

Millière, Jean-Baptiste, 195

Moltke, Count Helmuth von, 72, 73, 80, 84, 87, 101, 105, 112, 113, 120, 126, 132, 133, 146, 147, 163, 173, 175–9

Moniteur, 29, 50

Montijo, Count de, 9

Montijo, Countess de, 23, 94, 151, 152, 160, 230, 234

Monts, General, 206, 207

Mouchy, Duke de, 9

Mouchy, Duchess de (Anna Murat), 9, 86

Moulton, Charles, 88, 89

Moulton, Lillie, 68, 69, 88, 89

Napoleon I, Emperor of the French, 3, 15, 16, 17, 33, 34, 36, 37, 38, 52, 62, 73, 95, 124, 134, 159, 180, 189, 206, 207, 234, 245, 246

Napoleon II, Duke de Reichstadt, 16

Napoleon III, Emperor of the French; rebuilding of Paris, 3; early career and character, 15–22; and Liberal Empire, 42–8; and army reform, 49–54; search for alliances, 55–8; and republicanism, 59–62; health, 28, 67, 89, 107, 129, 149, 166, 235, 237; and Hohenzollern candidature, 78–88; leaves for the front, 95–6; at Metz, 103; at the battle of Saarbrücken, 105–7; hands over supreme command to Bazaine, 120; leaves Metz, 121; at Châlons, 127–31; decides to fall back on Paris, 131; forbidden to return to his capital, 139; sets out to relieve Bazaine 142; parts from Prince Imperial, 149–50; courts death at Sedan, 168; at the battle of Sedan, 165–74; orders hoisting of white flag, 172; meets Bismarck in cottage, 177–9; leaves for Wilhelmshöhe, 181; hears of fall of the Empire, 225; at Wilhelmshöhe, 206–7; and peace negotiations, 215–20; arrives in England, 221; at Camden Place, 222–8, 231;

Napoleon III—*cont.*
plans for restoration, 231–5; illness and death, 235–7; responsibility for fall of the Empire, 246–7

Napoleon, Prince Jerome (Plon-Plon), 6, 44, 45, 56, 140, 180, 234, 235, 239, 246, 247; character and career, 37–41; advises Napoleon III to fall back on Paris, 128–31

Napoleon, Prince Victor (*see* Victor)

Napoleon, Prince (present pretender), 239

Nicholas I, Tsar of Russia, 13, 17

Niel, Marshal, 51, 67

Nieuwerkerque, Count de, 38

Nigra, Count Constantine, 109, 197–200

Noir, Victor, 62–4

Normanby, Lord, 16

Offenbach, Jacques, 7, 8

Ollivier, Emile, 45–8, 53, 54, 65, 69, 81, 83–5, 87, 107, 108, 110, 115–19, 134, 190, 242, 244

Olly Farm, 164, 165, 168

Orleans, House of (*see also* Paris, Count de), 221, 233

Orphée aux Enfers, 8

Palikao, Count de, 119, 129, 134, 137, 138, 150, 153, 155–7, 167, 170, 185–7, 189, 193, 194, 196; appointed head of new ministry, 118; orders MacMahon to relieve Bazaine, 141; responsibility for fall of the Empire, 244

Parieu, M. de, 92

Paris, Count de, 43, 47, 232, 233

Pavia, La, 8

Pearl, Cora, 8, 9

Persigny, Duke de, 22

Petain, Marshal, 253

Petiet, M., 159

Petiet, Mme, 159, 165

Phoebus, 166

Picard, Ernest, 153, 196

Piennes, Marquis de, 116, 200

Pierre, Bonaparte, Prince, 62–4

Presse, La, 109

Prévost-Paradol, 59, 68

Prim, Marshal Juan, 77–81

Pyat, Felix, 60, 153, 195

Randon, Marshal, 89

Rappel, Le, 109

Regnier, M., 217–18, 220

Reille, General, 173

Renan, Ernest, 10

Réveil, 62

Rezonville, 125, 126, 131

Rigolboche, 7

Rochefort, Henri de, 7, 60–4

Roon, Count Albrecht, von, 72, 80, 84, 163

Rothschilds (bankers), 82, 215, 233

Rouher, Eugène, 87, 141, 142, 229, 234

Rowles, Emily, 223

Saarbrücken, 105–6, 110, 111, 113, 122, 239

Sadowa, 21, 28, 29, 50, 53, 70, 71, 247

Saint Haouen, Captain de, 170

Sainte-Beuve, C. A., 10

St Privat, 132, 133

Salmon, Yvan (*see* Noir, Victor)

Sass, Marie, 86, 115

Schmitz, General, 128

Schneider, Hortense, 8

Schneider, M, 194

Sedan, 158, 159, 161, 162–80, 183, 185, 186, 202, 231, 235, 237, 238, 241, 242, 244, 247, 248, 253, 254

Seé, Dr Germain, 67

Sheridan, General, 163, 173, 179

Solforino, 52, 177

Sophie, Queen of Holland, 28, 55, 61

Soumain, General, 186, 187

Spicheren, 112–13, 116, 122

Steinmetz, General von, 107, 112, 123, 124, 132

Strauss, Johann, 7

Strode, Mr, 223

Tascher de la Pagerie, Countess, 19

Temps, Le, 147, 154

Thérésa, 7, 9

Thiers, Adolphe, 22, 44, 60, 86, 185, 188, 189, 194, 221, 232, 233, 234; proposes Council of National Defence, 186; responsibility for the fall of the Empire, 244–5

Thompson, Sir Henry, 236

Times, The (London), 98, 100, 162

Treaty of Vienna, 248

Trochu, General Louis Jules, 130, 136, 137, 154–6, 185–8, 194, 195, 210, 211, 226, 246; career, 128–9; appointed governor, 131; character, 154; heads new government, 196; responsibility for fall of the Empire, 244

Twain, Mark, 7

Uhlmann (Prince Imperial's valet), 93

Vichy régime, 253

Victor-Emmanuel II, King of Italy, 38, 56, 57, 109, 114, 140, 248

Victoria, Crown Princess of Prussia, 10, 70, 72, 79, 97, 98, 99, 146, 163

Victoria, Queen of England, 9, 15, 18, 39, 54, 55, 56, 70, 79, 82, 90, 97, 98, 99, 145, 162, 224, 230

Victor-Napoleon, Prince (son of Plon-Plon), 239

Viel-Castel, Count H., 8

Waldteufel, 7, 61

Walewska, Mme, 66

Walker, Sir Beaumont, 179

Washburn, Elihu, 200

Waterloo, 253

Watrin, Lt, 158, 159, 203, 204

Wellington, Duke of, 18

Wilhelm, I, King of Prussia, 21, 54, 70–3, 82–4, 96, 98–101, 120, 162, 163, 171, 173, 176, 178–81, 219, 242; and Hohenzollern candidature, 78–80; meets Napoleon after Sedan, 180; proclaimed Emperor of Germany, 220

Wimpffen General, E. F. de, 167, 170, 172–177, 179, 244

Wissembourg, 111, 115